C'MON THE

Wrexham FC Yearbook 2008-09

Edited by Peter Jones

Photographs by the Evening Leader & Les Evans

We would like to thank the following people for their contributions to this project:

Kevin Baugh, Steve Cooper, Gareth M.Davies, Sandra Edwards, Les Evans, Paul Evans, Arfon Griffiths MBE, David Griffiths, John Humphries, Barry Jones, Bryn Jones, Jack Jones, Colm O'Callaghan, Geraint Parry, Carolyn Poole, Gary Pritchard, Richard Purton, David Roberts, Paul Sleeman, Haydn Taylor, Mark Williams, Mike Williams, Richard Williams, Tony Williams, Martin Wright & Rob Wynne.

Produced by Wrexham Supporters' Trust Sponsored by the Evening Leader

Subscribers

A warm thank you goes out to the following pre-subscribers without whom this book would never have been possible.

First published in Great Britain in 2008 by:
Wrexham Football Supporters' Society Limited, PO Box 2200, Wrexham, LL12 9WG.

Printed and bound in Great Britain in 2008 by:
Blueprint, 47 Carlton Crescent, Gwaun Miskin, Pontypridd, CF38 2RS.

ISBN: 978-0-9554179-2-4

Contents

Section 1: Introductions

Section 2: Season Preview 2008/09

Section 3: Wrexham FC History

Section 4: Wrexham's Supporters' Groups

Section 5: Season Review 2007/08

Back row L-R: Marc Williams, Silvio Spann, Andy Fleming, Mike Williams, Conall Murtagh, Christian Smith, Kyle Critchell, Michael Proctor, Wes Baynes, Chris Marriott.

Middle row L-R: Anthony Williams, Sam Aiston, Gareth Evans, Jefferson Louis, Steve Evans, Gavin Ward, Nat Brown, Darran Kempson, Lewi Mackin, Shaun Pejic, Chris Maxwell.

Front row L-R: Simon Spender, Simon Brown, Tom Kearney, Brian Little (Manager), Brian Carey (Assistant Manager), Martin Foyle (First Team Coach), Shaun Whalley, Neil Taylor, Carl Tremarco.

Brian Little

Welcome back to a new season after what has been a very hectic summer. After the disappointment of losing our Football League status last May, our aim is quite simply to bounce back at the first attempt. I'm looking to make us a completely different team – certainly one with far more pace. That's something we lacked last term and which is becoming more and more important in the modern game.

To that end we've been very active in the transfer market and have brought in seven new faces. So it's a warm welcome to Nat Brown, Simon Brown, Darran Kempson, Kyle Critchell, Tom Kearney, Jefferson Louis and Shaun Whalley. Meeting with each of the players, they all realise the potential of this club and are desperate to play a part in restoring the club's fortunes.

One pleasing factor is that we've managed to bring those players in early and so that has helped them gel during the demands of pre-season training. The build up to the new campaign has gone well and we have looked far more competitive in the friendly games we've played to date.

One thing you will have noticed already is that we are asking the midfield to play a little deeper than normal. Because we conceded a lot of goals last season this will help the defence and if we can tighten up at the back we won't need to score as many at the other end.

In doing this we are looking to hit teams on the counterattack so this is where fitness levels come in and we must get to a level that will carry us through the season. The players have responded to this, but the acid test will come with the start of the season proper.

I think Conference football, or the Blue Square Premier League as it's now called, has changed significantly from when I was at Darlington. I remember our plan of attack then was to be possibly the only fully professional side in it, so that was a massive advantage to us.

The biggest difference several years on is that we are now in a competition where there is a gaggle of ex-League clubs, and the gap has been breached by other sides that may not yet have been in the Football League, but have built a foundation behind them to make themselves competitive at this level.

You are automatically going in amongst ten clubs who are ready to go into the Football League. So getting there again is the most difficult part and I think it's proved in recent years that the teams that do get there are more than capable of holding their own in Division Two.

Everybody's first season after relegation from the Football League is one that is looked upon with great interest by the media and the fans. Everybody is getting used to a different type of challenge because the fans will be going to some grounds they've never been to before.

My message to everyone is that we all need to be pulling in the right direction. We've tried very hard on the playing side to pre-pare well for this season, but I would under-stand some fans who think I'll just see how it starts before I'll pop down there. But if we can get off to a good start, then one of the key ingredients to doing that is our fans being behind us and accepting that it is a good standard of football, it's a good league, that there are some good teams in it and that it's not going to be easy.

It is definitely a long season ahead of our-selves and there's some super competitions which we need to try and be competitive in. All in all we're perhaps looking at a competi-tive campaign of hopefully 60 plus games. If we do that then we've had a decent season.

Finally, my thanks to everyone involved in the production of The Supporters Trust Wrexham FC Yearbook. The passion which you, the fans, show is second to none and together we can get this club back to regaining its former glories.

Who's who ?

CONTACT
Wrexham Football Club (2006) Ltd
The Racecourse Ground, Wrexham, LL11 2AN

TELEPHONE
Match & Ticket sales 01978 262129 Ext 1
Catering, Hospitality & Functions 01978 262129 **Club Shop** 01978 262129 Ext 2
Commercial & Sponsorship Department 01978 262129 Ext 3 **Football in the Community** 01978 358545 **Collier's Park Training Ground** 01978 853223

WEBSITE AND EMAIL
Website **www.wrexhamafc.premiumtv.co.uk**
Enquiries **info@wrexhamfc.tv**
Sponsorship **sponsorship@wrexhamfc.tv**
Racecourse Lotto **lotto@wrexhamfc.tv**

CLUB OFFICIALS
Directors Paul Atkinson, Geoff Moss, Paul Retout, **Chief Executive** Anthony Fairclough, **President** Arfon Griffiths MBE, Senior Vice-President Nev Dickens **Vice-Presidents** Dave Bennett, Malcolm K. Davies, Dave Griffiths, John Marek & Wrexham Supporters' Trust.

BEHIND THE TEAM
Manager Brian Little, **Assistant Manager** Brian Carey, **First Team Coach** Martin Foyle, **Head Physiotherapist** Mel Pejic, **Reserve Team Manager** Joey Jones, **Reserve Team Coach** George McGowan, **Reserve Team Physiotherapist** Mike Williams, **Goalkeeping Coach** Gavin Ward, **Chief Scout (9-16yrs)** John Rearden, **Centre of Excellence Head of Youth** Steve Cooper, **Centre of Excellence Manager** Andy Davies, **Centre of Excellence Recruitment Officer** Stuart Webber, **Centre of Excellence Physiotherapist** Richie Buchanan **Centre of Excellence Physiotherapist** Ritson Lloyd, **Centre of Excellence Physiotherapist** Jen Taylor **Club Doctors** Hywel Hughes, Roger Van Heerden, **Groundsman** John Edwards / Paul Challoner

THE ADMINISTRATION STAFF
Club Secretary Geraint Parry, **Commercial Manager** Phill Sadler, **Safety Officer** Colin Edwards, **Function & Catering Manager** Phil Bennett **Accounts Manager** John Coats, **Accounts Assistant,** Sue Edwards, **Ticket Sales** Gill Dugan, **Administration** Marjorie Pike, **Centre of Excellence Administrator** Tricia Deary-Furber, **Club Historian** Peter Jones, **Club Shop Sales** Dave McGuire.

Trust President Arfon Griffiths' message
Llythyr Arlywydd grwp ymddiried, Arfon Griffiths

Since the last yearbook, a lot has happened. For the third successive year I am pleased to see that the Trust are continuing to produce a comprehensive yearbook that is the envy of many clubs. A lot of work goes into the production of such an annual, and I again wish the Trust every success with it.

Since the last yearbook there has been many tears shed, and I am as distraught as any Wrexham fan at losing our Football League status. It's no good looking for people to apportion blame, what's happened has happened, but I can rest assured no one connected with Wrexham FC wanted it to happen, and everyone is

Am y trydydd flwyddyn llwyddianus rwy'n hapus gweld fod y Trust yn parhau gyda'r Blwyddiadur. Mae yna lawer o waith yn mynd i fewn ir llyrf, a dwi'n dymuno pob lwc ir Trust wrth gwneud.

Ers y Blwyddiadur diwethaf mae llawer o wynebau digalon i weld, ac mi rydw i mor drallodus a unrhyw gefnogwyr Wrecsam ar golli ein statws yn y cynghair peldroed. Does dim da mewn edrych ar bobl i feio, mae beth sydd wedi digwydd wedi digwydd, ond gallaf esbonio fod neb sydd wedi cysylltu efo C.P.Wrecsam eisiau hyn ddigwydd, a mae pawb mor ymroddgar fyth i guro ein safle yn y cynghair peldroed yn ol, a dylai bob gefnogwr as committed as ever to win back our Football League place, and every fan should be behind the manager and team in doing so.

It is imperative that we can win promotion at the first attempt, as the longer we stay at this level the harder it will be to get out. Losing funding from our demise won't help, but it's great to see that the directors have made the decision to keep the Centre of Excellence on the same budget by raising funds from wherever they can to keep it running.

The last two years have been the worst I can remember watching a Wrexham side. We were fortunate to escape the drop in our first year out of Administration, but results speak for themselves, and last year we can have no excuses other than we were simply not good enough. You can say we were unlucky in the odd game not to win, but over a season results usually balance themselves out, and the league table at the end doesn't lie.

Although we gave a few youngsters first team experience, they were brought into the side at a difficult time. They showed promise, but you can't expect them to produce the required results in a struggling team. They needed help from the experienced players, but this was not forthcoming from the players we had at the club. The likes of Graham Whittle, Mickey Thomas, Joey Jones, Dave Smallman, etc, all came through the youth system, but they had players of the experience of Eddie May, Mel Sutton, Mickey Evans around them. However, the youngsters at the club today do have the best coaching facilities in the Blue Square Premier League, and a training ground far better than many Football League clubs.

The people I feel most sorry for are the supporters. Last season our support was

gefnogi'r rheolwr ar tim drwy gydol y cyfnod yma.

Mae'n hanfodo bwysig ein bod yn danfod ir cynghair peldroed ar yr ymgais gyntaf, am mai'r hirach rydym yn aros ar y lefel yma yr anoddach fydd o i ddianc. Dydi colli cyllid gan rhai ddim yn helpu ond mae'n wych gweld fod y cyfarwyddwr wedi penderfynnu cadw'r "Centre of Excellence" ar yr un cyllideb wrth godi arian o lle bynnag y gallent i gadw'n rhedeg.

Mae'r dau flwyddyn diwethaf wedi bod y gwaethaf gallaf gofio yn gwylio tim Wrecsam, roeddem yn lwcus dianc rhag alltudiaeth y tymor cyn diwethaf, a does dim esgusodion am y flwyddyn diwethaf ond ein bod 'im digon da. Bysan deg dweud ein bod wedi bod yn anlwcus mewn ambell gem i beidio curo ond ar diwedd y Dydd dydy bwrdd y cynghair ddim yn dweud celwydd.

Er ein bod wedi rhoi cyfle i ambell i chwaraewr ifanc yn y tim gyntaf, roedd yn amser anodd iddyn nhw ddod i fewn. Dangosodd rhai fod ganddynt dalent, ond gallem ni ddim disgwyl iddynt gynhyrchu y canlyniadau oedd yn angenrheidiol mewn tim oedd yn tangyflawni. Roedd y chwaraewyr ifanc angen help gan y chwaraewyr profiadol ar y cae ond ni ddigwyddodd digon o hyn. Daeth chwaraewyr fel Graham Whittle, Mickey Thomas, Joey Jones, Dave Smallman a Billy Ashcroft drwyr "Centre of Excellence", ond roedd ganddynt chwaraewyr profiadol o'i hamgylch i'w helpu fel Eddie May, Mel Sutton a Mickey Evans.

Beth bynnag, mae gan y chwaraewyr ifanc yn y clwb heddiw rhai or staff gorau yn y "Blue Square Premier" i weithio efo, ac hefyd safle ymarfer gwell na'r rhan fwyaf or timau yn y cynghair peldroed.

absolutely amazing, especially away from home. I travelled to a number of games last season, and it was great to see the support the team got, culminating in the final game of the season at Lincoln. Not many teams would have taken that following in similar circumstances. Lets hope that support continues in getting us back up.

I want to say a big thank you to Geoff Moss and Nev Dickens who financially, and using there business acumen, have kept the club going over the past two difficult years. Geoff's support has been immense, make no mistake of that, and I am more than satisfied that the club is in safe hands.

Nev Dickens has stepped down in the summer, and I'd like to thank him for his part in bringing the club out of Administration. I'm sure Nev would liked to have seen the proposed development materialise, but he always said he wanted to get out after two years, though only if people with the club at heart came in.

Finally, it's good to see new faces on the Trust Board, and I hope that they and the club's directors can sort their differences out. Both sides need to give and take. The club is more important than us all, and important to North Wales. We all need to get on to take this club forward.

**Arfon Griffiths
MBE**

Rhaid cyfaddef fy mod yn teimlo drost y cefnogwyr fwyaf, tymor dwythaf roedd ein cefnogaeth yn rhagorol, yn enwedig i ffwrdd o adref. Trafeiliais i nifer o gemau tymor diwethaf a roedd yn wych gweld y cefnogaeth cafodd y tim. Rhaid gobeithio fod y cefnogaeth am barhau ac am helpur clwb dychwelyd ir cynghair pel-droed.

Byswn yn hoffi dioch i Geoff Moss a Nev Dickens sydd yn ariannol wedi cadw'r clwb yn rhedeg drost y ddau flwyddyn diwethaf yma. Mae cefnogaeth Geoff wedi bod yn wych a dwi yn fwy na bodlon fod y clwb mwen dwylo saff.

Mae Nev Dickens wedi camu i lawr yn y Rhaf, a byswn yn hoffi dioch iddo am ddod ar clwb allan o weinyddiaeth. Dwi'n siwr buasai Nev wedi hoffi gweld y clwb datblygu ond dywedodd o hyd ei fod eisiau allan ar ol 2 flwyddyn.

Or diwedd, mae'n dda gweld gwynebau newydd ar y bwrdd "Trust", a dwi'n gobeithio fod nhw ar cyfarwyddwyr yn gallu sortio allan eu gwahaniaethau. Mae'r ddau ochr angen rhoi a cymeryd. Mae'r clwb yn fwy pwysig na ni i gyd, ac yn bwysig i De Cymru. Rydym i gyd angen mynd ar clwb yma ymlaen.

**Arfon Griffiths
MBE**

Edrych ymlaen wrth edrych yn ôl

Wrth edrych ymlaen at y tymor newydd yn y Conference, mae'n anorfod ein bod ni'n mynd i edrych yn ôl ar y tymor a fu. 'Dwi'n siŵr nad fi oedd yr unig gefnogwr oedd wedi rhagweld y cwymp yn gynnar iawn yn y tymor a 'dwi'n siŵr nad fi ydi'r unig gefnogwr sydd â barn ynghylch pwy sydd ar fai ... ond nid dyna bwrpas yr erthygl yma.

'Dwi'n mynd i edrych yn ôl ymhellach na'r tymor diwethaf, yn wir, 'dwi am fynd yr holl ffordd yn ôl i 1992. Roedd Wrecsam wedi gorffen tymor 1991/92 yn nythu rhwng Chesterfield a Walsall yng nghanol y bedwaredd adran. Steve Watkin oedd ein prif sgoriwr gyda Karl Connolly yn ail agos ond, wrth gwrs, uchafbwynt y tymor oedd y fuddugoliaeth dros Arsenal yn nhrydedd rownd Cwpan FA Lloegr.

Yn wir, dyma oedd prif stori bêl-droed Cymru ym 1992 ... ond roedd 'na stori chwyldroadol arall ar fin cychwyn hefyd - roedd Cymdeithas Bêl-droed Cymru wedi penderfynu sefydlu Cynghrair Bêl-droed Cenedlaethol.

Mae sefyllfa clybiau Cymru yn Lloegr yn un dyrys ond yn un hanesyddol. Byth ers i'r Derwyddon gyrraedd rownd wyth olaf Cwpan FA Lloegr yn 1883, roedd clybiau gorau Cymru yn edrych tua Lloegr am her bêl-droed.

Roedd sefydlu cynghrair cenedlaethol yn gam oedd bron i ganrif yn rhy hwyr gan Gymdeithas Bêl-droed Cymru, ond yn gam pwysig er mwyn diogelu annibyniaeth y Gymdeithas a'r tîm cenedlaethol. Er hyn, roedd sefydlu'r gynghrair yn achos cryn gur pen i Gymdeithas Bêl-droed Cymru gyda chlybiau fel Bangor, Caernarfon a'r Barri, oedd yn glybiau cymharol lewyrchus yn y pyramid pêl-droed Seisnig, yn gwrthod ymuno â'r sefydliad newydd.

Roedd Bangor, Bae Colwyn, Y Barri, Caernarfon, Casnewydd, Y Drenewydd, Merthyr a'r Rhyl - neu'r "Irate Eight", fel a'u gelwir gan y wasg Gymreig - yn bygwth mynd â'r Gymdeithas Bêl-droed i'r llys oni bai eu bod yn cael parhau i chwarae pêl-droed dros y ffin yn Lloegr.

Fe drodd y sefyllfa'n hyll iawn cydag ambell i aelod o'r Gymdeithas yn gwneud sylwadau haerllug am y clybiau a chydag ambell i glwb yn symud allan o Gymru'n gyfan gwbwl er mwyn cael parhau i chwarae dros Glawdd Offa.

Wedi hir a hwyr, ac er gwaetha'r fuddugoliaeth yn yr Uchel Lys, penderfynodd Bangor, Y Barri, Y Drenewydd, Y Rhyl a Chaernarfon ymuno â Chynghrair Cymru ond mae Merthyr, Casnewydd a Bae Colwyn - yr alltudion - wedi parhau i frwydro ym mhyramid Lloegr.

Camwch ymlaen 16 mlynedd ac mae Wrecsam bellach wedi ymuno efo'r alltudion fel pedwerydd clwb "non-lîg" Cymreig. Heb fod yn amharchus, mae'n deimlad od iawn clywed Wrecsam yn cael eu trin a'u trafod yn yr un straeon papur newydd ac yn yr un sgyrsiau pêl-droed â Merthyr, Casnewydd a Bae Colwyn? Pwy fyddai wedi dychmygu'r prynhawn hwnnw ar ôl trechu Arsenal, mai edrych ymlaen at deithio i Lewes, Crawley a Salisbury fyddai cefnogwyr Wrecsam yn 2008?

Ond wedi dweud hynny, beth ydyn ni, fel cefnogwyr, wedi ei ddathlu yn yr 16 mlynedd ers trechu'r Gunners? 'Does 'na'm llawer o ddigwyddiadau'n llamu i'r cof, mae'n rhaid i mi gyfaddef ... ambell i fuddugoliaeth yng Nghwpan FA Lloegr yn erbyn Ipswich a Birmingham ... un fuddugoliaeth ac ymddangosiad yn Stadiwm y Mileniwm ar gyfer Tlws yr LDV ... hyn oll mewn 16 mlynedd.

Gofynnwch i unrhyw gefnogwr Wrecsam dros ei 25 mlwydd oed pa gêm ydi ei uchafbwynt o wylio'r Robins - ia, Robins nid Dreigiau - a 'dwi bron yn sicr mai Anderlecht, Porto neu Real Zaragoza fyddai'r enwau fyddai'n cael eu crybwyll. Atgofion o Barry Horne yn rhwydo'n hwyr ym Mhortiwgal, seren ryngwladol yr Iseldiroedd, Robbie Rensenbrink yn torri ein calonnau yn rownd wyth olaf Cwpan Enillwyr Cwpanau Ewrop ac o gôl Chris Armstrong yn Lyngby . Go brin mai gemau yn erbyn Scunthorpe, Rotherham neu Halifax fyddai'n llamu i'r cof!

Y cwestiwn mawr felly, wrth baratoi i groesawu Crawley Town a Kettering i'r Cae Ras, ydi pam na ddylwn ni fod yn paratoi i groesawu Caersws a Chaernarfon? Pam na ddylwn ni ystyried symud yn ôl dros y ffin i fod yn glwb anferth yn Uwch Gynghrair Cymru? Wrth i Lanelli fwynhau eu tymor cyntaf yng Nghynghrair y Pencampwyr ac wrth i Fangor a'r Seintiau Newydd gystadlu yng Nghwpan Uefa unwaith eto, ydi hi'n deg gofyn pwy wnaeth y penderfyniad call yn ôl ym 1992 - Merthyr 'ta Bangor? Bae Colwyn 'ta'r Barri? Penderfynwch chi ...

Gary Pritchard - BBC Radio Cymru

Section 2:
Who's Who In The Blue Square Premier League 2008/09

Blue Square Premier League Clubs

Relegation to the Blue Square Premier League after 87 years as a Football League Club was a bitter pill to swallow, but now we are there, we look forward to visiting new and old haunts. The following pages gives an insight to those clubs we will be visting over the coming season.

Relegated with us was Mansfield Town, who themselves had been a Football League club for 77 years, while exchanging places with us, are former league clubs, champions Aldershot Town and Exeter City, who overcome Cambridge United in the play-off final, which hopefully gives us all heart that we can regain our Football League status at the earliest opportunity.

Former Football League clubs in the Blue Square Premier League are Barrow, Cambridge, Kidderminster Harriers, Mansfield Town, Oxford United, Rushden & Diamonds, Torquay United and York City. Let's hope for a good season.

WHO'S WHO IN THE BLUE SQUARE PREMIER LEAGUE

ALTRINCHAM

Formed in 1903 Altrincham won the Cheshire Amateur Cup in 1904, and a year later they won the Manchester League title and Cheshire Senior Cup.

After WW1 they became founder members of the Cheshire County League, but it wasn't until the 1930's that they won the Cheshire League Cup in 1933 and the Cheshire Senior Cup in successive years.

After WW2 little success came until Noel White and Peter Swales bought the club in the 60s. With Freddie Pye as manager, Altrincham won the Cheshire League Cup in 1964 and 1966, the latter year winning the League title for the first time and reachng the FA Cup 3rd round.

'The Robins' first appeared in the F.A. Cup competition proper in 1934, but it was during the 70's that they enjoyed much success; the highlights were drawing at Everton and winning the F. A. Trophy at Wembley in 1978.

They were founder members of the Alliance Premier League in 1979 winning the Title in its first two years and failing, by one vote, to gain election to the Football League in 1980.

Further success in the F. A. Cup came with a draw at Spurs, and a visit to Anfield in 1980/81. In 1986 they won the F.A. Trophy again and in the F.A. Cup became only the second non-league side to defeat a Division One club on its own ground, when they beat Birmingham at St. Andrew's

The 90's were a mixed period with the club being relegated for the first time in 1996-97, but two years later they won the Unibond Premier League.

Ground: Moss Lane
Capacity: 6,085
Founded: 1903
Nickname: The Robins
Manager:
Graham Heathcote
Last Season
Position: 21st
Points: 41
Average Att.: 1,176
This Season
Home: Mon 13th Apr
Away: Mon 25th Aug
Title Odds: 80/1
**How To Get There
From The Racecourse**:
A483 – A55 (s/p
Ellesmere Port) – M53
(to J11) - M56 (to J6) -
Go straight on at traffic
lights (Delahays Road
[A5144] is the right turn
at these lights) and take
third road on right
(Westminster Road) and
continue straight on for
half a mile or so, down
a slight hill with speed
humps, to Moss Lane.
Ground is on the right.
**Nearest railway
station:**
Altrincham (0.6 miles)

WHO'S WHO IN THE BLUE SQUARE PREMIER LEAGUE

BARROW

Barrow were founded on July 16th 1901 at the old Drill Hall in the Strand and played at the Strawberry Ground, Roosecote and Ainslie Street before moving to their current stadium, Holker Street, in 1909.

After early years spent in the Lancashire Combination, the club became founder members of the Football League Third Division North in 1921.where they remained until the reorganisation of that league in 1958 when Barrow found themselves in the Division Four.

The club achieved its first ever promotion in 1967 to Division Three, but the joy was short lived when in 1969 they lost manager Colin Appleton through ill health. Within three seasons they had been voted out of the Football League, being replaced by Hereford United.

They then played in the Northern Premier League, until they were elected to the Alliance Premier League in 1979, and where they remained until they were relegated back into the Northern Premier League in 1983.

Since then they have enjoyed two promotions into the Conference. One in 1989, only to be relegated to the then HFS Loans League in 1992. In 1998 they won promotion again, but after just one season they were relegated. They then achieved modest positions in the Premier Division without ever really threatening to return to the Conference, although they finished runners-up in 2003.

Much the same happened the following year when the club finished third and claimed a place in the new Conference North, where they remained until last season when they beat Stalybridge Celtic 1-0 at Burton to send the Bluebirds into the Blue Square Premier League.

Ground: Holker Street
Capacity: 4,006
Founded: 1901
Nickname: The Bluebirds
Manager: Dave Bayliss & Darren Sheridan
Last Season Position: 5th
Points: 76
Average Att.: 1,066
This Season Home: Thurs 1st Jan
Away: Fri 26th Dec
Title Odds: 66/1
How To Get There From The Racecourse: A483 – A55 (s/p Ellesmere Port) – M53 (to J11) - M56 (to J9) – M6 (to J36) - A590 (s/p Kendal) - Stay on A590 until it starts to rise, pass over railway line until the Travel Lodge in Barrow where you turn left.
Nearest railway station: Barrow (0.6 miles)

WHO'S WHO IN THE BLUE SQUARE PREMIER LEAGUE

BURTON ALBION

Burton Albion came the closest ever of becoming a Football League club last season, losing in the play-off semi-finals 4-3 on aggregate to Cambridge United.

One of Burton's principal industries is brewing, and hence the club's nickname is the 'Brewers'. Albion can claim line-age from Burton Swifts F.C., Burton Town F.C., Burton United F.C., and Burton Wanderers F.C., who were all failed football clubs.

Ground:
The Pirelli Stadium
Capacity: 5,000
Founded: 1950
Nickname:
The Brewers
Manager:
Nigel Clough
Last Season
Position: 5th
Points: 81
Average Att.: 2,913
This Season
Home: Tues 2nd Sep
Away: Sat 21st Feb
Title Odds: 14/1
How To Get There From The Racecourse:
A483 – A5 – M54 – A5 – A38 – Take the 2nd Burton exit onto the A5121 Burton/Clay Mills – over the 1st island at the next island turn right into Princess Way. The entrance to the stadium is 300 yards on the right.
Nearest railway station:
Burton on Trent (1 mile)

Albion began life at the Lloyds Foundry ground on Wellington Street in the Birmingham & District League, but high atten-dances meant that the club quickly searched for a more suit-able home.

Eton Park was built off Derby Road and officially opened on September 20, 1958, coinciding with their promotion to the Southern League. From then until its demolition in 2005 the Brewers played all of their home games at Eton Park (it was also used as the home ground for many Derby County reserve matches).

It was demolished to make way for housing, as the club had just completed a new stadium, at a cost of £7.2 million. It is situated directly opposite Eton Park and was named the Pirelli Stadium, situated as it was a short distance from Pirelli's factory in Burton.

In 1979 the club joined the Northern Premier League, rejoin-ing the Southern League in 1987, before switching back in 2001/02 and winning the Northern Premier League title and promotion to the Conference League.

WHO'S WHO IN THE BLUE SQUARE PREMIER LEAGUE

CAMBRIDGE UNITED

Initially formed as Abbey United after the Abbey district of Cambridge, the club played in local amateur leagues in its early years, moving grounds around Cambridge before settling at the Abbey Stadium. They changed its name to Cambridge United in 1951. Playing in the Eastern Counties League they were runners-up in 57/58, and promoted to the Southern League.

Three years later, they reached the Southern League Premier Division where they remained until election to the Football League in 1970, replacing Bradford Park Avenue.

The early 1990s, saw John Beck lead the U's to the first ever play-off final at Wembley, gaining promotion from Division 4, and reaching the FA Cup quarter-finals in 1990 and 1991;

They won Division Three in 1991, and reached the play-offs in 1992, but failed in their bid to become founder members of the Premier League. This was the club's highest final league placing to date. The following season saw them relegated.

Further relegation followed two seasons later. They returned to Division Two but were relegated in 2002. In 2005, after 35 years in the Football League, Cambridge United were relegated into the Conference.

The club filed for administration in 2005, but it took an eleventh hour bid and the intervention of then sports minister Richard Caborn, and the sale of their Abbey Stadium home for £1.9 million to keep the club afloat.

Last season saw them fail in their bid to return to the Football League when they lost to Exeter City at Wembley.

Ground:
The Abbey Stadium
Capacity: 9,617
Founded: 1912
Nickname: The U's
Manager:
Gary Brabin
Last Season
Position: 2nd
Points: 86
Average Att.: 3,551
This Season
Home: Sat 24th Jan
Away: Sat 6th Sep
Title Odds: 11/1
How To Get There From The Racecourse:
A483 – A5 – M54 (to J1) – M6 (to J1a) – A14 (head for Cambridge/Newmarket) – Leave A14 on B1047 – Turn right at top of slip road - Follow road through the village of Fen Ditton to T-junction and traffic lights - Turn right and go straight over at roundabout - Ground is on the left hand side after ½ mile.
Nearest railway Station:
Cambridge (4 miles)

WHO'S WHO IN THE BLUE SQUARE PREMIER LEAGUE

CRAWLEY TOWN

A conference club since 2004, Crawley Town was formed in 1896 and played their formative years in the West Sussex League. Five seasons later they entered the Mid-Sussex League and won the Senior Division in only their second season.

Crawley remained in Junior Football until they entered the Sussex County League in 1951, although they had played in an Emergency County League competition in 1945/46.

Ground:
Broadfield Stadium
Capacity: 4,996
Founded: 1896
Nickname:
The Red Devils
Manager:
Steve Evans
Last Season
Position: 15th
Points: 60
Average Att.: 1,042
This Season
Home: Sat 21st Mar
Away: Sat 31st Jan
Title Odds: 33/1
**How To Get There
From The Racecourse:**
A483 – A5 – M54 (to J1) – M6 (to J8) – M5 (to J4) – M42 (to J3a) – M40 (to J1a) – M25 (to J7) – M23 (to J11 Pease Pottage) – Take 4th exit and continue to roundabout (landmarked by a large football) – Take the 1st exit which enters the stadium car park.
Nearest railway station:
Crawley (2 miles)

Four seasons in Division One ended in relegation, but Crawley returned to the First Division immediately as runners-up. The club then switched to the Metropolitan League, a competition for both professional and amateur sides.

The club adopted professional status in 1962 and joined the Southern League the following year. For the next 20 years the 'Red Devils' played in the First Division in its various guises, apart from a brief taste of Premier Division football in 1969/70.

In 1983/84 the Sussex club finished as runners-up to RS Southampton and returned to the Premier Division, where they remained until 2003/04 when they won a Southern League treble; and promotion to the Conference League.

In July 2005 the club was sold to new owners, and a month later they made the historic decision to turn full-time.. However, the club went into Administration in 2006, but despite this set back and point reductions they have overcome off the field problems to remain in the Conference League.

WHO'S WHO IN THE BLUE SQUARE PREMIER LEAGUE

EASTBOURNE BOROUGH

Eastbourne Borough were formed in 1964 as Langney FC. They competed in the Eastbourne & District Football League Division 2. Prior to 1968/69 the name changed to Langney Sports F.C., having played on local recreation grounds before moving to Princes Park near the seafront.

1973/74 saw promotion to the Eastbourne & Hastings League Premier Division, and in 1983 elected as a founder member of Division 3 of the Sussex County League. At the same time moving to its current home ground at Priory Lane, in the heart of the residential area of Langney.

Langney Sports became Third Division champions in 1987, and a year later promotion to Division 1. They became Sussex County League Champions in 2000, and were promoted to the Eastern Division of the Southern League.

In 2001 the club was renamed Eastbourne Borough to be identified with the town of Eastbourne. In 2004 they were promoted to the Premier Division, but though they only finished 11th in their first season, they were elevated to the newly-formed Conference South for the start of 2004/5.

They missed out on a further promotion in 2006 by losing 2-1 to Altrincham in the North/South play-off final at Stoke City, but they reached the Blue Square Premier League for the first time with a 2-0 win over Hampton & Richmond in the Blue Square South 2008 Play-off final at Stevenage..

The club are regarded as a top non-league team which has won the sportmanship award several years running. The club is renowned for its very friendly atmosphere.

Ground: Langney Sports Club
Capacity: 5,664
Founded: 1964
Nickname: The Sports
Manager: Garry Wilson
Last Season
Position: 2nd
Points: 80
Average Att.: 871
This Season
Home: Sat 20th Dec
Away: Sat 7th Mar
Title Odds: 80/1
How To Get There
From The Racecourse:
A483 – A5 – M54 (to J1) – M6 (to J8) – M5 (to J4) – M42 (to J3a) – M40 (to J1a) – M25 (to J7) – M23 - A27 - from Brighton, turn left at Polegate traffic lights, and head eastwards on A27.At next roundabout, take 2nd exit A22; another roundabout shortly afterwards, take 1st exit s/p Stone Cross & Westham. Continue towards Stone Cross village, past Dittons Nursery on left. Go to crossroads, with Red Lion pub on the right. Turn right, on to B2104. At the end of Friday Street, turn left into Hide Hollow (B2191), passing Crematorium on right. Turn right at roundabout into Priory Road, and Priory Lane is about 200 yards down the road on the left.

WHO'S WHO IN THE BLUE SQUARE PREMIER LEAGUE

EBBSFLEET UNITED

Originally formed as Gravesend & Northfleet F.C. in 1946, after a merger between Gravesend United (originally formed in 1893) and Northfleet United (originally formed in 1890) with the new club retaining the red & white home colours (and the Stonebridge Road stadium) of Northfleet United.

In 1979, the team was one of the founder members of the Alliance Premier League (now the Blue Square Premier), but were relegated back into the Southern League Premier two seasons later.

Gravesend & Northfleet joined the Isthmian League in 1997/98, playing in the Premier Division of the league until 2001/02, when they finished as champions and earned promotion back into the Conference, where they have since remained.

Following a public consultation meeting on 1st May 2007 the club changed its name to Ebbsfleet United, gaining a sponsorship deal with Eurostar, whose trains serve Ebbsfleet International railway station.

Since February 2008, the club has been owned by the web-based venture MyFootballClub, whose members may vote on team selection and player transfers, instead of those decisions being made exclusively by the club's management and staff as at most other clubs.

Last season they beat Aldershot Town to reach the FA Trophy final, and secure the club's first trip to Wembley where they beat Torquay United 2-1. The club is currently looking to build a new stadium in the Ebbsfleet Valley.

Ground:
Stonebridge Road
Capacity: 5,011
Founded: 1946
Nickname:
The Fleet
Manager:
Liam Daish
Last Season
Position: 11th
Points: 69
Average Att.: 1,087
This Season
Home: Sat 13th Sep
Away: Sat 3rd Jan
Title Odds: 14/1
**How To Get There
From The Racecourse:**
A483 – A5 – M54 (to J1) – M6 (to J1) – M1 (to J7) – M25 (to J2) – A2 (to 2nd exit s/p Northfleet/Southfleet) – Follow B262 to Northfleet – then B2175 (Springfield Road) – Straight ahead at 1st roundabout – At 2nd roundabout take 2nd exit (Thames Way) – Follow signs to stadium.
Nearest railway station:
Northfleet (0.5 miles)

WHO'S WHO IN THE BLUE SQUARE PREMIER LEAGUE

FOREST GREEN ROVERS

Forest Green Rovers are based in Nailsworth, Gloucestershire. The club was founded in 1890 as Nailsworth & Forest Green and joined the Stroud & District League where they remained for the first 32 years of their existence.

They were founder members of the Gloucestershire Northern Senior League in 1922 which they were to win three times in 1935, 1950 and 1951. In 1968 they were founder members of the Gloucestershire County League where they remained for seven seasons with an average finishing position of 6th.

They joined the Hellenic League in 1975, and in 1981/82 they clinched the Hellenic League championship and the FA Vase. They moved into the Southern League where they finished third in their maiden season in the Midland Division.

However, in subsequent seasons they failed to make much impact, and in 1989 the club changed its name to Stroud F.C.. This highly opposed move failed to improve the club's fortune and the name was changed back to Forest Green Rovers for the 1992/93 season.

Two successive promotions in 1997 and 1998 to the Conference National where they finished 12th in their first season. A run to the final of the FA Trophy saw them lose 1-0 at Wembley Stadium to Kingstonian. Another appearance in the FA Trophy final in 2001 saw another 1-0 defeat, this time to Canvey Island at Villa Park.

In August 2006 they moved grounds just 300 yards up the road from the old ground to the New Lawn.

Ground:
The New Lawn
Capacity: 5,147
Founded: 1890
Nickname:
The Rovers
Manager:
Jimmy Harvey
Last Season
Position: 8th
Points: 71
Average Att.: 1,178
This Season
Home: Tues 18th Nov
Away: Sat 4th Oct
Title Odds: 28/1
How To Get There
From The Racecourse:
A483 – A5 – M54 (to J1) – M6 (to J8) – M5 (to J13) – A46 to Nailsworth – At mini roundabout in the town turn right up Spring Hill to Forest Green – The stadium is half a mile up the hill on the left.
Nearest railway Station:
Stroud (4 miles)

WHO'S WHO IN THE BLUE SQUARE PREMIER LEAGUE

Ground:
The New Recreation
Ground
Capacity: 4,500
Founded: 1890
Nickname:
The Blues
Manager:
Micky Woodward
Last Season
Position: 10th
Points: 70
Average Att.: 907
This Season
Home: Sat 14th Feb
Away: Sat 20th Sep
Title Odds: 14/1
**How To Get There
From The Racecourse**:
A483 – A5 – M54 (to J1)
– M6 (to J1) – M1 (to J7)
– M25 (to J30) – A13 (to
Tilbury) 2nd exit to
roundabout – 4th exit to
Chadwell St Marys and
Grays – 2nd right into
Bradleigh Avenue – Turn
right at end of road and
then left into Bridge
Road – Ground is 500
yards on right.
Nearest railway Station:
Grays (0.5 miles)

GRAYS ATHLETIC

Grays Athletic were established in 1890 and became founder members of the Athenian League, in which they briefly played before World War I (1912-14 and again since 1958).

In 1945 they were one of the nine founder members of the Corinthian League, which they won that first season. After playing in the Isthmian League between 1983 and 2004, they were founder members of the new Conference South, and became divisional champions at the first attempt.

They were also to win the FA Trophy two years in a row, first in 2005 with a 6-5 penalties win over Hucknall Town at Villa Park, and then with a 2-0 win over Woking in 2006 at Upton Park.

The 2005/06 season also saw them take an early lead in the Conference, remaining unbeaten for a record equalling 15 games, but they eventually finished in third place, and were beaten in the semi-finals of the promotion play-offs by Halifax Town.

Grays currently play at the New Recreation Ground, which has been their home since 1906. The future of this location has been proposed to be developed into residential properties, and in April 2008 chairman Micky Woodward announced that the club plan to move to a new 7,500 all-seater stadium located in Aveley, Thurrock - approximately five and a half miles away from their current home..

WHO'S WHO IN THE BLUE SQUARE PREMIER LEAGUE

HISTON

Histon FC is based in the twin villages of Histon and Impington, approx three miles north of Cambridge.

Last season they competed for the first time in the Conference National, after having won and been promoted from the Conference South in 2006/07, the highest level that the club has ever reached.

Nicknamed The Stutes, originating from the club's previous name Histon Institute, they play their home matches at Bridge Road in Impington. The club crest features a rose, the flower representing the rose-covered field given to the club by local firm Chivers. Chivers was a jam factory, and the major employer in Histon & Impington. The company's chairman, John Chivers, helped to found the Histon Institute in 1903, playing its early football in the Cambridgeshire League

In 1960 the club (which by now had dropped the "Institute" from their name) joined the Delphian League, but just three years later this league disbanded. Histon, along with most of the other member clubs, joined the Athenian League. In 1966 they switched to the Eastern Counties League, where they were to play for nearly 25 years. When the ECL adopted a two-division format, in 1988, Histon were placed in the Premier Division.

Histon's traditional rivals used to be Ely City, but the clubs have not met in recent years and Histon now consider nearer neighbours Cambridge City and Cambridge United as current-day rivals, as they are now in the same division as United, and one above City.

Ground: The Grassworld Stadium
Capacity: 3,800
Founded: 1904
Nickname: The Stutes
Manager: Steve Fallon
Last Season
Position: 7th
Points: 72
Average Att.: 1,063
This Season
Home: Sat 11th Oct
Away: Sat 28th Mar
Title Odds: 33/1
How To Get There
From The Racecourse:
A483 – A5 – M54 (to J1) – M6 (to J1a) – A14 (to M11) – M11 (J14 for A14 Eastbound s/p Newmarket) – A14 (take the first exit onto B1049 s/p Histon/Impington) – Take the 1st left off roundabout, go straight over traffic lights (Holiday Inn hotel on right) – Turn right into ground just before pedestrian crossing.
Nearest railway Station:
Cambridge (4 miles)

WHO'S WHO IN THE BLUE SQUARE PREMIER LEAGUE

KETTERING TOWN

Kettering Town were originally formed in 1872, turning professional in 1891. The club graduated through twelve different leagues from 1892 winning the Midland Football League title in 1896 and 1900.

The Southern League Championship was won on three occasions, in 1928 and 1957 under Tommy Lawton and in 1973 under the guidance of Ron Atkinson.

In the 1930s the club won the East Midlands League and in 1948 the 'Poppies' became Birmingham & District League champions. They became founder members of the Alliance Premier League (now Conference League) in 1979. However, the Football Conference title has so far eluded Kettering, having finished runners-up in 1981, 1989, 1994 and 1998.

The FA Cup has brought success and publicity to the club with the first round proper being reached on 41 occasions. In 1901 the club reached the last sixteen and in more modern times the Poppies reached the fourth round proper in 1988/89.

They have also made the FA Trophy Final at Wembley Stadium on two occasions; the first time was in 1979 when they lost 2-0 to Stafford Rangers; and 2000 saw the Poppies lose a closely fought final with Kingstonian 3-2.

The GMAC Cup was won in 1987 and runners-up in 1995, but the Poppies finally won the Blue Square North division title last season, and thus renew there local rivalry with nearby Rushden & Diamonds.

Ground:
A-Line Arena,
Rockingham Road
Capacity: 6,264
Founded: 1872
Nickname:
The Poppies or Kettles
Manager:
Mark Cooper
Last Season
Position: 1st
Points: 97
Average Att.: 1,497
This Season
Home: Sat 6th Dec
Away: Sat 18th Apr
Title Odds: 33/1
How To Get There
From The Racecourse:
A483 – A5 – M54 (to J1) – M6 (to J1a) – A14 (to J7) – A43 - Travel for one mile, turn right at first roundabout onto A6003 (Rockingham Road) - Ground is 800 yards on the left.
Nearest railway Station:
Kettering (1 mile)

WHO'S WHO IN THE BLUE SQUARE PREMIER LEAGUE

KIDDERMINSTER HARRIERS

Kidderminster Harriers were formed in 1886 from an athletics and rugby union club that had existed for nine years. They were founder members of the Birmingham and District League in 1889, but did not win it until 1938.

They moved to the Southern League the following year, but played just two games because of the onset of World War II, rejoining the Southern League in 1948, but in 1960 dropped back down to the Birmingham League. They were back to the Southern League by 1970, and in 1983 were promoted to the Alliance Premier League (now the Conference) after finishing second to AP Leamington, who were refused entry.

Harriers were Welsh Cup finalists in 1986 and 1989, but in 1994, they were Conference champions, although they were controversially refused promotion due to the Football League's tightened safety regulations for stadiums after the Bradford City fire disaster.

Aggborough's main stand was of wooden construction, and despite assurances a new cantilever stand would be ready for the new season (which was completed on time) the Football League rejected Harriers' promotion.

Former Liverpool star Jan Mølby was appointed manager for 1999/00, and he led the club to the Conference title at the first attempt, but after five seasons they were relegated back to the Conference. One recent bright spot was their trip to the FA Trophy Final at Wembley, but lost 3-2 to Stevenage Borough. It was the first competitive game to be played at the new Wembley. Harriers in doing so became the first team to play at both the old and new Wembley.

Ground: Aggborough
Capacity: 6,238
Founded: 1886
Nickname: Harriers
Manager: Mark Yates
Last Season
Position: 13th
Points: 67
Average Att.: 1,556
This Season
Home: Tues 24th Feb
Away: Sat 22nd Nov
Title Odds: 25/1
How To Get There
From The Racecourse:
A483 – A5 (to exit on Shrewsbury by-pass s/p A458 Bridgnorth) – A458 (to Bridgnorth s/p A442 Kidderminster) – A458 (Enter Kidderminster and follow town centre and s/p A449 Worcester) – A442 – A456 – A451 (to roundabout with A448 s/p Bromsgrove) - Take first right into Hoo Road – The ground is 500 yards up the hill on the left.
Nearest railway Station:
Kidderminster (0.5 mile)

WHO'S WHO IN THE BLUE SQUARE PREMIER LEAGUE

LEWES

Lewes Football Club was formed at a meeting at a local pub in 1885 and initially wore green shirts designed to evoke the surrounding South Downs. The present red and black kit was adopted in 1893.

The club have always played their home matches at the Dripping Pan (often just called The Pan). The ground itself is known to have been used for football matches prior to the formation of the current club.

Having won the championship of the Mid Sussex League twice before WWI, Lewes became founder members of the Sussex County League in 1920. They were runners-up four times, but it wasn't until 1964/65 that they finally won the title, and promotion to the Athenian League. After winning the Division 2 title in 1968, promotion to the Premier Division followed just two years later when the club won the Division One title.

In 1977 Lewes joined the newly expanded Isthmian League, initially in Division Two, and won promotion in 1980, but in 1991 the Rooks were relegated. They bounced back at the first attempt but could only manage one season at this level before two successive relegations saw them in Division Three.

1998/99 saw Jimmy Quinn as manager and the club claimed two consecutive promotions, taking them to the Isthmian League Division One South. In 2003/04 they were champions and stepped up to the Conference South via play-off's, and in effect jumping two divisions. Last season saw them win promotion as Conference South champions and reach the top division in non-league football for the first time.

Ground:
Dripping Pan
Capacity: 3,000
Founded: 1885
Nickname: The Rooks
Manager: Kevin Keehan
Last Season
Position: 1st
Points: 89
Average Att.: 857
This Season
Home: Sat 1st Nov
Away: Sat 7th Feb
Title Odds: 125/1
**How To Get There
From The Racecourse**:
A483 – A5 – M54 (to J1) – M6 (to J8) – M5 (to J4) – M42 (to J3a) – M40 (to J1a) – M25 (to J7) – M23 (to A23) – A23 (to A27) – A27 (After five miles to first roundabout take 1st exit to Lewes) – Follow road to traffic lights at Lewes Prison – Turn right into Winterbourne Hollow and Bell Lane to mini round-about – Turn left into Southover High Street – Cross two mini round-abouts to Mountfield Road – Ground is on your right.
Nearest railway Station:
Lewes (200 yards)

WHO'S WHO IN THE BLUE SQUARE PREMIER LEAGUE

MANSFIELD TOWN

Mansfield Town was founded in 1897 under the name of Mansfield Wesleyans. Like many football clubs, the Stags can trace their origins to a local church, in this case the Wesleyan church on Bridge Street.

The present name was adopted by the club in the summer of 1910. By this time Stags had moved to their present home, Field Mill. Football has been played at the ground since 1861 and is widely regarded as one of the oldest football stadiums in the world.

After several attempts, Stags finally won election to the Football League in 1931. They narrowly missed promotion to the Second Division in 1964/65, but the most successful period in Stags' League history came during the 1970s, when they claimed the Division Four title in 1974/75, and were then promoted to the second tier for the only time in their history in 1976/77.

The Stags reached Wembley for the only time in 1987 as they captured the Freight Rover Trophy by beating Bristol City 5-4 on penalties after a 1-1 draw. The club went into decline in the 1990s, being relegated back to the bottom division in 1991. In 1994/95 they made the play-offs, only to lose against arch-rivals Chesterfield and miss out on a place in the final.

The Stags gained promotion to Division Two in 2001/02, only to be relegated back after only one season. In 2003/04 they reached the play-off final, but lost in the Millennium Stadium on penalties to Huddersfield. The club has been in turmoil the past two years, with fans demanding the removal of owner, Keith Haslam. Last season, along with ourselves, they lost their Football League status after 77 years.

Ground:
Field Mill
Capacity: 8,000
Founded: 1897
Nickname: The Stags
Manager:
Billy McEwan
Last Season
Position: 23rd
Points: 42
Average Att.: 2,821
This Season
Home: Sat 4th Apr
Away: Sat 18th Oct
Title Odds: 10/1
How To Get There
From The Racecourse:
A534 (to Nantwich) – A500 (to Stoke on Trent) – A500 (to Brittania Stadium) - A50 (s/p Uttoxeter) A50 (s/p Derby) – A38 (s/p M1 North) – A38 – A617 – A38 (s/p Mansfield turn right onto A6009) – A6009 – A60 – Turn right into Bishop Street.
Nearest railway Station:
Mansfield on the Robin Hood Line from Nottingham (five minute walk)

WHO'S WHO IN THE BLUE SQUARE PREMIER LEAGUE

NORTHWICH VICTORIA

Northwich Victoria's records go back to 1874. They played at the same Drill Field ground for over 125 years, but after a ground sharing period with local rivals Witton Albion they started 2005/06 in their new stadium (Victoria Stadium) in Wincham, just outside Northwich and across the Trent & Mersey Canal which separates them from Witton Albion.

The club were briefly members of the Football League Division 2 from 1892-94, but otherwise played in various regional leagues until joining the newly formed Cheshire County League after WWI, wiining the title just once.

In 1968 they became founder members of the Northern Premier League, and in 1979 founder members of the Alliance Premier League (later the Conference), and were the last club to be ever-present in that league (1979-2005).

1984 saw the Vics win the FA Trophy with a 2-1 replay win over Bangor City. In 2005 the club went into administration, but were voluntarily demoted due to legal problems and FA deadlines over the transfer of their Conference membership to the club's new owners. The alternative would have been outright expulsion from the Conference, which would have forced them into starting again in one of the lower regional divisions.

2005/06 saw them crowned Conference North Champions, but in October 2007 the club again went into administration to stave off closure, but with the loss of ten points they still managed to escape relegation.

Ground:
Victoria Stadium
Capacity: 4,500
Founded: 1874
Nickname:
The Vics
Manager:
Dino Maamria
Last Season
Position: 19th
Points: 44
Average Att.: 908
This Season
Home: Tues 27th Jan
Away: Tues 9th Dec
Title Odds: 50/1
**How To Get There
From The Racecourse**:
A483 – A55 (s/p
Ellesmere Port) – M53
(to J11) - M56 (to J10) –
A559 – Follow the road
until the Renault
Garage on the left –
Turn left into Wincham
Avenue – The ground
is at the bottom of the
road on the right.
**Nearest railway
Station:**
Northwich (1 mile) or
Hartford (2 miles)

WHO'S WHO IN THE BLUE SQUARE PREMIER LEAGUE

OXFORD UNITED

Oxford United was formed as amateur club Headington in 1893, adding the suffix United the following year. It was created by Rev John Scott-Tucker, the vicar at the local church and a local doctor named Robert Hitchings.

Headington had no permanent home until 1913, when they were able to purchase Wootten's Field on London Road, but this was developed on in 1920. A permanent home was finally found in 1926, when they purchased the Manor Ground site, where they remained until 2001 when they moved to the Kassam Stadium.

Competing in local leagues, they were elected to the Southern League and becoming professional in 1949. In 1960, Headington United was renamed Oxford United in order to give it a higher profile, and two years later they were elected to the Football League after winning the Southern Premier League.

They reached the Division Two in 1968, but were relegated in 1976. Between 1984 and 1986 the club earned successive promotions into the First Division, and also won the League Cup, but were unable to enter the 1987 UEFA Cup because of the UEFA ban on English clubs in Europe.

Relegation from the top flight in 1988 began an 18-year decline which eventually saw the club relegated to the Conference in 2006, becoming the first team in the history of English football to have won a major trophy and to be relegated from the Football League.

Ground:
Kassam Stadium
Capacity: 12,500
Founded: 1893
Nickname:
The U's
Manager:
Darren Patterson
Last Season
Position: 9th
Points: 71
Average Att.: 4,581
This Season
Home: Thurs 21st Aug
Away: Sat 11th Apr
Title Odds: 9/1
How To Get There
From The Racecourse:
A483 – A5 – M54 (to J1) – M6 (to J8) – M5 – M42 (to J3a) – M40 (to J9) – A34 - A423 (s/p London) A4074 (s/p Reading) – Grenoble Road to ground
Nearest railway Station:
Oxford (5 miles) Special bus service to and from ground for league matches

WHO'S WHO IN THE BLUE SQUARE PREMIER LEAGUE

RUSHDEN & DIAMONDS

Rushden and Diamonds were formed on the 21st of April 1992 by a merger of Rushden Town and Irthlingborough Diamonds. The merger was the brainchild of Max Griggs, the owner of Dr. Martens.

The new club took Rushden Town's place in the Midland Division of the Sourthern League, but played at Irthlingborough's Nene Park as Rushden's Hayden Road was not good enough for promotion (they had been demoted from the Premier Division the previous season due to the state of their ground).

Rushden and Diamonds won promotion to the Southern League Premier Division in 1993 and Football Conference in 1996. Under Brian Talbot's guidance, after three near-misses they finally won promotion to the Football League in 2001 as champions.

In their first season they reached the Division Three play-off final but lost to Cheltenham Town. In 2003 they won the Third Division championship on the last day of the season - their third promotion/league title in eight seasons.

2003/04 saw the club start on a downward slope when they were relegated. In the summer of 2005, Max Griggs handed over the club and certain assets to a Supporters' Trust, along with an initial cash pledge, but the new regime couldn't stop the club being relegated to the Conference at the end of the season. Last season saw Rushden finish runners up of the Setanta Shield losing out to Aldershot after a penalty shoot out.

Ground:
Nene Park
Capacity: 6,441
Founded: 1992
Nickname:
The Diamonds
Manager:
Garry Hill
Last Season
Position: 16th
Points: 59
Average Att.: 1,586
This Season
Home: Tues 23rd Sep
Away: Sat 16th Aug
Title Odds: 9/1
How To Get There
From The Racecourse:
A483 – A5 – M54 (to J1) – M6   (to J1a) – A14 (to J10) – A6 (s/p Bedford) – B5348 (s/p Irthlingborough) - B571 to ground.
Nearest railway Station:
Wellingborough (6 miles)

WHO'S WHO IN THE BLUE SQUARE PREMIER LEAGUE

SALISBURY CITY

Salisbury City were founded as simply Salisbury F.C. in 1947. A previous club had existed under the name Salisbury City prior to World War II but the current club does not consider itself to be connected to this club and uses the 1947 date of formation.

The new club immediately entered the Western League and won the Second Division title at the very first attempt. They remained members of the Western League until 1968, winning the championship in 1958 and 1961. In 1968 the club was elected to the Southern Football League but met with little success until 1985/86 when Salisbury finished as runners up to Cambridge City and were promoted to the Premier Division, albeit only for a single season.

In 1993 the club's name was officially changed to Salisbury City, and in 1994/95 they won the Southern League Southern Division championship. After redevelopment work at the council-owned Victoria Park, the club was able to step up to the Premier Division, a promotion which had been denied them two years earlier due to ground gradings.

Salisbury lasted seven seasons in the Premier Division, but troubles off the field eventually led to relegation, coming close to being wound-up. 2003/04 saw Salisbury win promotion from the Southern League Eastern Division and the re-organisation of the pyramid system saw them placed in the Isthmian League Premier Division, although after one season they returned to the Southern League Premier Division, but won promotion to the Conference South at the first attempt.

In 2007 they won promotion to the Conference with a play-off win over Braintree Town.

Ground: The Raymond McEnhill Stadium
Capacity: 3,740
Founded: 1947
Nickname: The Whites
Manager: Nick Holmes
Last Season
Position: 12th
Points: 68
Average Att.: 1,543
This Season
Home: Sat 28th Feb
Away: Sat 30th Aug
Title Odds: 40/1
How To Get There
From The Racecourse: A483 – A5 – M54 (to J1) – M6 (to J8) – M5 (to J11a) – A417 (s/p Cirencester) – A419 (s/p Swindon) – A346 (s/p Marlborough) – A338 (s/p S'bury) – A303 (s/p Amesbury) - A345 (s/p S'bury) – pass the turn off for Boscombe Down on the left – Go up hill & through the traffic lights at High Post (hotel and night club on your right) carry on down to the Beehive roundabout – turn left, through the first small roundabout and then left into Partridge Way.
Nearest Rail Station: Salisbury (2.5 miles)

WHO'S WHO IN THE BLUE SQUARE PREMIER LEAGUE

STEVENAGE BOROUGH

Stevenage has had several early football clubs dating back to the 19th century, but the Borough side that we know today was formed in 1976 after the bankruptcy of Stevenage Athletic. The Broadhall Way pitch was dug up with JCB's in a determined effort to ensure it never saw football again.

Since then, with help from the local authority, there has been a continuous re-build of the stadium. The team started out playing in the Chiltern Youth league on a roped off pitch at the town's King George V playing fields and moved up to intermediate status joining the Southern Combination.

In 1980 the club moved back to the Broadhall Way Stadium and the name Borough was added. With the council as their landlords and a refurbished stadium, Stevenage Borough took on senior status and joined the United Counties League. In their first season as a senior club they won the double of United Counties Division One Championship and Cup before switching across the non-league pyramid into the Isthmian League Division Two winning the title in their first season and reaching the quarter-finals of the FA Vase.

The beginning of the 1990's saw Borough win successive titles to win promotion to the Conference in 1995/96. In only their second season they won the league, but were denied promotion to the Football League as their stadium did not meet the requirements for Football League grounds.

The closest they have come since was in a 1-0 defeat to Carlisle United in the 2004/05 Play-off Final. In 2002 Borough reached the FA Trophy Final for the first time in their history, but lost 2-0 to Yeovil at Villa Park, but they made amends in 2007 when they beat Kidderminster Harriers 3-2 in an exciting final at the New Wembley.

Ground:
Broadhall Way Stadium
Capacity: 6,546
Founded: 1976
Nickname:
The Boro
Manager:
Graham Westley
Last Season
Position: 6th
Points: 79
Average Att.: 2,225
This Season
Home: Sat 9th Aug
Away: Sat 29th Nov
Title Odds: 11/2
How To Get There From The Racecourse:
A483 – A5 – M54 (to J1) – M6 (to J1) – M1 (to J7) – M10 – A414 (s/p Hatfield) – A1(M) (to J7) A602 (s/p Stevenage) – follow dual carriageway to second roundabout, take the third exit and ground is 50 yards on the left hand side.
Nearest railway Station:
Stevenage (2 miles)

WHO'S WHO IN THE BLUE SQUARE PREMIER LEAGUE

TORQUAY UNITED

The original Torquay United was formed in 1899 by a group of school-leavers. They joined the East Devon League followed by the Torquay and District League where they won the league title in 1909.

Following a number or mergers, they became Torquay United, and entered the Southern League in 1927, and won their first league title. Capitalising on this momentum, the club succeeded in applying for league membership at the expense of Aberdare Athletic.

Throughout the 1930s Torquay struggled against financial problems, and they also failed to finish higher than 10th in twelve seasons. When league football was resumed in 1946, United continued to struggle.

Promotion to Division Three was gained in 1960, but after only two seasons they were relegated. Frank O'Farrell's appointment in 1965 saw them win a second promotion. Following a relatively uneventful decade they finished bottom of Division Four and applied for re-election for the first time since 1928. A year later the 'Gulls' had to apply for re-election again.

1987/88 saw Torquay reach the Play-Off Final where they lost to Swansea City. Since then they have reached Wembley four times; May 1989 losing 4-1 to Bolton in the Sherpa Van Trophy; Beating Blackpool in a play-off final in 1991 5-4 on penalties after a 2-2 draw; losing 1-0 to Colchester in a play-off final, and losing in last seasons FA Trophy final 1-0 to Ebbsfleet United

2003/04 saw United win promotion for the third time in their history, but lasted only one season. In 2006/07 the Gulls lost their 80 year Football League status.

Ground:
Plainmoor
Capacity: 6,283
Founded: 1899
Nickname: The Gulls
Manager: Paul Buckle
Last Season
Position: 3rd
Points: 86
Average Att.: 2,929
This Season
Home: Sat 27th Sep
Away: Sat 17th Jan
Title Odds: 6/1
How To Get There
From The Racecourse:
A483 – A5 – M54 (to J1) – M6 (to J8) – M5 (to A38) – A38 (until split into two) – A380 (head for Torquay) - Stay on this road, across the roundabout – Penn Inn through Kingskerswell – Across a 2nd roundabout, left hand lane of dual carriageway – After 3rd set of traffic lights follow signs to left for TUFC
Nearest railway Station:
Torre (30 mins on foot) & Torquay (on sea front)

WHO'S WHO IN THE BLUE SQUARE PREMIER LEAGUE

Ground: Wessex Stadium
Capacity: 6,500
Founded: 1890
Nickname: The Terras
Manager: John Hollins
Last Season
Position: 18th
Points: 46
Average Att.: 1,340
This Season
Home: Sat 25th Apr
Away: Sat 15th Nov
Title Odds: 66/1
**How To Get There From
The Racecourse:**
A483 – A5 – M54 (to J1) –
M6 (to J8) – M5 (to J15) –
M4 (to J19) – M32 (to J3)
– A4320 (follow s/p Bath)
– A4 (s/p Bath) – A4174
(s/p Shepton Mallett) –
A37 (s/p Shepton Mallett)
– A361 (s/p Yeovil &
Glastonbury) – A37 (s/p
Yeovil) – A303 – A37 (s/p
Yeovil) – A30 (s/p Chard &
Dorchester) – A37 (s/p
Poole) – A35 (s/p Poole) -
A354 from Dorchester –
Turn right at first round-
about onto Weymouth
Way – Go to next round-
about and turn right (s/p
Football Ground) – At next
roundabout take the third
exit into the ground.
Nearest railway Station:
Weymouth (2 miles)

WEYMOUTH

Weymouth Football Club were founded in 1890. Nicknamed 'The Terras' almost immediately, due to their terracotta strip, the team won the Dorset Junior Cup for the first three seasons, becoming a senior club as the team rose in stature.

Founder members of the Dorset League, Weymouth joined the Western League in 1907. The club became full-time in 1923 after joining the Southern League, but by 1928/29, with debts mounting, they withdrew from the Southern League to become amateur once again. They climbed back up the table and then folded for 5 years and reformed. WW2 saw an end to football in Weymouth as the Recreation Ground was requisitioned for the War effort in 1939.

The club reformed in 1947 on a semi-professional basis, and soon achieved promotion back into the Southern League. In successive seasons in the 60s the Terras were Southern League champions , sharing with Telford and Yeovil the distinction of playing all twenty seasons in the Premier Division prior to the re-organisation of the league structure at the time.

A move from the club's town centre ground to the new Wessex Stadium in 1987 brought initial success, but the club entered somewhat of a slump after relegation from the Conference, see-sawing between the Premier and Southern Divisions of the Southern League. Journalist and author Ian Ridley took control of the club in 2003/04 Within a season the club turned around from relegation fodder to just missing out on promotion to the Conference. Promotion to the Conference was secured in May 2006.

WHO'S WHO IN THE BLUE SQUARE PREMIER LEAGUE

WOKING

Woking Football Club was formed in 1889, and joined the West Surrey League in 1895/96. In 1911 the club joined the Isthmian League, maintaining their place in the top division for 72 years and finishing as runners-up to Wycombe Wanderers in 1956/57.

That achievement was eclipsed in the following season when, in front of a 71,000 crowd, the Cards beat Ilford F.C. 3-0 in the last FA Amateur Cup Final to be televised live. The club then went into decline, culminating in a first-ever relegation in 1982/83. By the end of 1984/85 the club had fallen further down the football ladder, being relegated to Division Two South of the Isthmian League.

Woking clinched the Division Two South title in 1986/87. After two third place finishes in Division One, they were promoted back to the Premier Division at the end of 1989/90. Promotion to the Conference was achieved in 1991/92 with the Isthmian League title.

The FA Trophy was won in 1994 when Runcorn were beaten, and twelve months later as Woking became only the second club ever to win successive finals when they beat Kidderminster Harriers. Wembley was revisited in 1997 and the FA Trophy was won for the third time, this time against Dagenham & Redbridge.

The Cards also achieved five successive top five finishes in the Conference, including being runners-up in 1994/95 and 1995/96. All this was followed by a downturn in the club's fortunes that led to a financial crisis, but they overcame that to turn professional in 2003, whilst continuing to ensure their Conference position.

Ground:
Kingfield Stadium
Capacity: 6,000
Founded: 1889
Nickname:
The Cardinals
Manager:
Kim Grant
Last Season
Position: 17th
Points: 53
Average Att.: 1,758
This Season
Home: Sun 28th Dec
Away: Sat 14th Mar
Title Odds: 50/1
How To Get There
From The Racecourse:
A483 – A5 – M54 – M6 – M5 (to J8) – M42 (to J3a) – M40 (to J1a) – M25 (to J11) – A320 (follow signs for Woking Leisure Centre) – A247 into Wych Hill Lane – Ground is third turning on right – Westfield Avenue—Opposite Woking Leisure Centre
Nearest railway Station:
Woking S.R. (1 mile)

WHO'S WHO IN THE BLUE SQUARE PREMIER LEAGUE

YORK CITY

York City was first founded in 1908 as an amateur side, although some sources state the roots of the club can be traced as far back as 1897 when the York and District League was formed.

The club joined the Northern League in 1908, but left after two seasons to form the Yorkshire Combination. They turned professional in 1912, joining the Midland League until 1914/15 before folding in 1917 during WW1.

The club was re-formed in 1922 by members of the former club, becoming a limited company and gaining admission to the Midland League until election to the Football League in 1929. They played in Division Three North until 1958, becoming founding members of Division Four.

Promotion was won in the inaugural season, only to be relegated a season later! Promotion in 64/65 was followed with instant relegation the next season. York's record of promotion every six years was maintained in 70/71, but this time they managed to stay in Division Three, albeit on goal average!

York were eventually promoted to Division Two in 73/74, and their first season in Division Two saw them finish in their highest ever league position - 15th. However, the following season relegation followed. The club dropped further still in 76/77, but 83/84, managed by former Wrexham boss Denis Smith, saw York win the Fourth Division title with a record 101 points - the first team to do so.

In 1993 York ended a five year spell in Division Three by gaining promotion via the play-offs, beating Crewe on penalties in the final at Wembley Stadium. In 2003/04 York were relegated to the Conference after 75 years of League membership. They reached the play-off semi-finals in 2006/07, but were beaten by Morecambe.

Ground:
Kit Kat Crescent
Capacity: 9,034
Founded: 1908
Nickname:
The Minstermen
Manager: Colin Walker
Last Season
Position: 14th
Points: 62
Average Att.: 2,258
This Season
Home: Tues 7th Oct
Away: Thurs 14th Aug
Title Odds: 25/1
**How To Get There
From The Racecourse**:
A483 – A55 (s/p E.Port) – M53 (to J11) - M56 (to J9) – M6 (to J21a) – M62 (to J12) – M60 (to J18) – M62 (to J29) - M1 (north to J45) – A64 (s/p York) – A1237 (turn left) - A1237 (outer-ring road for 5 miles to A19) – A19 (turn right into York & continue for one mile) – turning for ground on left opposite Grange Hotel.
Nearest railway Station:
York (20 minute walk)

First Team Fixtures 2008/09

Date			Time	H/A	Opponents	Competition
August	Sat	9th	15.00	H	Stevenage Borough	BSP
	Thurs	14th	19.45	A	York City	BSP
	Sat	16th	15.00	A	Rushden & Diamonds	BSP
	Thurs	21st	19.45	H	Oxford United	BSP
	Mon	25th	15.00	H	Altrincham	BSP
	Sat	30th	15.00	A	Salisbury City	BSP
September	Tues	2nd	19.45	H	Burton Albion	BSP
	Sat	6th	15.00	A	Cambridge United	BSP
	Sat	13th	15.00	H	Ebbsfleet United	BSP
	Sat	20th	15.00	A	Grays Athletic	BSP
	Tues	23rd	19.45	H	Rushden & Diamonds	BSP
	Sat	27th	15.00	H	Torquay United	BSP
October	Sat	4th	15.00	A	Forest Green Rovers	BSP
	Tues	7th	19.45	H	York City	BSP
	Sat	11th	15.00	H	Histon	BSP
	Sat	18th	15.00	A	Mansfield Town	BSP
	Sat	25th	15.00	TBC	TBC	FAC 4th Qual
November	Sat	1st	15.00	H	Lewes	BSP
	Sat	8th	15.00	TBC	TBC	FAC R1
	Sat	15th	15.00	A	Weymouth	BSP
	Tues	18th	19.45	H	Forest Green Rovers	BSP
	Sat	22nd	15.00	A	Kidderminster Harriers	BSP
	Sat	29th	15.00	A	Stevenage Borough	BSP
December	Sat	6th	15.00	H	Kettering Town	BSP (FAC R2)
	Tues	9th	15.00	A	Northwich Victoria	BSP
	Sat	13th	15.00	TBC	TBC	FAT R1
	Sat	20th	15.00	H	Eastbourne Borough	BSP
	Fri	26th	15.00	A	Barrow	BSP
	Sun	28th	15.00	H	Woking	BSP
January	Thurs	1st	15.00	H	Barrow	BSP
	Sat	3rd	15.00	A	Ebbsfleet United	BSP (FAC R3)
	Sat	10th	15.00	TBC	TBC	FAT R2
	Sat	17th	15.00	A	Torquay United	BSP
	Sat	24th	15.00	H	Cambridge United	BSP
	Tues	27th	19.45	H	Northwich Victoria	BSP
	Sat	31st	15.00	A	Crawley Town	BSP (FAT R3)
February	Sat	7th	15.00	A	Lewes	BSP
	Sat	14th	15.00	H	Grays Athletic	BSP
	Sat	21st	15.00	A	Burton Albion	BSP
	Tues	24th	19.45	H	Kidderminster Harriers	BSP (FAT R4)
	Sat	28th	15.00	H	Salisbury City	BSP
March	Sat	7th	15.00	A	Eastbourne Borough	BSP (FAT SF)
	Sat	14th	15.00	A	Woking	BSP (FAT SF)
	Sat	21st	15.00	H	Crawley Town	BSP
	Sat	28th	15.00	A/H	Histon	BSP
April	Sat	4th	15.00	H	Mansfield Town	BSP
	Sat	11th	15.00	A	Oxford United	BSP
	Mon	13th	15.00	H	Altrincham	BSP
	Sat	18th	15.00	A	Kettering Town	BSP
	Sat	25th	15.00	H	Weymouth	BSP

Key: BSP = Blue Square Premier League; FAT = FA Trophy; FAC = FA Cup.

BLUE SQUARE PREMIER LEAGUE FIXTURES 2008-09

	York C	Wrexham	Woking	Weymouth	Torquay U	Stevenage	Salisbury C	Rushden D	Oxford U	Northwich V	Mansfield T	Lewes	K'minster	Kettering T	Histon	Grays A	Forest GR	Ebbsfleet U	Eastbourne	Crawley T	Cambridge	Burton A	Barrow	Altrincham
Altrincham	27-1	25-8	21-2	14-3	24-1	28-2	6-9	29-11	11-10	1-1	23-9	20-9	11-4	16-8	1-11	18-4	3-1	4-10	7-2	28-3	22-11	20-12	12-8	
Barrow	13-4	26-12	4-4	22-11	7-2	30-8	31-1	2-9	8-8	28-2	23-8	21-3	24-1	20-9	29-11	21-2	1-11	27-9	18-10	18-4	3-1	7-10		27-1
Burton A	26-12	21-2	16-8	13-9	3-1	22-11	14-3	7-2	18-4	12-8	11-10	30-8	25-8	24-1	11-4	28-3	27-9	1-11	29-11	4-10	9-12		27-1	24-2
Cambridge U	18-11	6-9	17-1	11-10	13-9	28-12	20-12	1-11	27-1	24-3	14-2	7-10	12-8	25-8	1-1	27-9	4-4	1-11	11-4	28-2		15-11	16-8	25-4
Crawley T	9-8	31-1	1-1	7-3	23-8	13-4	21-2	14-3	24-1	30-8	13-9	24-2	12-8	27-9	25-4	2-9	4-4	18-11	11-4		15-11	4-4	11-10	6-12
Eastbourne B	24-1	7-3	15-11	4-4	9-12	11-10	18-11	9-8	3-1	6-12	31-1	26-12	20-12	7-10	13-9	13-4	2-9	24-2		14-2	23-8	21-3	25-4	30-8
Ebbsfleet U	7-3	3-1	11-4	6-12	18-10	23-8	25-4	17-1	3-1	4-4	9-8	13-4	1-1	22-11	7-10	26-12	2-9		23-9	27-1	2-9	14-2	15-11	21-3
Forest Green R	21-3	4-10	20-9	25-8	23-9	20-9	12-8	18-4	30-8	21-2	22-11	28-3	28-3	20-12	31-1	28-2		9-12	23-9	16-8	18-10	6-12	15-11	15-11
Grays A	4-4	20-9	11-4	27-1	29-11	23-9	11-4	18-11	7-3	16-8	22-11	4-10	18-4	12-8	28-12		28-2	26-12	13-4	2-9	27-9	28-3	21-2	18-4
Histon	9-12	28-3	18-10	7-2	9-8	21-3	4-10	13-4	15-11	20-9	3-1	4-10	18-4	15-11		28-12	7-3	27-1	28-2	12-8	17-1	4-4	25-8	16-8
Kettering T	13-9	18-4	6-12	1-11	21-2	2-9	17-1	23-8	22-11	4-10	26-12	29-11	18-10		15-11	1-11	11-10	26-12	21-2	9-12	22-11	24-1	24-2	31-1
Kidderminster H	23-9	22-11	30-8	17-1	2-9	4-4	6-12	30-8	7-2	14-2	9-12	9-8		24-1	18-11	3-1	26-12	11-10	24-3	3-1	21-2	23-9	18-11	23-8
Lewes	25-4	7-2	21-3	11-4	27-1	6-12	16-8	13-9	13-9	18-10	24-1		9-8	29-11	18-10	1-11	14-3	13-9	23-8	2-9	20-9	29-11	6-9	4-4
Mansfield T	7-2	18-10	20-12	20-12	28-3	25-4	15-11	27-1	27-9	25-8		24-1	9-12	26-12	3-1	22-11	14-3	9-8	31-1	13-9	14-2	11-10	23-8	23-9
Northwich V	23-8	9-12	4-10	27-9	21-3	7-3	28-12	28-3	6-12		25-8	18-10	14-2	4-10	20-9	16-8	21-2	4-4	6-12	30-8	24-3	12-8	28-2	1-1
Oxford U	1-11	11-4	31-1	12-8	28-2	20-12	1-1	4-10		25-4	27-9	13-9	7-2	22-11	15-11	7-3	30-8	3-1	3-1	24-1	27-1	18-4	8-8	11-10
Rushden & D	24-2	16-8	25-8	28-12	11-10	1-1	4-4		2-9	20-12	18-4	18-4	13-4	24-2	14-2	14-3	24-1	12-8	28-3	21-3	20-9	28-3	7-3	27-9
Salisbury C	29-11	24-2	25-4	2-9	13-4	18-10		3-1	21-3	22-11	27-9	18-11	6-12	27-1	14-2	23-8	7-2	25-8	10-3	23-9	28-2	20-9	1-1	7-10
Stevenage B	27-9	29-11	7-2	16-8	18-4		18-10	26-12	26-12	15-11	25-4	6-12	4-4	2-9	21-3	23-9	20-9	28-12	28-3	13-4	28-12	22-11	30-8	28-2
Torquay U	28-8	17-1	12-8	1-1		4-10	25-8	7-3	7-10	24-1	28-3	27-1	2-9	21-2	9-8	29-11	23-9	18-10	9-12	23-8	13-9	3-1	7-2	24-1
Weymouth	28-2	15-11	18-11		1-1	14-2	10-3	21-2	9-12	27-9	20-12	11-4	17-1	1-11	7-2	27-1	16-8	6-12	4-4	7-3	11-10	13-9	22-11	14-3
Woking	11-10	14-3		18-11	12-8	1-11	23-9	9-12	13-4	24-1	20-12	21-3	30-8	6-12	18-10	11-4	20-9	1-1	15-11	1-1	17-1	16-8	4-4	21-2
Wrexham	7-10		28-12	25-4	27-9	9-8	28-2	23-9	21-8	3-1	18-4	7-2	22-11	18-4	28-3	20-9	4-10	3-1	7-3	31-1	6-9	21-2	26-12	25-8
York C		14-8	6-9	28-2	15-11	31-1	20-9	18-10	21-2	11-4	2-9	17-1	16-8	14-3	16-8	6-12	14-2	20-12	18-4	6-12	4-10	28-12	25-8	28-12

Gavin John Ward (1)

Vastly experienced shot-stopper who became Brian Little's second permanent signing as Wrexham manager from old adversaries Chester in January 2008. A veteran of over 400 appearances, spanning 19 years, and more clubs than he would care to imagine, the 38 year old joined a rare group of 'goalkeeper goalscorers' in 2006 when he netted from a free-kick just outside his area whilst playing for Tranmere Rovers. As well as fighting it out with Anthony Williams for the number 1 jersey this term, Gavin will also be spending time coaching the next generation of goalkeepers coming through the ranks at Colliers Park.

Previous clubs: Aston Villa, Shrewsbury Town, West Bromwich Albion, Cardiff City, Leicester City, Bradford City, Bolton Wan'ers, Burnley (Loan), Stoke City, Walsall, Coventry City, Barnsley (Loan), Preston North End, Tranmere Rovers, Chester City.

Position	Goalkeeper
Nationality	English
Birthplace	Sutton Coldfield
Date of Birth	30/06/1970
Height	6ft 3in (190.5 cm)
Weight	14st 12lbs (94.43 kg)

Wrexham Career Statistics

	League		FA Cup		WPC		Carling		JPT		Total	
	apps	gls	apps	gls	apps	gls	apps	gls	apps	gls	apps	gls
07/08	22	0	-	-	1	0	-	-	-	-	23	0
Total	22	0	-	-	1	0	-	-	-	-	23	0

Kyle Adrian Ross Critchell (2)

A full-back who can also play in midfield joined the Red Dragons after a nominal fee was agreed with Blue Square rivals Weymouth. The 21-year-old joined Southampton as a trainee after being spotted playing for Weymouth reserves, before making his league debut during a loan spell at Torquay. He eventually earned a move to Chesterfield, before returning to Weymouth where he impressed the Wrexham coaching staff enough during the recent Four Nations semi-pro tournament to offer him a 2-year contract. Also capped by Wales at Youth level, and made his debut for the under-21's against Austria in 2005. He will be hoping a move to the principality will earn him a return to Brian Flynn's plans.

Previous clubs:
Southampton, Torquay United (Loan), Chesterfield, Weymouth.

(No appearances to date for Wrexham FC)

Position	Defender
Nationality	Welsh
Birthplace	Dorchester
Date of Birth	18/01/87
Height	6ft 0in (183 cm)
Weight	12st 2lbs (77.18 kg)

Carl Tremarco (3)

Brian Little agreed to take over the remainder of his contract from Tranmere Rovers during the January transfer window. Having come through the ranks at Prenton Park he made his professional debut against Hornchurch in an FA Cup tie in 2003 – going on to make over 50 appearances for the club before his switch to North Wales. The classy left back impressed in his first few games, although injury hampered the remainder of his season. Despite interest from Chester and Rotherham during the close season, the 22 year old penned a 2-year contract with the Red Dragons and will be hoping to make the left back berth his own this time out.

Previous clubs: Tranmere Rovers

Wrexham Career Statistics

	League		FA Cup		WPC		Carling		JPT		Total	
	apps	gls	apps	gls	apps	gls	apps	gls	apps	gls	apps	gls
07/08	10	0	-	-	-	-	-	-	-	-	10	0
Total	10	2	-	-	-	-	-	-	-	-	10	0

Position	Defender
Nationality	English
Birthplace	Liverpool
Date of Birth	11/10/85
Height	5ft 11in (180 cm)
Weight	12st 3lbs (77.63 kg)

Darran Kaya Kempson (4)

Described by manager Brian Little as a signing he could "not afford to miss", the former Shrewsbury Town player penned a 2-year deal after falling down the pecking order at the Prostar Stadium. A commanding central defender who at 23 years of age has already built up a wealth of experience having turned out for Accrington, Morecambe, Crewe and Bury before his switch to Shrewsbury in 2007. A former England semi-professional international, the pacy centre-half has first hand experience of life in the Conference from his time with Morecambe where he attracted praise for his no-nonsense approach. With strength and positional play also amongst his list of attributes, the new capture will add competition for places at the heart of the defence.

Previous Clubs: Preston North End, Accrington Stanley (Loan), Morecambe (Loan), Morecambe, Crewe Alexandra, Bury (Loan), Shrewsbury Town, Accrington Stanley (Loan).

(No appearances to date for Wrexham FC)

Position	Defender
Nationality	English
Birthplace	Blackpool
Date of Birth	06-12-84
Height	6ft 2in 188(cm)
Weight	13st 0lbs (82.6 kg)

Position	Defender
Nationality	Welsh
Birthplace	Wrexham
Date of Birth	26/02/79
Height	6ft 5in (195 cm)
Weight	13st 10lbs (87.18 kg)

Steve James Evans (5)

A towering, uncompromising centre back, many Wrexham fans were glad when 'Big Steve' finally put pen to paper in the summer and signed a new one year contract, with an option to another 12 months. A giant of a centre-half who causes opposing defenders problems at set pieces. No doubt Steve himself will want to get playing to lay some of the ghosts from last season to rest. There isn't a doubt that the lad lacks passion and Reds fans want to see the Steve of two seasons ago, which catapulted him to gain six full Welsh international caps.

Previous clubs:
Crewe Alexandra, West Bromwich Albion, TNS Llansantffraid, Oswestry Town (Loan).

Wrexham Career Statistics

	League		FA Cup		WPC		Carling		JPT		Total	
	apps	gls	apps	gls	apps	gls	apps	gls	apps	gls	apps	gls
06/07	34/1	2	3	0	-	-	1	0	1	0	39/1	2
07/08	29/1	3	-	-	1	0	1	0	1	0	32/1	3
Total	63/2	5	3	0	1	0	2	0	2	0	71/2	5

Position	Defender
Nationality	English
Birthplace	Sheffield
Date of Birth	15/06/81
Height	6ft 2in (186 cm)
Weight	12st 5lbs (78.5 kg)

Nathaniel Brown (6)

A powerful towering centre-half, Nat became Wrexham's sixth summer signing, having had the remaining year of his contract with Lincoln cancelled by mutual consent. After working his way through the ranks at Huddersfield Town, where he made over 80 appearances, Nat signed for Lincoln in 2005. 100 games in his three seasons with the Imps followed, as did play-off semi-finals in successive seasons. It is this kind of experience that manager Brian Little will be hoping to build his team around as we go in search of promotion at the first attempt. Brown is a very versatile player who, as well as playing in central defence, can also operate in a central midfield role, as well as up front.

Previous clubs:
Huddersfield Town, Lincoln City

(No appearances to date for Wrexham FC)

Wesley Baynes (7)

Another product of the succcesful youth set-up at Colliers Park, Wes has been at the club for over ten years having progressed through the ranks from the under 8's to making his first team bow in the 2-2 draw against Chester in Brian Little's first game in charge. The 19 year-old already has himself a reputation as a free-kick specialist – mainly down to his two strikes against Lincoln on the last day of the season – not to mention a wonderful strike against Championship outfit Wolves during pre-season. Equally adept at right back or on the right wing, he recently signed an extension to his contract keeping him at the club until 2010. After an impressive start to his career, Baynes will be hoping to keep the momentum going this time around.

Previous clubs: None

Wrexham Career Statistics

	League		FA Cup		WPC		Carling		JPT		Total	
	apps	gls	apps	gls	apps	gls	apps	gls	apps	gls	apps	gls
07/08	10/2	2	-	-	1	0	-	-	-	-	11/2	2
Total	10/2	2	-	-	1	0	-	-	-	-	11/2	2

Position	Right Back/Midfielder
Nationality	English
Birthplace	Chester
Date of Birth	12/10/88
Height	5ft 11in (180 cm)
Weight	10st 10lbs (68.1 kg)

Simon Alexander Brown (8)

A recent signing from fellow Blue Square Premier League side Mansfield, the 25 year old striker will be looking to emulate his form from previous seasons when he netted 11 times in 16 appearances for the Stags in 2005/06. He also holds Mansfield's club record for the fastest ever hat-trick, when he scored three goals in 14 minutes in a 5-0 win over Macclesfield! Began his career at West Bromwich Albion, but failed to make a first team appearance before joining Kidderminster Harriers following a loan spell, when he made his Football League debut for them. Mansfield paid out £50,000 for Simon in December 2004. A lot is expected from this pacey marksman as the Dragons look to improve our goals per game ratio.

Previous clubs:
West Bromwich Albion, Kidderminster Harriers, Mansfield Town

(No appearances to date for Wrexham FC)

Position	Midfielder
Nationality	English
Birthplace	Wednesbury
Date of Birth	18/09/83
Height	5ft 7in (170 cm)
Weight	11st 0lbs (69.92 kg)

Jefferson Lee Louis (9)

Jefferson is a much travelled striker, who has spent the majority of his career to date playing the non-league circuit. Some fans may recall that he hit the national headlines in 2002 when, after scoring the winning goal in an FA Cup game for Oxford, he was caught on camera celebrating wildly (dressed only in a towel!) when United were drawn to play his boyhood heroes Arsenal in the next round. Capped by Dominica in a World Cup qualifier in 2008, he was snapped up on a two-year contract after spending a short spell at Mansfield last season. The 29 year-old from Harrow is renowned as a strong and powerful striker and standing at 6' 2" he should bring a much needed physical presence to Wrexham's attack this term.

Position	Forward
Nationality	Dominican
Birthplace	Harrow
Date of Birth	22/02/79
Height	6ft 2in (186 cm)
Weight	14st 5lbs (91.25 kg)

Previous clubs:
Thame United, Oxford United, Woking (Loan), Ebbsfleet United (Loan), Forest Green Rovers, Woking, Bristol Rovers, Hemel Hempstead, Lewes, Worthing, Stevenage Borough, Eastleigh, Yeading, Havant & Waterlooville, Weymouth, Maidenhead United, Mansfield Town.
(No appearances to date for Wrexham FC)

Shaun James Whalley (10)

Shaun is the son of former Preston North End captain, Neil Whalley. He agreed a one-year deal in the summer after being released by Accrington Stanley. Whalley scored against Wrexham in a 3-1 win for his former club back in April - hopefully the first of many more goals he will score at the Racecourse! He started his career with the youth teams at Southport and from there he joined Chester City. Impressive spells with non-league outfits Runcorn and Witton Albion followed before his move to then Football League newcomers Accrington in 2006. Lightning quick and skilful on the ball, Shaun is sure to give a few defenders a tough time this time out.

Position	Forward
Nationality	English
Birthplace	Whiston
Date of Birth	07-08-87
Height	5ft 9in (175 cm)
Weight	10st 7lbs (66.7 kg)

Previous clubs:
Southport, Chester City, Runcorn Halton, Witton Albion, Accrington Stanley.

(No appearances to date for Wrexham FC)

Neil John Taylor (11)

A promising youngster who signed professional forms in the summer of 2007. He first featured in first team action in a pre-season friendly match at Port Vale in July 2006. A former pupil of Ysgol Bryn Hyfryd in Ruthin, where he represented Denbighshire at county level and North Wales schoolboys. He has since been capped by Wales at under 17 and 19 levels in Victory Shield matches, and now at under-21 level. He is equally at home playing at either left-back or on the left side of midfield. Neil has continued to make excellent progress. He'll be looking to cement his position in the team this year.

Previous clubs: None

Wrexham Career Statistics

	League		FA Cup		WPC		Carling		JPT		Total	
	apps	gls	apps	gls	apps	gls	apps	gls	apps	gls	apps	gls
07/08	22/5	0	-	-	1	0	0/1	0	-	-	23/6	0
Total	22/5	0	-	-	1	0	0/1	0	-	-	23/6	0

Position	Left Back/Midfielder
Nationality	Welsh
Birthplace	St. Asaph
Date of Birth	07/02/89
Height	5ft 9in (175cm)
Weight	11st 3lbs (71.21 kg)

Levi Alan Mackin (12)

Despite Levi being loaned out last season to Droylsden in January where he made 12 appearances, Levi is back! Often described by Denis Smith as the young player with the most potential this could be the season when he finally makes an impact on the first team. A central midfielder player, able to play a holding role or break forwards, he returned to us in April 2008 and scored his first goal in a 4-2 win at Lincoln City. It's strange to think that Levi first made his Club debut way back in 2003 in a 1-1 draw with Wycombe Wanderers.

Previous clubs: Droylsden (Loan)

Wrexham Career Statistics

	League		FA Cup		WPC		Carling		JPT		Total	
	apps	gls	apps	gls	apps	gls	apps	gls	apps	gls	apps	gls
03/04	1	0	-	-	-	-	-	-	-	-	1	0
04/05	5/5	0	-	-	1	0	0/1	0	-	-	6/6	0
05/06	3/13	0	-	-	0/1	0	0/1	0	0/1	0	3/16	0
06/07	1/6	0	0/1	0	1	0	0/2	0	-	-	2/9	0
07/08	9/1	1	-	-	1	0	2	0	-	-	12/1	1
Total	19/25	1	0/1	0	3/1	0	2/4	0	0/1	0	24/32	1

Position	Midfielder
Nationality	Welsh
Birthplace	Chester
Date of Birth	04/04/86
Height	6ft 0in (183 cm)
Weight	12st 0lbs (76.2 kg)

Thomas James Kearney (14)

A summer signing from Halifax, Kearney will be looking to add much more stability to our ever-changing midfield. The former Everton trainee has signed a two-year contract and will hopefully bring a combative role to the midfield. He was instrumental in Halifax overcoming their 10 point deduction last season, and Reds fans will be looking for the same sort of flair and determination this time round. He certainly impressed Reds fans when he signed; "It will be a great challenge. Every player is going to make it clear that promotion is the one thing that we are looking for." Just what we all want to hear! He added: "Being in a competitive environment here is a challenge I am looking forward to." Tom's sister is Gillian Kearney has appeared in Brookside, Shameless and Casualty.

Position	Midfielder
Nationality	English
Birthplace	Liverpool
Date of Birth	07/10/81
Height	5ft 9in (175 cm)
Weight	10st 12lbs (68.9 kg)

Previous clubs: Everton, Bradford City, Halifax Town.

(No appearances to date for Wrexham FC)

Michael Paul John Williams (15)

The third post war player to play for Wrexham with the name Mike Williams! The Welsh Under 21 cap looked impeccable at centre-half last season. With some players we keep expecting and waiting for them to deliver, but in Mike's case he already has! Equally comfortable at left back, or in the centre of defence, Williams made his debut in a miserable 4-0 defeat at Wycombe in September 2007, but has since made a good impression with his solid performances when he's had the chance. Described by Denis Smith as "...quick, strong and has a good left foot." Still only 21, he has been a major influence in Brian Flynn's successful under-21 team.

Previous clubs: None

Wrexham Career Statistics

	League		FA Cup		WPC		Carling		JPT		Total	
	apps	gls	apps	gls	apps	gls	apps	gls	apps	gls	apps	gls
05/06	7/5	0	-	-	1	0	-	-	-	-	8/5	0
06/07	20/11	0	3	0	1	0	2	0	1	0	27/11	0
07/08	15/3	0	-	-	1	0	-	-	1	0	17/3	0
Total	42/19	0	3	0	3	0	2	0	2	0	52/19	0

Position	Defender
Nationality	Welsh
Birthplace	Bangor
Date of Birth	27/10/86
Height	5ft 11in (180 cm)
Weight	12st 0lbs (76.2 kg)

Silvio Reinaldo Spann (16)

Silvio is a versatile midfielder who is known for his hard work, stamina and his ability to shoot from long distance. In fact, it was striking the ball from distance that led him to 'You Tube' fame when he scored a spectacular free-kick more than 40 yards out whilst playing for Trinidad & Tobago against El Salvador in 2007. Spann had been named in the Soca Warriors' squad for the 2006 World Cup, but had to drop out after suffering injury in the run-up to the tournament. Having signed for Wrexham from homeland club W-Connection in 2007 after spells in Italy, Japan and Croatia, the 27 year-old was another player made available for transfer in the summer.

Previous clubs: St. Benedicts College; Vibe CT 105; W Connection; Doc's Khelwalaas; 2000 W Connection (All Trinidad); 2001 AC Perugia (Italy); Jan 2002 San Benedettesse Calcio (Italy); 2002 W Connection (Trinidad); Apr 2004 Dinamo Zagreb (Croatia); Jan 2005 Yokohama (Japan); 2006 W-Connection;

Position	Midfield
Nationality	Trinidadian
Birthplace	Couvo, Trinidad
Date of Birth	21/08/81
Height	5ft 9in (175 cm)
Weight	10st 10lbs (68 kg)

Wrexham Career Statistics

	League		FA Cup		WPC		Carling		JPT		Total	
	apps	gls	apps	gls	apps	gls	apps	gls	apps	gls	apps	gls
07/08	7/2	1	1	0	-	-	-	-	1	0	9/2	1
Total	7/2	1	1	0	-	-	-	-	1	0	9/2	1

Simon Spender (17)

At just 22 years of age, Mold born Spender is the second longest serving player on the club's books having made his debut against Plymouth Argyle in 2004. A former Welsh Under-20 and 21 cap, 'Spends' is now in his sixth season with the club after coming through the youth ranks at Colliers Park. Now a 'veteran' of over 100 appearances, it was during the closing stages of the 2006/07 season that he cemented his place in the team after a string of impressive performances. The energetic right-back continued this form into last season – culminating in him being voted Wrexham Supporters' Trust's Player of the Season.

Previous clubs: None

Position	Defender
Nationality	Welsh
Birthplace	Mold
Date of Birth	15/11/85
Height	5ft 11in (180 cm)
Weight	11st 0lbs (69.9 kg)

Wrexham Career Statistics

	League		FA Cup		WPC		Carling		JPT		Total	
	apps	gls	apps	gls	apps	gls	apps	gls	apps	gls	apps	gls
03/04	3/3	0	-	-	-	-	-	-	-	-	3/3	0
04/05	9/4	0	2	0	0/1	0	0/2	0	2	0	13/7	0
05/06	15/3	2	1	0	1/2	1	-	-	1	0	17/5	3
06/07	23/2	2	-	-	-	-	1	0	-	-	24/2	2
07/08	31/1	1	1	0	0/1	0	2	0	-	-	34/3	1
Total	81/14	5	4	0	1/4	1	3/2	0	3	0	91/20	6

Michael Anthony Proctor (18)

After initially being brought in on a month's loan in March 2007, the former Hartlepool striker signed a three-year deal after playing a pivotal role in retaining our Football League status during the remainder of that campaign. Despite slipping down the league structure last time out, the clever striker still chipped in 12 goals to finish as the club's top scorer. Now in the second year of his contract, manager Brian Little made him available for transfer in the summer. Having started his career with Sunderland, he finished York's top scorer in 2001/02 while on loan with 14 goals.

Previous clubs: Sunderland, Hvidore (Loan) (Sweden), Halifax Town (Loan), York City (Loan), Bradford City (Loan), Rotherham United, Swindon Town (Loan), Hartlepool United.

Position	Forward
Nationality	English
Birthplace	Sunderland
Date of Birth	03/10/80
Height	5ft 11in (180 cm)
Weight	12st 0lbs (76.2kg)

Wrexham Career Statistics

	League		FA Cup		WPC		Carling		JPT		Total	
	apps	gls	apps	gls	apps	gls	apps	gls	apps	gls	apps	gls
06/07	9	2	-	-	-	-	-	-	-	-	9	2
07/08	20/17	11	-	-	1	0	2	1	0/1	0	23/18	12
Total	29/17	13	-	-	1	0	2	1	0/1	0	32/18	14

Andrew Lee Fleming (19)

Another product of the of the Centre of Excellence at Wrexham, cultured midfielder Fleming is highly rated by the Racecourse coaching staff, but last season, his first as a professional, saw him suffer with injury. He made his first team debut as an early substitution at Darlington in January 2007, and then manager Brian Carey handed him his first start in the goal-less derby draw against arch rivals Chester City at The Racecourse the following month, and showed maturity beyond his years. He will be hoping to add to his appearances this season, and make an impact in the Dragons midfield, having shown plenty of potential so far, but can he command a regular first team place?

Previous Clubs: None

Position	Midfielder
Nationality	English
Birthplace	Liverpool
Date of Birth	05/10/87
Height	6ft 0in (183 cm)
Weight	11st 5lbs (72.1 kg)

Wrexham Career Statistics

	League		FA Cup		WPC		Carling		JPT		Total	
	apps	gls	apps	gls	apps	gls	apps	gls	apps	gls	apps	gls
06/07	1/1	0	-	-	-	-	-	-	-	-	1/1	0
07/08	2/2	0	-	-	-	-	-	-	-	-	2/2	0
Total	3/3	0	-	-	-	-	-	-	-	-	3/3	0

Shaun Melvyn Pejic (20)

A Welsh under-21 international, and currently the club's longest serving player. Shaun still has one year left on his contract, though last season saw him make sporadic appearances for the Dragons, but still managing 23 appearances in all competitions. All Reds fans will be hoping for a return to form from two seasons ago where he and Steve Evans were beginning to forge an excellent partnership at the heart of our defence.

Previous Clubs: None

Wrexham Career Statistics

	League		FA Cup		WPC		Carling		JPT		Total	
	apps	gls	apps	gls	apps	gls	apps	gls	apps	gls	apps	gls
00/01	1	0	-	-	-	-	-	-	-	-	1	0
01/02	11/1	0	-	-	1	0	-	-	-	-	12/1	0
02/03	23/4	0	1	0	1	1	2	0	2	0	29/4	1
03/04	20/1	1	-	-	-	-	1	0	1	0	22/1	1
04/05	30/5	0	2	0	2	0	2	0	4/1	1	40/6	1
05/06	26	0	-	-	2/1	0	-	-	1	0	29/1	0
06/07	33	0	3	0	1	0	1	0	-	-	38	0
07/08	17/2	0	0/1	0	0/1	0	2	0	0/1	0	19/5	0
Total	161/13	1	6/1	0	7/2	1	8	0	8/2	1	190/18	3

Position	Defender
Nationality	Welsh
Birthplace	Hereford
Date of Birth	16/11/82
Height	6ft 0in (183 cm)
Weight	12st 2lbs (77.1 kg)

Marc Richard Williams (21)

A Welsh under-21 international like his brother Mike. He made his first team debut for the Dragons in a 2-0 win at Rushden in January 2006 alongside his brother Mike and almost marked the occasion with a goal, hitting the bar early in the second half. They are the seventh pair of brothers to represent the club. Marc is at a stage in his career where he will be hoping to make the step up this season to become a permanent fixture in the first team. His non-stop running; enthusiasm; and not to mention his ability to hold up the ball, have endeared him to the Racecourse crowd, and many have likened his style of play to that of a certain Andy Morrell!

Previous Clubs: None

Wrexham Career Statistics

	League		FA Cup		WPC		Carling		JPT		Total	
	apps	gls	apps	gls	apps	gls	apps	gls	apps	gls	apps	gls
05/06	2/2	0	-	-	-	-	-	-	-	-	2/2	0
06/07	11/5	1	0/1	0	-	-	-	-	-	-	11/6	1
07/08	11/9	3	0/1	0	-	-	0/2	0	0/1	0	11/13	3
Total	24/16	4	0/2	0	-	-	0/2	0	0/1	0	24/21	4

Position	Forward
Nationality	Welsh
Birthplace	Bangor
Date of Birth	27/07/88
Height	5ft 10in (178 cm)
Weight	11st 12lbs (75.3 kg)

Connell Francis Murtagh (22)

Former Hearts midfielder Conall Murtagh became Brian Carey's third summer signing after putting pen to paper on a 2-year contract. The Northern Ireland Under-21 international had originally agreed to join Southport after a successful season in the Welsh Premier League with Rhyl, where he was voted in the league managers' team of the season. However, as soon as Wrexham's interest became known the 'Sandgrounders' agreed to tear-up the contract to allow Murtagh to resurrect his professional career. Murtagh still has a year to complete of a biomedical sciences course at Manchester University, which he will do with full support from the 'Dragons'.

Previous Clubs: Hearts, Raith Rovers, Altrincham, Connah's Quay Nomads, Rhyl, Droylsden.

(No appearances to date for Wrexham FC)

Position	Midfielder
Nationality	Northern Irish
Birthplace	Belfast
Date of Birth	29/06/85
Height	5ft 11in (180 cm)
Weight	11st 7lbs (73 kg)

Wrexham Career Statistics

	League		FA Cup		WPC		Carling		JPT		Total	
	apps	gls	apps	gls	apps	gls	apps	gls	apps	gls	apps	gls
07/08	3/1	0	-	-	-	-	1/1	0	-	-	4/2	0
Total	3/1	0	-	-	-	-	1/1	0	-	-	4/2	0

Samuel James Aiston (23)

Predominately a winger, he was used in a more central midfield role last season. Sam was Brian Little's first signing as Wrexham manager after arriving from Northampton last November. His debut for the club soon followed in the 2-2 draw with Chester – a club he had previously represented during two loan spells from Sunderland. During a career that has spanned over 300 games, he has also turned out for Stoke, Shrewsbury, Tranmere and Burton. Another player made available for transfer during the close season, the 31 year-old Geordie will be hoping his displays during pre-season will force him back into Brian Little's plans for the forthcoming campaign.

Previous clubs: Newcastle United, Sunderland Chester City (Loan), Stoke City (Loan), Shrewsbury Town, Tranmere Rovers, Northampton Town, Burton Albion.

Position	Midfielder/Winger
Nationality	English
Birthplace	Newcastle-upon-Tyne
Date of Birth	21/11/76
Height	6ft 2in (186 cm)
Weight	12st 0lbs (76.2 kg)

Wrexham Career Statistics

	League		FA Cup		WPC		Carling		JPT		Total	
	apps	gls	apps	gls	apps	gls	apps	gls	apps	gls	apps	gls
07/08	13/6	0	-	-	-	-	-	-	-	-	13/6	0
Total	13/6	0	-	-	-	-	-	-	-	-	13/6	0

Gareth David Evans (24)

Gareth was spotted while playing with the Cefn Druids Academy and subsequently switched to become a scholar at the Racecourse. A promising young centre back, 'Gaz' was actually released prior to the 2006-7 season, but funding was subsequently found to offer him a reprieve. He made his first team debut as a late substitute in the memorable 4-1 beating of Sheffield Wednesday at Hillsborough in August 2006.

He had loan spells last season with Northwich Victoria and Tamworth. Could be nicknamed 'Ronseal' as he always does what it says on the tin- a tough, no-nonsense centre half who is good in the air!

Previous Clubs: Northwich Victoria, Tamworth.

Wrexham Career Statistics

	League		FA Cup		WPC		Carling		JPT		Total	
	apps	gls	apps	gls	apps	gls	apps	gls	apps	gls	apps	gls
06/07	9/3	0	-	-	-	-	0/2	0	-	-	9/5	0
07/08	11/2	0	1	0	-	-	-	-	-	-	12/2	0
Total	20/5	0	1	0	-	-	0/2	0	-	-	21/7	0

Position	Defender
Nationality	Welsh
Birthplace	Wrexham
Date of Birth	10/01/87
Height	6ft 1in (185 cm)
Weight	12st 2lbs (81.6 kg)

Anthony Simon Williams (26)

A former Welsh under-21 international, Williams joined Wrexham on a permanent basis in May 2007, signing a two year contract, after impressing during his loan spell at the club when he kept five clean sheets in nine games, but following our relegation to the BSP in May 2008, he was transfer listed by the club. He has since stated in the press that he wishes to stay and fight for his place and this is exactly the sort of attitude we need at the club right now!

Previous clubs:
Blackburn Rovers, QPR (Loan), Macclesfield Town (Loan), Huddersfield Town (Loan), Bristol Rovers (Loan), Gillingham (Loan), Macclesfield Town (Loan), Hartlepool United, Swansea City (Loan), Stockport County (Loan), Grimsby Town, Carlisle United, Bury (Loan).

Wrexham Career Statistics

	League		FA Cup		WPC		Carling		JPT		Total	
	apps	gls	apps	gls	apps	gls	apps	gls	apps	gls	apps	gls
06/07	9	0	-	-	-	-	-	-	-	-	9	0
07/08	22	0	1	0	-	-	-	-	1	0	24	0
Total	31	0	1	0	-	-	-	-	1	0	33	0

Position	Goalkeeper
Nationality	Welsh
Birthplace	Maesteg
Date of Birth	20/09/77
Height	6ft 2lbs (188 cm)
Weight	13st 9lbs (86.3kg)

Christopher Ethan Maxwell (27)

A promising goalkeeper, Chris was one of two YT's offered a professional contract in the summer. He has been with Wrexham's Centre of Excellence since the age of ten, having played his early football in his home town of Llandudno at Ysgol John Bright and Ysgol Glan Wydden schools, while representing Conwy & District schoolboys. He was playing for Penrhyn Bay United junior team when he was signed up by Wrexham. He has since gone on to represent Wales at both under 16's and under-17's levels. Although not having featured much in the reserve team last season, Chris has worked hard at his game to earn himself a professional contract, and will be hoping to put pressure on Gavin Ward and Anthony Williams for a first team opportunity.

Position	Goalkeeper
Nationality	Welsh
Birthplace	St.Asaph
Date of Birth	30/07/90
Height	5ft 11in (180 cm)
Weight	11st 3lbs (72.28 kg)

Previous clubs: None

(No appearances to date for Wrexham FC)

Christopher Michael Marriott (28)

A left-back, who was equally at home playing in the centre of defence for both the youth and reserve teams. Chris joined Wrexham's Centre of Excellence at the age of 14, having been spotted playing for Newton in the Wallasey Junior Sunday League. Having attended Overchurch junior and Caldy Grange Secondary school - a rugby only school, he played football for Green Leaves in the Wallasey Junior League from the age of six! He played representative football for the Wirral under-11's from where he was spotted by Tranmere Rovers, spending two years with Rovers before leaving. The second of the two YT's who were offered professional contracts in the summer, he was a regular in the reserve team last season, even captaining the side despite a number of senior professionals being alongside him. He first appeared for the first team in the summer of 2007 in a pre-season friendly with Newtown.

Position	Left-Back
Nationality	English
Birthplace	Birkenhead
Date of Birth	24/09/89
Height	5ft 8in (173 cm)
Weight	10st 7lbs (66.59 kg)

Previous clubs: None

(No appearances to date for Wrexham FC)

Centre of Excellence 2008/09

Relegation from the Football League has not just been a set back to the first team, but it has had a great knock on effect for the excellent youth policy we have at the club, which has produced many players over the years, players such as Steve Watkin, Waynne Phillips, Gareth Owen, Lee Jones, Chris Armstrong, Bryan Hughes, Dave Brammer, Craig Morgan, Mark Jones, Simon Spender, Shaun Pejic etc plus many many more.

Make no mistake the School of Excellence is under severe threat, and need to raise at least £100,000 to keep the current system as it is. The reason for this is that relegation from the Football League immediately cuts our grant aid by 50%, and if we do not return within two years, we lose it all. The School of Excellence needs help now and quickly.

Following the introduction of the Football Associations 'Charter for quality' in 1997, Wrexham established their youth department. This department built on work already under-way to develop youth players which the late Cliff Sear and Brian Flynn had been driving forces behind. Over the past ten years the Wrexham Centre of Excellence has grown into one of the most productive and respected examples of youth development in the country. Recently the centre was rated as a model of good practice and one of the best examples of youth development outside of the Championship.

Youth Coaching Team

Head of Youth Steve Cooper, Centre of Excellence Manager Andy Davies, Head of Recruitment Stuart Webber, Physiotherapists Ritson Lloyd, Stuart Tunnicliffe, Jamie Gardner Administrator Tricia Deary- Furber, Chief Scout John Rearden, Regional Scout Ron Parry, Education & Welfare Jonathan Miller.

Steve Cooper, Head of Youth

The current programme caters for 140 players from the ages of 8 to 18, some of whom now train five times a week on our brand new state of the art field turf at Colliers Park. We have a training syllabus that matches anything in the UK and have the staff struc-ture, all fully qualified, to implement it on a daily basis. At present the captains of the Wales under 16, 17 and 19s are all Wrexham players of who have been in the pro-gramme for more or less their entire career to date. In the last four years, 16 players have broken through from our youth system to the professional ranks, some of which are now playing championship football along with others progressing as far as full internationals.

Please feel free to visit Colliers Park at any time and see for yourself the service we provide. We don't just develop footballers, we also work hard in giving our boys val-ues, morals, and an ethic that will last with them forever. We provide a measure for life.

I appeal to you and anyone else to sit up and take note of what could happen to the heart beat of Wrexham Football Club. If not, the future of one of the most productive and well run youth systems in the UK is in danger of losing existence.

So how can you help? You can make a donation or sponsor a player and watch how that player grows in stature and follow his career.

Steve Cooper
Head of Youth, Wrexham FC

Youth Team Squad 2008/09

Second Year Training Scheme

Obi Anoruo	Striker
Luke Carding	Left Winger
Kai Edwards	Defender
Mark Head	Striker
Johnny Hunt	Left Back
Matt Hurdman	Midfielder
Jack Jones	Midfielder
Rob Pearson	Midfielder
George Stewart	Right Winger

First Year Training Scheme

Tom Bainbridge	Goalkeeper
Leon Clowes	Centre Half
Jordan Kane	Striker
Aaron Malton	Midfielder
Josh Marsh	Centre Half
Edward Moss	Midfielder
Nick Rushton	Striker
Declan Walker	Right Back

Centre of Excellence Squads 2008-09

Under 9's: Coach Danny Copnall
Ben Barratt, Angus Crayston, Alexander Downes, Niall Freeman, Luke Gallagher, Lewis Jones, Elgan Pugh, Connor Spencer-Wilson.

Under 10's: Coach Paul Williams & Neil Taylor
Josh Abbott, Llan Ap Gareth, Nathan Brown, Ben Burrows, Owen Goodenough, Ryan Harrington, George Harry, Aaron Jones (GK), Peter Rhys Jones, Callum McCann (GK), Brady McGilloway, Cameron Meadows, Jack Pennington, James Saul, Jake Vanschie, Ryan Williams.

Under 11's: Coaches Dave Lloyd & Stuart Webber
Nathan Paul Broadhead, Sean Cavanagh, Jack Chambers, Matthew Clewley, Jordan Davies, Kieran Joseph Evans, Cameren Gardner, Jacob McLaughlin, Rakim Yasir Newton, Alex Tiernan, Shaun William Trousdale, Thomas Vickers.

Under 12's: Coach Ben Heath & Steve Cooper
Jonathan Crump, Thomas Edwards, Sam Faulkner, Jake Fernandez-Hart, Matthew Graham-Hammons, Connor Hughes (GK), James Jones, William Marsh, Jake Phillips, Daniel Reynolds, Ben Richards, Francisco Rowlands, Jonathan Salisbury, Jonathan Smith, Edward Speed, Michael Vaughan-Muscat.

Under 13's: Coach, Ian Davies & Andy Davies
Thomas Batten, Iwan Cartwright, Ryan Crump (GK), Jordan Evans, Max Jenks-Gilbert, James Littlemore, Danny Myers, Aaron Simpson, Jack Smith, Curtis Strong, Richard Tomassen, Ross Weaver, Cory Williams, Jordan Williams.

Under 14's: Coaches Kevin Quigley & Andy Davies
Wesley Bennett, Oliver Bentley, Luke Douglas, Robert David Evans, Conor Patrick Fay, Tom Freeman, Conner Luke Kendrick, Gregory Patrick Mills, Kyle Parle, Jonathan Parry, Robbie Parry, Jonathan Royle, Alex Toward.

Under 15's: Coaches Roger Preece
Jared Bennett, Ryan Edwards. Max Fargin, Elliott Hewitt, Edward Marsh, Jamie McDaid, Jamie Morton, Kieran Murphy, Leon Newell, Nathan Nicholls, Matthew Owen, Joe Rigby, Matthew Regan, William Roberts, Robert Salathiel, Anthony Stephens, Stephen Tomassen.

Under 16's: Coach Tony Merola & Steve Lanceley
Niall Challoner, James Colbeck, Joseph Culshaw, Jack Dearman, Stephen Ferrigan, Michael Jones, Iwan lewis, Louis Moss, Danny Murphy, Max Penk, Liam Rice, Daniel Ward (GK).

Under-18s Coach Steve Cooper
Goalkeeping Coaches Tim Roberts & Fred Price.

Mike Williams

The Evening Leader's Richard Williams interviews Wales' under-21 'veteran' Mike Williams on the current UEFA qualifying campaign.

MIKE WILLIAMS has already experienced highs and lows in his relatively short football career. The 21-year-old centre-back, equally at home on the left of defence, has played his part in the upturn in fortunes experienced in Welsh football at under 21 level.

Five wins in six qualifying matches left Brian Flynn's young guns on the brink of qualification for the UEFA European under 21 Championships, and at the time of writing require just one victory from the double header against Romania to progress to the play-offs.

Wales have earned plaudits for both results and performances, and the resurgence of the national team is in stark contract to the lows Williams experienced last season with club side Wrexham who were relegated from the Football League. And Williams is delighted with Wales transformation.

"I think anyone playing for their country is going to be proud to put on that shirt, especially this last year as we have been doing so well," said Williams.

"Previously we have been bottom of the group in qualifying and it has been a case of making the numbers up. But not now. We have had a good 12 months and the team spirit has been great. If we qualify it will be brilliant for Welsh football. I have enjoyed it immensely. Wrexham were at the bottom last season so there was no enjoyment there. When you are winning it makes it that much better, especially this last year with Wales. I don't think it has sunk in yet."

The double header against Romania, to end the qualifying campaign, was always going to be a tough test for group leaders Wales. Regardless of what Wales have achieved, Williams - 22 in October - stressed the need to build on their recent exploits.

"We have put ourselves in a great position, with just the two games against Romania to go, Romania was always going to be tough because they are a good side, but we just wanted to win straight away to make the last game more enjoyable. There is still a long way to go and we have done nothing yet, but for the time being we are sitting nicely."

Wales put themselves in with an excellent opportunity of qualifying by beating much fancied France 4-2 at Ninian Park, and Williams has happy memories about that result.

"The win over France stands out. We were losing 2-1, but came back to win so well and that showed the character and spirit in the squad. That is the one which made people sit up and take notice. It was live on television and we showed everyone that Wales had a good under 21 side. That really put us in a good position and a chance to qualify."

Williams had not missed a minute of Wales' qualifying campaign before Lewin Nyatanga replaced him in the back four for the friendly defeat against England at The Racecourse in May. Disappointed to miss out against the likes of Theo Walcott as Flynn brought in experience from the senior side, Williams insists there is excellent spirit in the camp.

"I was pretty disappointed I did not get a chance against England, but there was a lot of quality in the squad. Lads came in from the senior squad and Lewin plays in my position. Lewin is a good player at a club in a higher league so there was nothing I could do but wait for my chance, come in and do well. You have to show what you can do when you get in."

"There is a lot of spirit in the squad. Players have come in and done well, and others on the side have performed when they have come in. It seems everyone is helping each other out and it is brilliant to be part of this squad. Everyone has played their part to get to here."

Although Williams thoroughly enjoys his time on international duty, he is eager to help Wrexham mount a promotion challenge this season. After deciding to revamp the Wrexham squad, manager Brian Little has brought in a number of new signings and Williams is hoping to play his part in what he hopes will be a more enjoyable campaign.

"It is a big season after the disappointment of last year. We were all gutted. But this is a new team and all the new signings have settled in. The gaffer will decide whether I am playing. Everyone wants to play but if not, hopefully when my chance comes I take it.

"Hopefully we will challenge for promotion - that is the aim. We need to win a lot more games than last year. Home form will be the key and we have to be stronger at The Racecourse. And hopefully by the end of the campaign we are at the opposite end of the table to last season."

50% off!

If you are in receipt of a Disability Living Allowance, Attendance Allowance or Work Tax Credit Disability Element you are eligible to apply for a DASH card.

This give you half price access to many leisure and fitness facilities, including gym memberships from £12.50 a month.

To find out more contact your local leisure and activity centre:

Chirk Leisure and Activity Centre	01691 778666
Clywedog Leisure and Activity Centre	01978 262787
Darland Leisure and Activity Centre	01244 571077
Gwyn Evans Leisure and Activity Centre	01978 754394
Morgan Llwyd Leisure and Activity Centre	01978 314693
Plas Madoc Leisure and Activity Centre	01978 821600
Queensway Leisure and Activity Centre	01978 355826
Rhiwabon Leisure and Activity Centre	01978 822978
Rhosnesni Leisure and Activity Centre	01978 358967
Waterworld Leisure and Activity Centre	01978 297300

50% i ffwrdd!

Os ydych yn derbyn Lwfans Byw i'r Anabl, Lwfans Gweini neu Gredyd Treth Gwaith Elfen Anabledd rydych yn gymwys i wneud cais am gerdyn DASH.

Mae hwn yn rhoi mynediad hanner pris i lawer o gyfleusterau hamdden a ffitrwydd, yn cynnwys aelodaeth campfa o £12.50 y mis.

I wybod mwy cysylltwch â'ch canolfan hamdden a gweithgareddau lleol:

Canolfan Hamdden a Gweithgareddau Y Waun	01691 778666
Canolfan Hamdden a Gweithgareddau Clywedog	01978 262787
Canolfan Hamdden a Gweithgareddau Darland	01244 571077
Canolfan Hamdden a Gweithgareddau Gwyn Evans	01978 754394
Canolfan Hamdden a Gweithgareddau Morgan Llwyd	01978 314693
Canolfan Hamdden a Gweithgareddau Plas Madoc	01978 821600
Canolfan Hamdden a Gweithgareddau Queensway	01978 355826
Canolfan Hamdden a Gweithgareddau Rhiwabon	01978 822978
Canolfan Hamdden a Gweithgareddau Rhosnesni	01978 358967
Canolfan Hamdden a Gweithgareddau'r Byd Dŵr	01978 297300

The Wrexham FC Collectors' And Historians' Society

Formed September 2007

THE WREXHAM FC COLLECTORS' AND HISTORANS' SOCIETY was formed in September 2007 for the purpose of preserving and promoting the history and heritage of Wrexham FC. It was formed to bring together all those fans who are interested in any and every aspect of the football club's colourful past. The ultimate goal being the establishment of a football museum.

Following its formation last August, Wrexham FC Chief Executive Anthony Fairclough, gave the group his blessing when he said: "An archive of Wrexham material and memorabilia down the seasons is the perfect way to preserve the history of our proud club. I fully support the aims of the Society, which will endorse the role of Wrexham C as a cherished local institution."

Official Club Historian Peter Jones said of the group; "The intention of WCHS is to look at preserving historical material relating to the 'Dragons'. That includes programmes, hand-books, fanzines, memorabilia, newspaper cuttings, photo-graphs, postcards, badges, replica shirts, statistics, audio/video material, etc.; in fact, anything at all uniquely related to the club."

Glyn Davies

"The Society are not looking to requisition supporters' col-lections. Instead it is attempting to register them, thereby compiling a database of memorabilia so that interesting items can be lent for display at exhibitions or for publishing."

"We would also ask that fans think twice before throwing away any items related to Wrexham Football Club, and think about donating them to the Society. If they wish, supporters can donate or bequeath their collections in the knowledge that they will be looked after by the Society. As part of our aims we are looking for the WCHS to be bound to keep two original copies of items whenever pos-sible, with numbers in excess of this to be sold on to collectors to boost Society funds. This would be the case particularly with donations of programmes, for instance. Funds raised would be used to purchase historical material, picture frames, the framing of shirts, and exhibition cases etc to display the artefacts we collect."

Already the Society has made an impact, with Society and Trust Member Glyn Davies having taken up the task of working on establishing the Racecourse Ground to be recognised as the oldest international venue, still in use, in the world.
This has now been recognised by the Guinness Book of Records, and a delighted Glyn said; "It is over 130 years ago, in 1877, that the first ever international was played on the Racecourse against Scotland, which Wales lost 2-0. There was a misconcep-tion that Wales played there early games at Acton Park, but that is untrue."

"Wales are the third oldest football association behind England and Scotland, but both of them played there early matches like Wales on cricket grounds, but the Racecourse was to become, and still is a ground that football has been continually played on."

Glyn's idea of highlighting the Racecourse as the olest international stadium still used came about when he saw that Hallam FC were in the Guinness Book of records as having the oldest ground in the world. "I believed that the Racecourse had a case and approached Guinness, but the bone of contention with Guinnes was whether interna-tionals were still being played on the Racecourse, otherwise they saw Hampden Park in Glasgow has being the record holder."

"The fact that Wales had played Norway on the Racecourse in a full international last February didn't seem to matter, so I wrote to the FAW for confirmation that Wales intended to play more games on here in the future. David Collins the FAW secretary replied; 'the Racecourse still figures as a venue for internationals involving Wales, subject to the required standards for international stadia being kept up to date, but it is still our intention to use the Racecourse as an international ground.' The news Glyn had been waiting for came on 17th June from Ralph Hannah, the Records Manager of Guinness World Records. In his email he confirmed Wrexham's world record; "After receiving confirmation from the FAW that the Racecourse will still be used for senior international matches we are delighted to confirm that the Racecourse is indeed the holder of the Guinness World Record for 'Oldest international football ground'."

Further work by the Collectors' and Historical group has seen a trophy returned to its rightful place.- the trophy cabinet at the Racecourse. The trophy was presented to the club in 1948, following the club's first ever overseas tour. They travelled to Germany to play three teams from the British Army on the Rhine at the end of the 1947/48 season. One of those matches was played against the Western Command, and it was from this game that the trophy was presented to the club.

However, it is not known what happened to the trophy until it turned up on eBay earlier this year. The Society bid for the trophy and thankfully were successful and have since returned it to its rightful place.

One other project that the Society have undertaken has been to raise funds to have framed photographs/shirts placed around the Racecourse. Club historian Peter Jones said; "Although the Racecourse is steeped in history, there is very little to show of our history in and around the ground itself. I approached the Club's Chief Executive, Anthony Fairclough, about being able to show our history around the club, and he was in total agreement with the idea."

"With the refurbishment of the Centenary Club, and the renaming of the room upstairs as the 'Bamford Suite', after the club's greatest ever goalscorer, Tommy Bamford, it

The Wrexham FC travelling party pictured at the Belsen concentration camp memorial in May 1948, while on there three match tour of Germany.

was agreed to honour all former players and man agers who feature in the club's 'Hall of Fame' within the room, and we have since started to fill the room with framed photographs and a small biography on each player. It really has given the room a new out look, and hopefully fans will enjoy the pictures."

"One of our next projects is to start on the downstairs room at the Centenary Club, and place framed shirts around the walls. We already have a number of shirts promised to frame and display, but to make it happen a lot quicker, would be for fans/businesses to sponsor a frame, and in doing so, they would have there name shown within the frame as the sponsor. The cost of sponsoring each frame would be £100."

"Finally, the biggest project that the Society has undertaken is to put together an on-line museum, which will take years to put together. We envisage the Society becoming the main source of information on the history of the club, and an active force in researching, recording and preserving all aspects of the 'Dragons', with Society members participating in these projects. I would call upon anyone interested in joining the Society, or who would to donate items of interest to it, or to even just registering an item to please e-mail Peter at shreds@wafc123.freeserve.co.uk or contact him via the Football Club.ut this has already been started, but more help would be appreciated for anyone with scanners and who is computer literate.

Racecourse Nights To Remember

Watching Holland's thrilling performances at the 2008 European Championships, brought back memories of the night when the Dutch masters came to Wrexham's Racecourse Ground as the 1988 European Champions. The game was a World Cup qualifying match, and the Dutch not surprisingly comprised a side full of world class players. We look back on another 'Racecourse Night to Remember'.

Wales: (Coach: Terry Yorath) Neville Southall (Everton), Clayton Blackmore (Manchester United), Mark Bowen (Norwich City), Peter Nicholas (Chelsea), Jeff Hopkins (Crystal Palace), Gavin Maguire (Portsmouth), Dean Saunders (Derby County), David Phillips (Norwich City), Iwan Roberts (Watford) *replaced by sub Andy Jones (Charlton Athletic)*, Geraint Williams (Derby County) *replaced by sub Colin Pascoe (Sunderland)*, Malcolm Allen (Norwich *City)*.

Holland: (Coach: Thijs Libregts), Hans Van Breukelen (PSV Eindhoven), Berry Van Aerle (PSV Eindhoven), Graeme Rutjes (KV Mechelen), Ronald Koeman (Barcelona), Addick Koot (PSV Eindhoven), Jan Wouters (Ajax), John Van't Schip (Ajax), Wim Hofkens (KV Mechelen), Wim Kieft (PSV Eindhoven), Frank Rijkaard (AC Milan) *replaced by sub Johnny Bosman (KV Mechelen)*, Rob Witschage (St. Etienne) *replaced by sub Mark Van Basten (AC Milan)*.

Referee: Mr Helmut Kohl (Austria)

Wales 1 Holland 2
World Cup Qualifier Group Four: 11th October 1989

Terry Yorath's sides hopes of qualifying for the 1990 World Cup finals in Italy had already ended before this game with a 1-0 defeat in Finland. The Dutch however, were fighting neck and neck with West Germany to the right for automatic qualication, while the runners-up could qualify has one of the two best runners-up from the seven four team groups.

The Dutch had a huge following of over 3,000 fans all seemingly wearing different ranges of orange clothing. The ferry company Townsend Thorensen, had obviously ferried many fans over, as the orange overalls that there workers wear, had clearly been 'borrowed' as they were on full view at the Racecourse.

Holland had come to Wales to impress, and even without the skill and artistery of the injured Ruud Gullit, the Dutch side made an impression on the home crowd.

However, the orange men were not to have it all there own way, as Wales put up a spirited, gutsy and typical Welsh performance against the silky skills of Koeman, Rijkaard and Van Basten.

Terry Yorath's side knew they were up against it early on as the Dutch found there rhythm, and after only twelve minutes they took the lead when Ronald Koeman's free-kick was met with a bullet header from defender Graeme Rutjes that gave Neville Southall no chance.

Holland went close again when Gavin Maguire cleared off the line from John Van't Schip as the Welsh battled to stay in the game.

But Wales fought back, and twice came close from Gavin Maguire free-kick's that were both parried by ex-

Forest 'keeper, Hans Van Breukelen, while Malcolm Allen should have lobbed the PSV Eindhoven shot-stopper instead of allowing the ball to drop. However, the same player did have the ball in the net, but it was disallowed for a foul.

After the break, Holland almost doubled there lead when Koeman's thunderous shot came back off the post in the 48th minute.

Wales should have equalised in the 65th minute when Dean Saunders blazed the ball across the face of the goal.

However, the Welsh were left to rue that missed chance in the 79th minute when Berry Van Aerle's cross in from the right was met by a thunderous header from substitute Johnny Bosman to secure the top spot in the group for the Dutch.

However, two minutes from time the spirited Welsh side scored a deserved consolation when following a uncharacteristic mistake by the Dutch 'keeper Hans Van Breukelen, Mark Bowen took advantage to stab the ball home.

Wales manager Terry Yorath was philisophical after the defeat when he said; "It was a better performance from us after our last game in Finland, but Holland were a very classy outfit."

"We did show more passion in this game than we did against Finland, but it is difficult to play against them when they are playing keep ball."

The Welsh team line-up back row (L-R)t Mark Aizlewood, Neil Slatter, Gareth Hall, Andy Holden, Iwan Roberts, Tony Norman, Neville Southall. Middle row (L-R); Ron Stitfall (Kit), Clayton Blackmore, Mark Bowen, Colin Pascoe, Geraint Williams, Malcolm Allen, Mark Hughes, Dr. Graham Jones (Medic), Peter Shreeves (Coach). Front row (L-R); Peter Nicholas, Barry Horne, David Phillips, Terry Yorath (Manager), Kevin Ratcliffe, Ian Rush, Dean Saunders.

"Our younger players found the going very tough, but there were some good points for us. I thought Malcolm Allen, Mark Bowen, and Jeff Hopkins all did very well for us, but at the end of the day you have to put your hands up and say that the Dutch were just too good for us".

Dutch striker Marco Van Basten, who came on as a substitute, said; "I think we are close to qualifying now, but Wales made it very difficult for us. We were lucky to get an early goal, and after that I thought we controlled the game."

Holland in fact went on to beat Finland 3-0 in there last game, and thus qualify for Italia '90, while Wales were beaten 2-1 in Colgne against a strong West German side, who also qualified for Italia '90.

In the finals, Holland were to be knocked out of the group stages by England and the Republic of Ireland, while the Germans actually went on to beat Argentina 1-0 in the World Cup final.

Left: Holland & Barcelona star Ronald Koeman in action at the Racecourse, Wrexham.

Wrexham Lager Sports & Social Club

Good food, excellent beers, and a warm welcome guaranteed.

Big screen showing Sky Sports

Supporters' Trust members free entry on matchday

Wrexham FC
Former Players Association

One bright spot last season for Wrexham Football Club was the formation of the Wrexham FC Former Players' Association, which has been long overdue. The Association was launched on 30th September 2007 at the Bamford suite in the Centenary Club at the Racecourse, with the aims of; promoting the good name and tradition of Wrexham Football Club; representing the interests of former players; organising sporting and social activities among former players; and to support and assist charitable organisations.

From that inaugural meeting a committee was made up of Nick Hencher (Wrexham FC 1977-1979 & 1985-1988), John Lloyd (1965-1967), Arfon Griffiths (1959-1961 & 1962-1979), Tecwyn Lloyd-Jones (1959-1964), Dixie McNeil (1977-1982 & 1985-1989) and Waynne Phillips (1989-1998 & 1999-2003).

At that inaugural meeting it was great to see former players from all era's in attendance, and acquaintances renewed. Charles Kelsall, who played in the late 40s was there; Eric Littler from the 50s; Reg Holland and Alan Fox from the 1961/62 promotion winning side; Bobby Park, Alan Bermingham, Dave Gaskell, Bernard Purdie, Brian Price, and Arfon Griffiths reminisced of the promotion season of 1969/70; while Mike Williams and Stuart Parker recalled the great European games with FC Porto and AS Roma, to name but a few.

The creation of the Wrexham FC Former Players Association is to provide comprehensive representation, support and benefits to all of its members. It is a non profit-making association governed by constitution and managed voluntarily by former players and others with specific skills.

Players at the inaugural meeting of the Wrexham FC Former Players Association in September 2007

Wrexham FC Former Players Association has been formed to provide the platform for former players of the club to renew friendships and make new ones through its annual calendar of sporting and social events. The Association are looking to include charity football matches; masters football; Golf Days; Re-unions; tribute dinners; Q & A answer forums and other events to complete a full and varied pro-gramme.

Whilst participating in many of these events, former players are also support-ing a primary objective of the association, which is their commitment to raise funds for charities and worthy causes.

The Association has already held a number of events, including a reunion for players of the 1950s, 1960s and 1970s; a

Tecwyn Lloyd Jones & Wyn Davies meet up at the Golf Day having been part of the 1962 promotion winning side under Ken Barnes.

golf day at Clays Golf Club, 30th Anniversary reunion of the 1977/78 Third Division Championship team; and a team entering the supporters groups annual end-of-season 8-a-side football tournament for the first time.

Events planned for the forthcoming season are a football match against former players of our rivals Chester City; a day at the races for members; a reunion of players from the 80s and 90s; while the biggest and most important event will be a reunion dinner that every former player is invited to at the Lion Quays Hotel on Sunday 28th September 2008, with Duncan McKenzie as guest speaker.

Thanks to Wrexham FC directors Neville Dickens and Geoff Moss, who have fully backed the for-mation of the Association, which hopes to continue to promote the name of Wrexham FC and to enjoy excellent links and reciprocal arrangements with the Club.

Wrexham FC has a proud and illustrious his-tory, and despite the set back of last season, the Former Players Associat-

Welsh Legend Dean Saunders and former Wrexham man-ager Brian Flynn, are stopped in there tracks by Colin Holt.

ion wish to play there part in helping Wrexham Football Club get back to where they rightly belong - the Football League.

The Golf Day was held at Clays Golf Club on the Wrexham Industrial Estate, and helped raise funds not only for the Centre of Excellence at Wrexham FC, but Air Ambulance Wales.

With over twenty teams taking part, there was a good turn out of Former Player members, while former Welsh Legend, Dean Saunders also took part. Everyone was then thoroughly entertained in the evening by former Racecourse favourite Gary Bennett.

The tenth annual Wrexham Supporters end of season 8-a-side football tournament took place at Colliers Park on the morning of the clubs last home game against Accrington.Nine supporters teams took part, and for the first time a Former Players team represented the Association. It was a fantastic experience for those supporters who had the opportunity to play against there heroes, wjilst also being watched and encouraged from the touch line by former Wrexham Legends Arfon Griffiths, Mike Williams and Graham Whittle.

Playing against teams who were more than half Billy Ashcroft's age, the former striker, was a rock in defence as the Former Players Association side lost just one of the four group games to reach the final on goal difference.

In the final they met the previous years winners Rhos & District Reds, but the former players weary legs got the better of them as the younger more vibrant 'Jacko' side went on to win the trophy for the second successive year.

The Wrexham FC Former Players side that finished runners-up in the tenth annual Supporters 8-a-side end of season football tournament; Back L-R: Arfon Griffiths, Nick Hencher, Billy Ashcroft, Andy Edwards, Steve Watkin. Front L-R: Ian Griffiths, Steve Buxton, Waynne Phillips, John Muldoon.

The 30th Anniversary of Wrexham Football Club's Third Division Championship side: Wrexham's greatest!

Wrexham FC 1977-78 Third Division Championship winning squad. Standing L-R; Mickey Evans, Dixie McNeil, Alan Hill, Wayne Cegielski, Steve Buxton, Dai Davies, Les Cartwright, Gareth Davies, George Showell, Arfon Griffiths and Nick Hencher. Sitting L-R; Graham Whittle, Bobby Shinton & Alan Dwyer.

Last March saw the 30th Anniversary of what was the most memorable season in the club's history - 1977/78. A packed Bamford Suite witnessed all the camaraderie and humour that was evident. The players laughed and joked as if it was only yesterday that they had finished playing, when in fact the likes of Bobby Shinton and Mickey Evans hadn't met each other since Bobby left Wrexham to join Manchester City in the summer of 1979.

That move was in fact the first ever move under the 'freedom of contract', and it was hotly discussed by Bobby and his manager of the time Arfon Griffiths during the reunion, which was excellently hosted by the BBC Match of the Day commentator, and Wrexham fan, Ian Gwyn Hughes.

Those lucky enough to have attended the evening were shown highlights of that memorable season, before recollecting there memories and telling stories of a what was without doubt the greatest ever season in Wrexham's history. The

Les Cartwright

only players missing from the side on the night were Mel Sutton, John Roberts, Mickey Thomas, Eddie Niedzwiecki and of course the late John Lyons, but they were all certainly remembered during the evening, as the players recalled those great times.

That team not only won the league in style, but they reached the quarter-finals of both the FA Cup and the Football League Cup knocking out First Division sides such as Bristol City and Newcastle United, while also winning the Welsh Cup to earn a place in the European Cup-Winners' Cup.

Manager Arfon Griffiths summed up the achievement of that Wrexham side perfectly, when he said: "I was so disappointed in 1977, when we missed out on going up. I was determined to kill off the old myth of 'they don't want to go up!'

"It wasn't easy as we only had a squad of 16 to 18 players, as Stuart Lee, Billy Ashcroft and Brian Lloyd only played a few games at the start of the season before moving on.

"It is without doubt the best Wrexham side I have ever seen. We played over sixty games that season, but the players knew that if they were injured or lost there place, they'd struggle to get back into the team; but as any manager will tell you, 'it's not the team that takes you up, its the squad.

Wrexham Pioneers

We continue to track those early Wrexham players who also represented Wales in full international matches, and following on from the previous yearbooks, Welsh and Wrexham Football Historian Gareth M. Davies this time continues with the 'stars' from the 1890's decade who wore the Welsh shirt.

William Haighton Turner accumulated five appearances for Wales between 1887 and 1891, but was sadly on the losing side on every occasion! One of three brothers, who also played for Wrexham and Wales (see a little further on), Wrexham born Bill was a utility forward who preferred the centre forward role. Football hacks of the time described him thus; 'A dashing centre forward who passes well to his wings', and 'had a fair shot, but rather rash'.

He had previously played for Wrexham Victoria and Wrexham Lever, before joining Wrexham for whom he appeared in two Welsh Cup finals, but again success eluded him, losing 1-0 to Chirk in 1890, and 5-2 to Shrewsbury a year later.

In March 1891 he made a guest appearance for Everton, who at the time were playing at Anfield (and would not be moving to a new ground at Goodison Road until twelve months later), but was not taken on. Bill was often in demand for representative football for Denbighshire.

Oswald Davies was a Classics Master at Grove Park school in Wrexham, and had previously played rugby for Stroud and Gloucester in 1885, before changing codes to soccer. 'Os' took up the round ball with Llangollen in 1887, whilst also appearing for the Grove Park School XI. Wrexham FC took an interest in him, and he joined them for the start of the 1889/90 campaign, although initially his employers had objected to him playing.

Wales team v. Ireland (5th April 1893): The two in the centre on the middle row are Sam Jones and Arthur Lea.

The outside-right impressed so much with the Racecourse club that he was chosen for Wales against Scotland at Paisley in March 1890, but it proved to be his only cap following a 5-0 defeat.

Noted to have 'a good command of the ball; a good shot; any amount of pluck; and would tackle the biggest back or half-back'. Another assessment was 'a brilliant footballer, but needs a little weight'. He appeared in the same two Welsh Cup finals as Bill Turner, losing them both.

The FA of Wales at the time he played believed he was born in Llangollen, but further research shows that he is more than likely to have originated from Clifton, near Bristol!

Along with Job Wilding, who was featured in last years yearbook, *Abel Hayes* was one of the first to join the newly formed Wrexham Olympic club in 1884. Noted as 'a tireless half-back who covered lots of ground, he also possessed great pace (a predessor of Kevin Ratcliffe perhaps!).

Hayes had begun with Wrexham Crown, and then Olympic before Everton recruited him in October 1885. After a spell Hayes moved to Bootle (then Prominent) between 1886 and 1888, and back home to Wrexham 1889/90 and Wrexham Hibernian. He then had a five year stint with Wrexham when his two Welsh caps were recorded both against Ireland, winning 5-2 in 1890 at Shrewsbury, and 4-1 in 1894 at Swansea.

The experience of Hayes was of great benefit to his hometown club in their first few seasons of organised league competitions, while he played in four Welsh Cup finals, winning once in 1893, when Wrexham beat Chirk 2-1 at Oswestry.

After leaving the Racecourse club in 1895, Abel moved to Rhostyllen for a couple of years, while Rhos Eagle Wanderers (Rhosllanerchrugog) was his last port of call before retiring in 1898. In the 1920's and 30's Abel Hayes was seen regularly at the Racecourse alongside his pal and Welsh international colleague Jack Powell. He made one appearance for North Wales against Staffordshire in 1889 when these types of regional representative games were common place. He died in Wrexham on 21st July 1941 when in his mid seventies.

Arthur Lea had only one arm, however, even with such a disadvantage he was an accomplished footballer. Lea overcame his handicap due to his all-round skill and natural flair with the ball, and was noted for his 'tremendous and powerful kick'.

After helping to form Wrexham Grosvenor in 1881, he eventually joined Wrexham in 1883 where he was to remain for eleven years. As a professional he received five shillings (25p) a week, but when making guest appearances his fee rose dramatically to ten shillings (50p), and was reputedly the highest paid player in Wales.

Arthur fulfilled his greatest ambition in 1893 when he captained Wrexham to victory over Chirk in the Welsh Cup final, and in the same year was made skipper for Wales against Ireland in Belfast, which was his fourth and final cap for his country. Shortly after Lea fell seriously ill and at one point it looked as if he could lose a leg.

Arthur recovered to start playing again, but his comeback was short lived, following a Soames Charity Cup final against Druids, which Wrexham won 1-0. He and the other players were roughly handled by some of the spectators and they had to hurriedly leave the field and make their way home by themselves! Lea remarked that 'if that's what football was all about, it was the end for him'.

He had combined playing with his every day work as a postman, sometimes reporting for work at 5.30am; then did a 18 mile round; before catching the 9.20 train to an away match. In the evening he would return to Chester after the last train to Wrexham, walk home and be back on duty by 5am! By 1900, he was reckoned to have travelled over 80,000 miles on foot in the service of the Post Office. After retirement he became land-lord of the Wrest Hotel, Marchwiel.

Arthur was also a useful cricketer, playing for Wrexham Cricket Club, mainly as a bowler, but also a good batsman, making a number of half-centuries. This remarkable character died in March 1945 at Wrexham when almost into his eighties.

Returning to the Turner brothers, *Joseph Hudson Turner* was a forward like brother Bill, who won his only Welsh cap against England at the Racecourse in May 1892 (Lost 0-2).

Joe who played for Wrexham (1890-93), Chester (1893-95) and later Wrexham Gymnasium was called up to stand in for Joseph Davies (Ardwick), and was described in the match reports as 'a novice on the left wing'.

The Turner's father was Borough Surveyor of Wrexham for over 50 years, and owned much property in the town. Joe who was a brother-in-law of Horace Blew (who was a great Wrexham and Welsh international of the early part of the 20th century, and who we will come to as this series progresses) always maintained his sporting activities, including instructor in the Wrexham Gymnasium for a long period.

In business, Joseph Hudson was a master plumber, but towards the end of his working life became the Licensee of the Crown Inn, Caergwrle. Won a Welsh Cup winners' medal with Wrexham in 1893, and a runners-up medal in 1891.

Richard E Turner was the youngest of the three Wrexham/Welsh caps and while his brothers were forwards he was a 'custodian' winning his Welsh place against Ireland and England. However, he had to pick the ball out of the net eleven times in all, as Wales lost 7-2 in Belfast, and 4-1 in Sunderland in February/March 1891.

Dick had begun playing as an out-fielder, and it was said; 'undoubtedly he would have been capped at half-back, but for a premature smash to an ankle'. This saw him take up 'between the sticks' and with the departure of incumbent Sam Gillam, he slotted well into the Wrexham vacancy.

Rated a 'very cool keeper who showed wonderful form and did his work in an easy manner'. In his first international he captained Wales and despite a hesitant start was retained against the English.

Before his seven years with Wrexham (1885-92) had played for the Victoria and Lever clubs in the Town. Appeared in two Welsh Cup finals in 1890 and 1891, and made one other appearance for Wales against the Canadians in 1891.

Dick, along with his brother Bill, eventually emigrated to South Africa.

Caergwrle born *Robert Davies* began his playing career at rivals Chester in December 1888 before returning home to Caergwrle Wanderers for the 1891/92 season, from where he attracted the attention of Wrexham, who he joined soon after.

The Welsh selectors spotted the forwards potential where the orthodox wingman showed pace and neat skills, and he was selected by Wales for the game with Ireland at Bangor (1-1) and England at the Racecourse (0-2).

Robert played in the Wrexham team that beat Chirk at Oswestry in the Welsh Cup final in 1893, and won a runners-up medal in the 1895 final defeat by Newtown at Welshpool. He resumed with his village club after this, and during the summer was a notable bowler for Caergwrle Cricket Club.

He was employed as a coal miner, and was later re-instated in the game as an amateur. He was still playing local football in 1913 when well in his forties!

A regular goalscorer and 'effective passer', *Ben Lewis* was said to possess 'admirable judgement and a well directed shot'. The F.A.W. player assessment described the young Lewis as 'a very good forward, works well but did not combine well with Robert Roberts (Rhosllanerchrugog)'. Ben won ten caps for Wales, seven of which when with Wrexham, two with Middlesbrough and one, his first with Chester.

Lewis enjoyed three spells with Wrexham, 1891-92, 1893-95 and 1896-99. Lewis played most of his football with Chester and Wrexham in the Combination League, and one season in the Northern League with Middlesbrough.

Controversially, Wrexham dropped Saltney born Lewis on the eve of the 1899 Welsh Cup final replay against Druids (which they lost), where the press described it a 'great mistake by the committee' and Ben severed his connection with the club. He did win one Welsh Cup Winners' medal in 1897 v. Newtown. A scorer of two goals in his ten matches for Wales, he also appeared in the first of two matches with the Canadian touring team in September 1891.

A product of the Wrexham reserve team *Samuel Jones* was a stocky but agile goal-keeper who understudied the regular Welsh custodian Jim Trainer in the 1890's. Sam won six caps in all, two with Wrexham, three at Burton Swifts and the latter one with Druids all between 1893 and 1899.

After his spell at the Racecourse, which included a Welsh Cup winners' medal in 1893, he joined Burton Swifts and remained with the Second Division club for three seasons where he was described as a 'Beacon of reliability' in a poor side. Sam was expected to move to a bigger club, but this did not materialise and eventually settled for the Combination League with Druids.

A member of the Denbighshire Militia, he interrupted his football activities to fight in the Boer War. A Collier, he was attached to the Royal Welch Fusiliers as a Volunteer for over twenty years.

A man of many talents *Joseph Rogers* was noted as a very strong, aggressive player and reputedly 'one of the fastest defenders Wrexham ever possessed'. A sharp tackler and cool under pressure, his great speed brought him local fame as an athlete and many sprint trophies.

Rogers gained all three of his caps for Wales in 1896 after moving to Wrexham from Brymbo Institute, and his three appearances were something of a roller coaster! At the end of February on the Racecourse, he helped Wales to a 6-1 win over Ireland. Two weeks later against England at Cardiff he and Sam Jones were in the team who lost 1-9, while five days later in Dundee, he saw defeat again, this time 4-0.

A Welsh Cup finalist with Wrexham in 1896-98 and 99, Joe was one of those players whose love of the game saw him playing into his forties with local Junior teams, among them Coedpoeth. Following his retirement from the game he retained these links with Wrexham and was employed on the Racecourse turnstiles for over 30 years.

He spent his working life as a coalminer. First at Gatewen Colliery (35 years), and later Plas Power Colliery. Rogers was also a talented musician and successful choir conductor.

John Taylor is a member of the 'one cap' brigade wearing the Welsh jersey for the only time in March 1898 against England on the Racecourse in a 0-3 reverse. A native of Shotton, he spent five years with Mancot and Pentre United before turning professional with Wrexham in October 1896.

After a slow start Taylor turned in some fine displays resulting in his cap and a move to Southern League club Reading. It was the 'wrong move' for him as he 'failed to deliver'. His wages were cut and he was offered a free transfer and £5 to leave. He was eventually taken on by Crewe and by 1902 was back in his home area with Chester.

Described as a 'fearless tackler and one of their best players'. The enigmatic Taylor ended the 1902/03 season by failing to turn up for matches and the Chester club sacked him. Won a Welsh Cup winners in 1897 and a loser's medal in 1898.

Another product of Mancot and Pentre United to join Wrexham and become a Welsh international was *Frederick Charles Kelly*. A native of Sandycroft, near Chester, Fred was the son of William Kelly, an F.A.W. committeeman, and was one of a number of players who understudied Billy Meredith.

Kelly won three caps, two with Wrexham in 1899 against Scotland and Ireland, and another against Ireland during 1902 after moving to Druids. At one time he was described as 'one of the very best forwards in Wales'. 'A forward who combines well and takes every opportunity of shooting for goal, in fact a player who has to be reckoned with'.

However, the winger was inconsistent which was why both Wrexham and Druids discarded him, and he eventually moved to Chester, Barnsley and later back to Druids in 1903/04. Fred Kelly followed the profession of Engineer. He died in Flixton, Lancashire at the age of 80 in July 1980.

Gareth M. Davies.

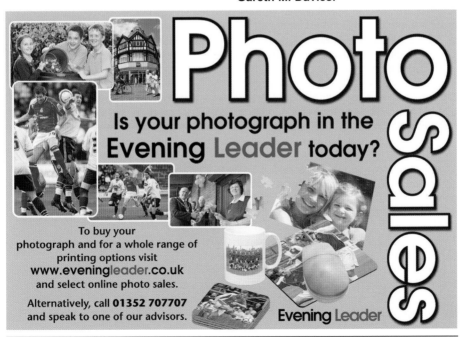

Wrexham FC Hall of Fame

Wrexham Supporters' Association honours the legends of the club through its Hall of Fame.The Hall of Fame was launched on September 20th, 2003 when twenty of Wrexham FC's all-time greats were inducted as its inaugural members on a very special evening at The Racecourse. Five new names have been added to the Hall of Fame each year since 2003, to further recognise the achievements of the club's greatest servants. To date the Supporters' Association has inducted forty three members.

Brian Flynn

Last season five more 'Legends' were chosen for the Hall of Fame, but due to unforseen circumstances, they were not actually inaugarated, but will be on 5th September 2008.

The players chosen last year were Alan Dwyer, who played an inmeasurable part in the 1977/78 Third Division championship team, having already been part of a side that had reached the quarter finals of the European Cup Winners' Cup, the FA Cup and the League Cup. A fantastic achievement.

The second selection was George Godding, who played in goal in the clubs first ever Football League match against Hartlepool in 1921, and went on to become the first ever player to make 100 appearances for the club, as well as being twice capped for Wales in 1923.

Another entrant was Steve Watkin who finished leading scorer in 1991/92, and went on to form a lethal goalscoring partnership with Gary Bennett to take the club to promotion in 1992/93. However, Steve will always be remembered for his goal against Football League Champions Arsenal in January 1992, which caused one of the greatest upsets in FA Cup history.

Big Jim Steel was the fourth entrant. His displays in european competition for the club brought him to the attention of a number of top european clubs. He will always be remembered for his winning goal against FC Porto on the Racecourse and the memorable battle with Real Zaragoza, that saw Wrexham go out on the away goals rule.

The final entrant into the club's Hall of Fame is Darren Ferguson who made over 350 appearances for Wrexham, playing a major part in the 2002/03 promotion winning side and playing in the successful the 2005 LDV final side, scoring an extra time goal to put the final nail in Southend's coffin.

There was certainly a lively debate when the five were chosen, but there are many players who quite clearly have still to force debate on being chosen.

The next inauguration will take place on 5th September 2008 at the Centenary Club, please give your support to this fantastic night of nostalgia. All Hall of Fame entrants are invited.

Alan Dwyer

Wrexham FC Hall of Fame

2002 Award
Tommy Bamford (1929 - 1934)
Albert Kinsey (1966 - 1973)
Gary Bennett (1992 - 1995 & 1997)
Cliff Lloyd (1937 - 1939)
Horace Blew (1897-1911, 1913-1927 & 1932-1936)
Eddie May (1968 - 1976)
Dai Davies (1977 - 1981 & 1985-1986)
Dixie McNeil (1978 - 1982 & 1985 - 1990)
Gareth Davies (1967 - 1982)
Aly McGowan (1953 - 1965)
Alan Fox (1954 - 1964)
John Neal (1967 - 1977)
Arfon Griffiths (1959 - 1961 & 1962 - 1981)
Ted Robinson (1894 - 1943)
Pryce Griffiths (1984 - 1986 & 1988 - 2003)
George Showell (1966 - 1991)
Alf Jones (1923 - 1936)
Mel Sutton (1972 - 1982)
Joey Jones (1971 - 1975, 1978 - 1982 & 1987 to present)
Billy Tunnicliffe (1947 - 1953)

2003 Award
Billy Ashcroft (1970 - 1977)
Mickey Evans (1966 - 1979)
Brian Lloyd (1971 - 1977)
Kevin Russell (1987 - 1989 & 1995 - 2007)
Graham Whittle (1972 - 1982)

2004 Award
Ken Barnes 1961 - 1965)
Karl Connolly (1991 - 2000)
Tommy Bannan (1951 - 1955 & 1957 - 1959)
Tommy Matthias (1912 - 1928)
Bobby Shinton (1976 - 1980)
Ron Chaloner (Special Award)

2005 Award
Phil Hardy (1990 - 2001)
Ron Hewitt (1951 - 1957 & 1959 - 1960)
Sammy McMillan (1963 - 1967)
Denis Smith (2001 - 2007)
Mickey Thomas (1971 - 1978 & 1991 - 1993)
Carroll Clark (Special Award)

2006 Award
Brian Carey (1991 - 1992 & 1996 to present)
Ray Smith (1967 - 1972)
Brian Flynn (1988 - 2001)
Bert Goode (1910-1911, 1913-1922 & 1923-1926)
Mike Williams (1984 - 1991)
Wrexham Supporters Trust (Special Award)
Johnny Edwards (Special Award)

2007 Award
Darren Ferguson (1999 - 2007)
George Godding (1921 - 1926)
Jim Steel (1983 & 1984 - 1987)
Alan Dwyer (1973 - 1981)
Steve Watkin (1989 - 1997)

George Godding

Darren Ferguson

Steve Watkin

Jim Steel

Where are they now?

It's always nice to keep in touch with old friends. So we thought we'd track down former Wrexham players who are still involved in the game in whatever capacity they now are. In fact it's quite surprising to find former Reds involved all over the world from the Hyundai A League in Australia to the Major Soccer League in America!

Name	Current Team	League (Position)
Danny Allsopp	Melbourne Victory	Hyundai A League (Australia)
Scott Barron	Millwall	League One
Steve Basham	Exeter City	Blue Square Premier League
David Bayliss	Barrow	Blue Square Premier League (Manager)
Dan Bennett	Singapore Armed Forces Football Club	Singapore S-League
Dean Bennett	Kidderminster Harriers	Blue Square Premier League
Michael Blackwood	Mansfield Town	Blue Square Premier League
Phil Boersma	Llangefni Town	Cymru Alliance League (Assistant Manager)
Phil Bolland	Cambridge United	Blue Square Premier League
Deryn Brace	Carmarthen Town	League of Wales (Player/Manager)
Dave Brammer	Millwall	League One
Mark Cartwright	Colwyn Bay	Unibond First Division South (Director)
Michael Carvill	Linfield	Irish Premier League
Steve Charles	Gainsborough Trinity	Blue Square North (Manager)
Karl Connolly	Prescot Cables	Unibond League Premier Division (Coach)
Terry Cooke	Colorado Rapids (USA)	Major Soccer League
Tom Craddock	Middlesbrough	Premier League
Malcolm Crosby	Middlesbrough	Premier League (Assistant Manager)
Matty Crowell	Northwich Victoria	Blue Square Premier League
Shaun Cunnington	Willenhall Town	North Prem League Div 1 South (manager)
Kevin Dearden	Millwall	League One (Goalkeeping Coach)
Matt Derbyshire	Blackburn Rovers	Premier League
Andy Dibble	Peterborough United	League Two (Goalkeeping Coach)
Matty Done	Hereford United	League One
Rob Duffy & Paul Hall	Newport County	Blue Square Conference South
Carlos Edwards	Sunderland	Premier League
Jake Edwards	Burton Albion	Blue Square Premier League
Paul Edwards	Port Vale	League Two
Stuart Elliott	Grays Athletic	Blue Square Premier League
Craig Faulconbridge	Haddenham United	Aylesbury District League Premier Division
Darren Ferguson	Peterborough United	League One (Manager)
Brian Flynn	Wales Under-21 manager	National Team
Ben Foster	Manchester United	Premier League
Steve Futcher	Colwyn Bay	Unibond
Carl Griffiths	Brentwood Town	Isthmian League Div One North (Manager)
Kevin Hannon	Warrington Town	Unibond League Division One (South)
Jimmy Harvey	Forest Green Rovers	Blue Square Premier League (Manager)
Seamus Heath	Northern Ireland Youth Developmen Officer	
Keith Hill	Rochdale	League Two (Manager)
Joe Hinnigan	Accrington Stanley	League Two (Physio)
Shaun Holmes	Finn Harps	League of Ireland
Andy Holt	Northampton Town	League One
Richard Hope	Grimsby Town	League Two
George Horan	Rhyl	League of Wales
Bryan Hughes	Hull City	Premier League
Tony Humes	Ipswich Town	Championship (Academy Manager)
Clayton Ince	Walsall	League One
Michael Ingham	York City	Blue Square Premier League
Jason Jarrett	Oldham Athletic	League One
Lee Jones	NEWI Cefn Druids	League of Wales (Joint Manager)

Name	Current Club	League (Position)
Michael Jones	Northwich Victoria	Blue Square Premier League
James Kelly	Rhyl	League of Wales
Chris Killen	Celtic	Scottish Premier League
Craig Knight	Mynydd Isa	Cymru Alliance League
Dennis Lawrence	Swansea City	Championship
Stuart Lee	FC Seattle Storm (USA)	Director of Coaching
Chris Llewellyn	Grimsby Town	League Two
Paul Linwood	Chester City	League Two
David Lowe	Derby County	Premier League (Academy Head Coach)
Andy Marriott	Exeter City	League Two
Lee McEvilly	Cambridge United	Blue Square Premier League
Mark McGregor	Altrincham	Blue Square Premier League
Jim McNulty	Stockport County	League One
Craig Madden	Stockport County	League Two (Youth Team Manager)
Paul Mitchell	MK Dons	League One
Maheta Molango	Lucena CF	Segunda B (Spain)
Craig Morgan	Peterborough United	League One
Andy Morrell	Bury	League Two
Jon Newby	Greenock Morton	Scottish League Division One
Eddie Niedzwiecki	Manchester City	Premier League (Assistant-Manager)
Armand One	Turun Palloseura	Finland Premier League
Gareth Owen	Rhyl	League of Wales
Waynne Phillips	NEWI Cefn Druids	Welsh Premier League (Joint Manager)
Paul Raynor	Crawley Town	Blue Square Conference Premier (Assistant Manager)
Jamie Reed	Rhyl	League of Wales
Kevin Reeves	Swansea City	Championship (Chief Scout)
David Ridler	Prescot Cables	Unibond League Premier Division
Neil Roberts	Rhyl	League of Wales
Paul Roberts	Bangor City	League of Wales
Steve Roberts	Walsall	League One
Lee Roche	Droylsden	Blue Square Conference North
Kristian Rogers	Port Talbot Town	League of Wales
John Ruddy	Everton	Premier League
Kevin Russell	Peterborough United	League One (Assistant Manager)
Mike Salmon	Arsenal	Premier League (Reserve Team Coach)
Mark Sertori	Newcastle United & England	Premier League (Club & Country Masseur)
Ron Sinclair	Stoke City	Premier League (Assistant Academy Director)
Alex Smith	Southport	Blue Square Conference North
Kevin Smith	Raith Rovers	Scottish League Division Two
Andy Thomas	Airbus UK	League of Wales
Lee Trundle	Bristol City	Championship
Graham Turner	Hereford United	League One (Manager)
Xavi Valero	Liverpool	Premier League (Goalkeeping Coach)
John Vaughan	Huddersfield Town	League One (Goalkeeping Coach)
Neil Wainwright	Morecambe	League Two
Richard Walker	Macclesfield Town	League Two
David Walsh	Mynydd Isa	Cymru Alliance League
Jon Walters	Ipswich Town	Championship
Peter Ward	Stockport County	League One (Assistant Manager)
David Warren	Waterford	League of Ireland
Steve Weaver	Wolves	Youth Team Coach
Paul Whitfield	Cammell Laird	Unibond Premier Division
Danny Williams	Rhyl	Welsh Premier League
Mark Wilson	Doncaster Rovers	League One
Tommy Wright	Norwich City	Championship (Goalkeeping Coach)

Obituaries

Keith Matthews (1934 - 2008)

A local lad in every sense of the word, Keith Matthews completed his education at the Llay Central School and the Wrexham Technical College, which is now Glyndwr University, followed by working at the old Thomas' timber yard next to Wrexham General Station.

As for football, he gained representative honours with Wrexham & District and Denbighshire Schoolboys, as well as playing for the Great Britain Youth Clubs' side. Keith was playing for Llay United in the Welsh National League when he was handed the opportunity to sign for Wrexham in December 1952, aged 18.

Keith made his Football League debut for the 'Robins' the following month at home to Tranmere Rovers, stepping into the side at outside-right after Billy Tunnicliffe had left the Racecourse to join Bradford Park Avenue. Wrexham won 1-0, and Keith kept his place for the following match, a 4-2 defeat at Oldham. However, he then found his first team chances in either of the wide berths limited, with the form of Glyn Hughes, and later Phil Gwatkin, stopping Keith from making progress.

Further progress was stifled in March 1955 when Keith was called up for his National Service, and he played his last match for the reserves in a Cheshire County League game at Stockport County on 12th March 1955. However, he was mainly based at RAF Cosford, which meant he could return home to play at weekends.

Upon his return from National Service in 1957 Keith found that he was to be released by Wrexham manager Cliff Lloyd at the end of the season, and during the summer he joined Cheshire County League side Witton Albion, where he spent a short spell before signing for fellow Cheshire County League side, Runcorn.

In April 1960 Keith moved on to Welsh League (North) side Blaenau Ffestiniog, where he picked up a Championship and Cup winners' medal. He signed for Holyhead Town in July 1962, where he was to end his playing career.

After hanging up his boots Keith took up employment as a wood cutting machinist, followed by working for an Insurance company for a number of years having settled in the Wrexham area. He later kept the newsagents and general store in Shones Lane, Llay, until he retired in November 1997. Keith sadly passed away at his home in Summerhill on 9th January 2008, aged 73.

Wrexham Career Statistics

Position: Outside-right/left
Birthplace: Llay, Denbighshire
Birthdate: 07/03/34
Appearances: 9
Goals: 0
Also represented: Llay United, Witton Albion, Runcorn,
                  Blaenau Ffestiniog & Holyhead Town.

Appearances and Goals

	League		FA Cup		Welsh Cup		Total	
	apps	gls	apps	gls	apps	gls	apps	gls
52/53	2	0	-	-	-	-	2	0
53/54	1	0	-	-	-	-	1	0
54/55	6	0	-	-	-	-	6	0
Total	9	0	-	-	-	-	9	0

BEGBIES TRAYNOR
CORPORATE RESCUE & RECOVERY

Proud to be associated with Wrexham Football Club

1 Winckley Court, Chapel Street, Preston PR1 8BU
Telephone: 01772 202000   Fax: 01772 200099

Section 4:
Wrexham's Supporters' Groups

Wrexham Supporters' Trust

2007/08 was a period which most Wrexham fans want erased from the annals of the club's history. When one considers the club's fortunes it is perhaps pleasantly surprising that the Trust have managed to keep its membership just above 700, and it is a figure which compares favourably with most other Trusts. However, it is difficult to predict what effect relegation will have on membership numbers this season, but if ever there was a time to be associated with supporters groups it is the present; so if you are not a member of Wrexham Supporters Trust perhaps now is the time to join.

The Trust Board has undergone considerable change over the past season with a number of resignations. I am sure that members appreciate the contribution made to the WST by Bruce Clapton (Chairman), Rob Griffiths (Chairman & Vice Chairman), Dave Preece (Secretary) and board members Kevin Bough, Terry Heath, Graham Matthias, Richard Purton, Sally Poppit and Phil Wynn. We thank you all.

Wrexham Supporters' Trust

Wrexham Supporters' Trust, PO Box 2200, Wrexham, LL11 9WG.
Telephone: 07981 151958
Website: http://www.wst.org.uk
Email: info@wst.org.uk

Following elections at the 2008 AGM, the Trust now has a number of new members on its board, and they will be responsible for taking the Trust forward, and maintaining the Trust's aim of achieving shares in Wrexham FC; and gaining board representation. The level of shareholding will be a matter for negotiation, as will the level of representation on the football club's board.

At the 2008 AGM members backed a board recommendation that despite the club's relegation there was an appetite for continued fundraising, and a new target of £500k was set. It is a considerable figure to aim for, but members do feel it is achievable and will provide the Trust with a good financial base for an equity purchase should the opportunity arise.

Most money raised by the Trust goes towards equity purchase, but over the years £108k of funds have also been donated to club projects. At present the fund for equity purchase stands in the region of £340k, which means the Trust has actually raised the grand total of almost £450k. Quite an achievement, and says much about those supporters who

have organised fund raising events as well as those who have supported them. In the last year the Trust have donated a new minibus for use at the Centre of Excellence at Colliers Park. The bus carries the Trust logo, and has already saved the centre 75% of their annual costs for hiring coaches.

The Trust have continued to take an active roll in the organisation of the Junior Dragons, and the main event last year was the Christmas party at Brymbo Social Club. A new committee has been formed to lead JD's events into 2008/09, and early indications look promising.

On match days the Trust run an office next to the Turf Hotel on Mold Road, in which we stock a selection of Trust and club merchandise, and has become a focus for both Wrexham and visiting fans in the run up to matches. The shop also sells, in an arrangement with Wrexham Football Club, family tickets for the Mold Road stand. The shop is run by volunteers so, if you have never been in the shop why not pop in and say hello.

The WST Christmas raffle is becoming an

institution, and we are grateful to those who donate so many fantastic prizes; and of course thank the people who help sell or purchase tickets. The Trust has recently launched its 200 club scheme which we hope will take off and become a big winner for both WST and those whose numbers are drawn, with half the money raised going back in to prizes.

The use of the Trust website continues to grow, and it contains a great deal of information about Trust activities. There is also an active and growing on line community of almost 200 members in the members forum. This has become a pop-ular way for members to discuss and exchange ideas as well as to interact with board members, who are always interested to receive feedback on this site.

The Trust need to be patient in our quest for part ownership of Wrexham Football Club, but in the meantime both members and the board of WST will continue to fund raise and plan for the day when share ownership and board representation becomes a reality. The Trust is determined to play its part in the regeneration of our football club and look forward to a successful business relationship with the club in a spirit of mutual respect.

SUPPORTERS' FEDERATION

WREXHAM SUPPORTERS FEDERATION

Wrexham Supporters Federation

Many fans will be unaware of the Wrexham Supporters Federation and what it is, but the committee's of all supporters groups are fully aware of the Federation having for the past twelve months held discussions that would be of benefit to the supporters groups movement and Wrexham FC who have been fully behind the aims and function of the Supporters Federation.

The Federation brings together all recognised supporters groups under one umbrella, but maintains the individuality of each group who will remain being run by their own elected committee's, who make up the Federation committee.

Aims of the Federation

The three aims of the Federation are as follows;
a) to reflect the primary importance of Wrexham FC to everyone connected with it and to develop the Football Club's fan base by encouraging greater, more positive, support.
b) to promote and encourage all Supporters Groups to join the Federation for the benefit of Wrexham FC and its

Supporters Groups.
c) to participate in joint fund raising and sponsorship activities to generate finances to the benefit of the Supporters groups and in particular, Wrexham FC.

Membership of the Federation

Participation in 'Wrexham Supporters Federation' is available to any of the recognised Football Club's Supporters' groups who agree to abide by its constitution and who fulfil the required criteria to join.

Benefits of Joining A Supporters Group

The Wrexham Supporters Federation encourage all Wrexham supporters to join a supporters group where you will be able to take advantage of the following benefits that have been agreed with the Football Club;

a) Priority match tickets for 'big' matches after season ticket holders and sponsors.
b) 10% discount in the club shop when you spend over £20 upon showing your membership card.

Chairman: Carroll Clark - Wrexham Supporters Association

Secretary: Chris Dimmick - Kings Mills Reds

Treasurer: Brian Davies - Shropshire Reds

Members :-
Wrexham Supporters Association, London Reds, Shropshire Reds, Holywell & District Reds, Buckley & District Reds, Rhos & District Reds, Kings Mills Reds, Mold & District Reds.

c) Regular meetings and events with fellow fans and the chance to meet players and other Wrexham related personnel.
d) Access to Wrexham FC memorabilia and other unique prizes.
e) Insurance benefits to away matches.
Plus much, much, more.

Other benefits are also being looked at, and other ideas and suggestons from members are most welcome. Please inform one of your committee members.

How Do I Join A Supporters Group?

Over the next few pages you will find the member groups of the Wrexham Supporters Federation with details about each group. Please contact your nearest group to become a member. All Wrexham fans are made welcome to join each of the supporters group's.

We Want to Form A New Supporters Group?

Wrexham Supporters groups are now established in a number of area's, but there have been one or two that have fallen by the wayside over the years; groups such as the

Ynys Mon Reds; the Vale of Clwyd Reds and even the Yorkshire Reds. There is still lots of support in those areas, but the people to run a supporters group are very few and far between because of the dedicated work it entails. Its not just about setting it up; its about carrying it on.

The Wrexham Supporters Association was the first established group in 1926; And it wasn't until 1993 that the first independent supporters group was set up with the London Reds, quickly followed a year later with the Shropshire Reds. All these groups have gone on to raise thousands of pounds for Wrexham Football Club.

If you are looking to form a new group to be officially recognised by the club then you need to be fully constitued. You will need at the very least an elected Chairman, Secretary and Treasurer.

The Federation groups have all at one time or another worked, helped and encouraged each other along. Contact any group for information on setting up a new group, and becoming a Federation member. They are here to help you.

Wrexham Supporters' Association

Wrexham Supporters' Association, c/o Wrexham FC
Telephone: 01978 266602
Website: http://www.wrexhamdragons.co.uk
Email: carroll.clark@btopenworld.com

The History of Supporters' Clubs in Wrexham

Wrexham AFC Supporters' Club (as it was then known) was born in August 1926 at the Black Lion pub in Wrexham. The driving force behind Wrexham AFC's first supporters' club was Jack Williams who was born in Summerhill in 1898. Jack saw his first Wrexham match in 1910, a Birmingham League encounter with Hednesford Town and was inspired to form a supporters' club. He was a man of great vision who recognised the importance of fans working together and with Tom Hodgson of Northampton Town, formulated the idea of the National Federation of Football Supporters' Clubs, which was inaugurated in 1927.

Wrexham Supporters' Association, as we are now known, owes a great debt to its founder Jack Williams. In recognition of his achievements we named our Player of the Season award after him. The Jack Williams Player of the Season was first awarded to goalkeeper Brian Lloyd at the end of the 1975/76 and has been awarded every year since by the Supporters' Association on behalf of Wrexham Football Club. Last season we made this prestigious award to Neil Roberts at the

final home match against Accrington Stanley, when we also presented Neil Taylor with the Young Player of the Season Award.

Our role within Wrexham Football Club
Over the years the Association helped to fund and build the old stand on the Kop and ran the Centre Spot club shop in the old Mold Road stand, the official Away Travel Scheme and the Junior Reds supporters' group. In recent years we have purchased equipment for Johnny Edwards to keep the Racecourse pitch in tip-top condition and last season purchased heart monitors for Mel Pejic to support fitness work with the players. We continue to provide practical day-to-day support as requested by the football club.

Last season we offered all fans an opportunity to join a supporters' club through our free membership scheme. This initiative boosted our membership to over 230 fans during the 2007/08, something we intend to build on in the coming season. Once again, all fans travelling on official away travel buses will automatically be signed up to our free membership

Membership Adults £5, Over-60s £3,
Under-16s £2

scheme, providing them with free insurance should an away match be cancelled within 6 hours of kick-off.

Looking to the future

The retirement of Phil Davies, who raised almost £100,000 from the 50/50 competition over a ten year period, left a big hole in our fundraising capacity. However, we're delighted that the competition has gone from strength to strength under the stewardship of Kevin Hughes who has brought some fresh ideas and enthusiasm to its organization. In total, the 50/50 competition raised £1740 last season of which 50% was donated to Wrexham Football Club in the form of cash and items of equipment such as the heart monitors.

For example, last season the Association purchased a short-wave electrotherapy machine for Mel Pejic in addition to sponsoring Michael Jones' match kit. In addition we sponsored the last home game in the Football League against Accrington Stanley and provided small donations to help the club to print fixture lists and teamsheets for Wrexham FC's sponsors and fans on matchdays. The Association will continue to raise money and support the club in its efforts to bounce back to the Football League at the first attempt.

There is much to look forward to this season, despite our relegation. In particular, the Association is proud to be a key member of a new collaboration of Wrexham FC Supporters' Groups, which aims to provide a strong and co-ordinated voice within the football club. The new Federation of Wrexham FC Supporters' Clubs will be chaired by Carroll Clark, who will bring his wealth of experience of working at national level as Treasurer of the Football Supporters' Federation to bear in the new organisation.

Supporters' clubs such as the Association will retain their identity within the new organisation, but collaborate to ensure that we all work in the same direction. As such we're still looking to bring new people onto the committee, so if you are interested in getting involved please get in touch with our Chairman Carroll Clark at carroll.clark@btopenworld.com. We will be writing to all members two weeks before the AGM inviting nominations and will publish the date in the local press and on our website, as we do every year.

Shropshire Reds

Shropshire Reds, PO BOX 547, Shrewsbury, Shropshire, SY3 8YY
Website: http://www.shropshirereds.co.uk
Email: shreds@wvtc123.freeserve.co.uk

The Shropshire Reds

You don't need to be Albert Einstein to conclude that last year was not one of the truly great chapters in the history of the Shropshire Reds. Coming, as it did, straight on the heels of "The Great Escape" near-fiasco of 2006-07 our fortunes have continued to slump alarmingly: membership has dwindled yet again, attendances at meetings have been well below the levels of previous years, and we have struggled to maintain our - traditionally - very impressive fund-raising record.

Undoubtedly this malaise is almost entirely due to the problems on the field of play. As the team spluttered and struggled through the season so did we, and try though we did to keep the interest alive things just kept on going downhill. If you accept that relegation from the Football League was pretty much inevitable before any Xmas presents were wrapped then you begin to understand the size of the task we faced in lifting everyone's spirits.

So what of the future? Well, there's non-League football for starters, something none of us thought would ever happen - but there are also a number of reasons to be (at least cautiously) optimistic. Contrary to what some "fans" might have you believe the Football Club is now more receptive to supporters' suggestions than it has been at any time that I can remember (nearly 50 years a Red). Constructive ideas will always capture Anthony Fairclough's attention, and he has proved to be the major success story of Wrexham's post-Administration history.

To give sensible opinion a proper voice the Shreds have been pleased to play their part in the creation and development of the Wrexham Supporters' Federation, a group made up of representatives from each of the Club's supporters' groups. Meetings are held regularly, many of them with Anthony in attendance, and the quality of the input and debate thus far has been very encouraging. At long last the Club's genuine fans are organising themselves properly so that both enthusiastic suggestions and constructive criticism may be presented in a proper manner.

Chairman	John Humpreys
Secretary	David Mainwaring
Treasurer	Brian Davies
Webmaster	Wyn Griffiths
Committee Members	Gary Coombes, Mark Drury, Andy Faulks, Dave Jones, Pete Jones, Darren Morris, Richard Watkin
Meeting Venue	Lion Quays Hotel, Moreton
Membership Cost	£6 Adults, £3 Children £13 Family
Meeting Frequency	Bi-monthly

Our immediate priority is to focus EVERYBODY on the one big task that stands before us - our return to the Football League. It's hard to imagine that anyone would disagree with that, and so - on behalf of not just the Shreds, but of all the Supporters' groups - I would urge you to link up with your local branch. There are a growing number of us these days, so it shouldn't be too difficult to find one on your doorstep. No excuses, now!!

The Shropshire Reds will continue to meet every other month, and to invite key personnel from Wrexham's past and present to share their memories and stories with us. We'll also look to expand our range of social activities as we try to build up our membership back to the levels we enjoyed just a few years ago. Members' suggestions are always welcome: I've always maintained that our greatest achievement has been to give the ordinary fan on the terrace the belief that he or she really is a very important part of the Club they love.

Finally, sad goodbyes and sincere best wishes to some good friends: Neil Roberts, Danny Williams and Shropshire lad Matty Done have all given us some of their spare time. Neil, in particular, deserves special thanks for attending one of our meetings on crutches, having undergone an operation on his injured ankle the same day that we got together; and, as Club captain, he was always happy to assist with the arrangements for making players available to us for our Club Nights. The very best of luck to you all.

Keep the faith. We can bring the glory days back to The Racecourse - but we've ALL got to do it TOGETHER.

JOHN HUMPHREYS.
Chairman, Shropshire Reds.

L-R; Simon Spender, Alex Stepney and Shreds Chairman John Humphreys.

Rhos and District Reds

The Coach & Horses Inn, Vinegar Hill, Rhosllanerchrugog, Wrexham, LL14 1EH
Telephone: 01978 841 749 (Ian Phillips, Secretary & Landlord of Coach & Horses)
Website: http://uk.groups.yahoo.com/group/rhosanddistrictreds/
Email: rhosanddistrictreds@yahoogroups.co.uk

Membership

Formed in April 2006 the Rhos and District Reds now have over 100 members. Our aims are to bring together fans from the local area and to support Wrexham FC. This year membership for under 16's is free, whilst adult membership is just £5 and forms can either be downloaded from our website http://uk.groups.yahoo.com/groups/rhosanddistrictreds/ or collected from the Coach & Horses on Vinegar Hill in Rhos. If you need to contact us, our Secretary's number is 01978 841 749.

Meeting Venue / Events

The Coach and Horses on Vinegar Hill in Rhos has become the home to the group and the support provided by the licensees Ian & Lynne Phillips has been crucial in the growth of the group. We organise regular meetings and have hosted very successful events including Quiz and Race nights which have been actively supported by the other Wrexham Supporters groups.

Last season we again ran a number of successful away trips and provided free travel for all members to the Shrewsbury game. Although local derby's are at a premium in the Blue Square Premier League, we will definitely be running some trips- see the quarterly newsletters for further details.

After winning the Supporters 8-a-side tournament in 2007 in our first season, we were pleased to enter two teams this year. Both Rhos 'A' and Rhos 'B' performed extremely well, both beating the team of ex-Wrexham players.

Rhos Reds 'A' managed to retain the Trophy for the second successive year, which was won with no-nonsense defending followed by quick counter-attack football to again see off the opposition!

Sponsorship

Last year the Rhos & District Reds sponsored Rhos lad, Mark Jones' home shirt for 2007/08, and we will again be looking to support Wrexham FC by sponsoring a player shirt this season.

We also donated £100 from our funds to help cover the cost of the WST Junior Dragons Children's Christmas party and

Chairman	Rob Wynne
Vice Chairman	Derek Andrews
Secretary	Ian Phillips
Treasurer	Emma Jones
Webmaster	Rob Wynne
Committee Members	Paul Richards, Chris Purvis, Aneurin Venables, Gavin Jones, Mike Garrigan.
Meeting Venue	Coach about Horses, Rhosllanerchrugog
Membership Cost	Adults, £5 Children Free!
Meeting Frequency	Bi-monthly

Rhos Reds: Winners of the Wrexham Supporters 8-a-side Competition 2008

also hosted a Poker night that raised £190 for Nightingale House.

Aims for 2008/09

Our aim is to ensure that all Wrexham supporters in the Rhos, Penycae, Johnstown, Ruabon and Cefn areas have an opportunity to meet up and help support Wrexham FC, organising regular meetings, having already held very successful Question and Answer sessions with both Mark Jones and Stevie Evans.

Relegation was a devastating blow for all Wrexham fans, but we are committed to ensuring that our group continues to grow. All money that is raised by the Rhos & District Reds is used to put on new events for our members and to help support Wrexham FC financially. Now is the time when Wrexham FC need our support most; lets back into the Football League as soon as possible, so please join your local supporters group!

C'Mon The Town!

Manchester Reds

The Manchester Reds were founded in November 1997 after there was enough interest to form as a supporters club.

Since formation The Manchester Reds have contributed over £1,500 to Wrexham FC in the form of sponsorship. As a supporters club the Manchester Reds main function is to arrange travel to home and away games within the Greater Manchester area and further afield, and also hold meetings which are open to all Wrexham fans.

It costs just £5 for waged fans to join the Manchester Reds, and £1 for unwaged fans. We welcome all Wrexham fans from the Greater Manchester area. So if you already live in Greater Manchester, or you know of Wrexham fans that do, then give us a shout and travel to matches with fellow Reds. Contact the Manchester Reds at:

feed_me_till_i_want_no_more@hotmail.co.uk

Buckley & District Reds

Buckley and District Reds, PO BOX 182, Buckley, CH7 9BR
Telephone: 07783430301
Website: www.buckleyreds.co.uk
Email: admin@buckleyreds.co.uk

The Buckley & District Reds were formed in January 2006 when 29 people attended the very first meeting which was held at the Hope & Anchor pub in Buckley. By June 2007 we had reached 110 members, with members from as far afield as London & Glasgow!

Aims and Objectives

The club was formed with the following aims in mind:-

1. To bring fans from the Flintshire area & beyond together to raise funds for the benefit of WREXHAM (A) FC
2. Give fans a feeling of involvement in the future of WREXHAM (A)FC
3. To interact with other fans groups
4. Work with other fans groups & WST for the benefit of WREXHAM (A)FC
5. To encourage increased support for WREXHAM (A)FC in the area
6. To promote a friendly atmosphere and to have fun at our fund raising events

Sadly in August 2006 Paul Antrobus, our founding member passed away aged 42, we have raised over £1,500 for the Macmillan Nurse charity in his memory,

Since our formation we have sponsored Danny Williams for 2006/07 season, donated £300 to the Centre of Excellence at Colliers Park, donated £100 towards the Junior Dragons Christmas party, taken out a loan note with the WST for £500 towards buying equity in the football club and taken part in the 'Be A Red for a Day' initiative which put £500 into the football club.

For the 2007/8 season we committed to sponsoring Danny Williams' home shirt and Anthony Williams' away shirt, and when Brian Little came on board in October, we agreed to sponsor his training equipment.

We also donated £100 towards the

Chairman	Bryn Jones
Secretary	Tony Williams
Treasurer	Dave Kelsall
Webmaster	Stuart Cooper
Committee Members	Stuart Cooper, Chris Haynes, Daz Jones, Andy Kelsall
Meeting Venue	Buckley Cricket Club
Membership Cost	£5 Adults, £1 Under 16s
Meeting Frequency	Monthly

Junior Dragons Christmas party, and donated £100 towards equipment for the newly formed group 'DEUD-DEGFED DYN' - The 'TWELFTH MAN'.

We also have our website and message board where our members can discuss anything to do with Buckley & District Reds, Wrexham FC or the Welsh national side.

Our aim is to raise funds to benefit Wrexham FC directly or indirectly through WST, but to have some fun in doing so!

Our committee members the past season have been involved in the setting up of 'Wrexham Supporter's Federation' and look forward to its launch in August. We see this as bringing extra benefits to Buckley & District Reds members, while also and forming new friendships with fellow Wrexham supporters from different areas, while also increasing the fundraising efforts for Wrexham FC

L-R: Player of the Season Simon Spender, Alex Stepney & Chairman Bryn Jones

London Reds Cochion Llundain

Address: c/o 18 Minster Road, Bromley, Kent BR1 4DZ
Telephone: Barry Jones on 07973 512258
Website: http://www.londonreds.co.uk

The London Reds

The London Reds Cochion Llundain was formed after the famous promotion game at Northampton way back in 1993. Following the match it was noticeable that many Wrexham fans were travelling south not north on the train. We started talking and in June 1993 the London Reds was formed.

Meeting Venues

Our meeting venue has changed in the past year as fewer pubs in central London have upstairs rooms available for hire. The lure of cramming in extra drinkers at the expense of a quiet function room has been too much at two of our favourite haunts. Please check our website or contact Barry Jones for details of our next meeting.

Events

For the sixteenth year in succession we will be running a bus to the last home game of the season. Relegation has meant that we have a lot more games within easy reach of London and we anticipate seeing more! As well as train journeys to home and away games we also hope to repeat the highly successful 'evening with Brian Little' at some stage during the new season.

Sponsorship

We will again be sponsoring a match ball and a player during the season, while we will support the newly formed Federation when required. We run a 50/50 draw club, which has a top quarterly prize of over £200, as well as a club pin badges, polo shirt and ceramic mugs.

Membership

Application forms; sponsorship activity; details of the 50/50 draw; trips and meeting places at home and away games are available from our Secretary Barry Jones on 07973 512258 or on our web site: **www.londonreds.co.uk.** Membership costs just £8 per year.

Contact Details:
Chairman: Dave Harris
Secretary: Barry Jones
07973 512258 wbarryjones@mac.com
Treasurer: Dave Jones
07804 444122 jones.dm@btinternet.com
Webmaster: Stuart Roberts

Mold & District Reds

Address: c/o Mold Delivery Office, 18 Earl Road, Mold CH7 1AA
E-mail: moldreds@hotmail.co.uk
Website: http://www.moldreds.co.uk

Mold & District Reds

The Mold & District Reds were formed in August 2007, with only a handful of people turning up at our very first meeting. Despite this a committee was formed, and they worked on building up support, with press releases, placing posters around the local area, to reach as many people as possible.

By the end of this season, even though it has been a disastrous one for the club, we enrolled over eighty members, and our aim this season is to take that over 100.

Mold and District Reds strive to run coaches to games whenever possible. Last season we took coaches to several away matches, as well as to the home games with Shrewsbury and Chester.

Our meetings are held every month, and we alternate venues between Mold Ex Service Men's Club, and the Bryn Griffiths Club (known locally as the Top and Bottom club). Our meetings usually concluding with a fun quiz put together by our very own quiz master Eddie Pritchard, and some light refreshments.

Both Simon Spender and Neil Taylor have been guest speakers at our meetings, and at the bottom club an estimated hundred people attended a successful question and answer evening with Brian Little and Martin Foyle. Brian Little commenting on how our support, and it was continued support like ours that helped the club along.

We have held a very successful race night at the bottom club where an evening was enjoyed by more than a hundred people. We have also donated some funds to charity, when we entered the fun horse race to celebrate 200 years of sport on the Racecourse, and money received for our participation was handed over to The Mold Daffodil's Group, which helps children with special needs.

Chairperson: Sandra Edwards
Treasurer: Paul Bryan
Secretary: Rita Florio
Committee members: Eddie Pritchard, Glyn Hayes, Rob Hughes, Adam Phillips, Jeff Green, Ron Owen.

Membership Fees for 2008/09 are £6 for adults, £3 juniors and OAPs, £12 family (2 adults and 3 juniors)

Kings Mills Reds

Address: c/o Kings Mills Public House, Kingmills Road, Wrexham LL13 0NS
E-mail: bpcam1952@yahoo.co.uk or
Bazzaedwards@aol.com

Kings Mills Reds

The Kings Mills Reds were formed in April 2007 by the locals of the Kings Mills public house in Wrexham, who have used the pub as a meeting place for years before Wrexham home and away games.

With the growth of other independent supporters groups, it was felt by some that having our own independent supporters group would enhance the support for our home town club in the Kings Mills and Hightown area, while also helping to raise funds for the club.

Meeting venue

Although our first full season as a group wasn't a successful one on the pitch, we have managed to bring together over sixty members, and have regular meetings at the Kings Mills pub, which is situated just off the Whitchurch Road out of Wrexham on Kings Mills Road. Meetings are held every last Wednesday of the month.

Sponsorship

As a group we have so far sponsored Danny Williams' away shirt last season, and will again be looking to sponsor a player for the new season, as well as looking at other new ways in which we can help to support Wrexham Football Club.

Most Improved Player of the Season

The Kings Mills Reds first ever 'Most Improved Player of the Season' was Simon Spender as voted for by our members. We wish Simon the very best for the new season and hope he continues the improvement in his game that we saw last season.

Main Aim

The main aim for the Kings Mills Reds is to promote Wrexham FC in the Kings Mills and Hightown area's of Wrexham, and we welcome all new members young and old. We would also like to invite members from the Marchwiel, Bangor-on-Dee, Overton areas to please come along and join us. All support is welcome.

Chairman: Brian Cameron
Secretary: Barry Edwards
Treasurer: Chris Dimmich
Committee: Ray Rondel, Pete Fisher, Glyn Davies, Mark Edwards, Chris Lee.

Holywell & District Reds

E-mail: evans-p1@sky.com or
shaunholden11@hotmail.co.uk

Holywell & District Reds

Seven years ago, two brothers from Holywell decided to form the area's first Wrexham supporters' club.

John and Paul Evans' initial idea was to bring together the vast amount of Wrexham fans that the district offers to organise coach trips to away games. Ironically, our first trip as a supporters' group turned out to be, the then manager, Brian Flynn's last, as Wrexham were beaten 5-0 at Tranmere in October 2001.

Although Wrexham were relegated that season, the Holywell & District Reds status grew and by the end of the campaign had attracted over 50 members.

Since then the group has sponsored a match every season as well as backing various players' kits and getting involved with club initiatives.

In the last of the club's 87-year stint in the football league, the Holywell Reds oversaw the St. David's Day 1-1 draw against fellow relegation victims Mansfield as match sponsors and also funded Eifion Williams' away strip.

As a group we aim to do our utmost in taking Wrexham higher and that will be essential again this year as we embark on what hopefully will be our only season outside of the Football League.

Once more the Holywell & District Reds will be pouring support into our beloved club and we want everybody from in and around the area to join us in our common goal of seeing Wrexham back onto a successful road, both on and off the pitch.

We hold monthly meetings at the Abbot Arms in Pen-Y-Maes, Holywell, and membership is £5 for adults and £3.50 for kids.

So if you're enthusiastic about getting further involved with your football club then please get in touch with us or keep an eye-out on the Wrexham FC website and in the local press for details of our meetings.

We'd be delighted to hear from you!

Chairman: Paul Evans
Secretary: John Evans
Treasurer: Barry Davies
Committee Members: Shaun Holden & Tracy Tanner

Junior Dragons

Wrexham Supporters Trust runs the Junior Dragons on behalf of the football club and our aim is to encourage youngsters to support Wrexham Football Club.

Being a young Wrexham fan is tough. Those of us over the age of 20 can at least off-set the current gloom with happy memories of famous wins, glorious cup runs and great players, to at least provide some comfort to the down in the mouth Wrexham fan.

Kids have nothing like this to fall back on, in truth the last five years, barring one great afternoon in Cardiff, have been grim viewing. We support a club that has lost more games than it has won of late. With our clubs relegation it is more important than ever that we work to encourage the youngsters to stick with it, and support the club in its current misfortunes. The Junior Dragons is hoping to play a major part in this neces-sary work. We do not want to see a lost generation.

As a result of this we are stepping up our activity this season. A new steering commit-tee has been formed to run the Junior Dragons, from which they will be represented at WST board level to underline the importance that the Trust places on the JD role. New members will receive a membership card, a team photo and their very own match-by-match record book, and during the season every member will receive four newsletters; be invited to four members meetings; as well as the annual Christmas party; and other exclusive Junior Dragon events. We are also hoping to organise travel to specific away matches.

JD's queue for autographs at the Open Day

The Junior Dragons will have their own MySpace page, and a regular column in the Evening Leader, as well as the clubs award winning match day programme. Certain matches during the season will be designated Junior Dragons games and

e-mail: juniordragons@wst.org.uk
Junior Dragons, c/o PO Box 2200, Wrexham, LL11 9WG.

members will have the opportunity to become mascots at home games.

The club are supporting us 100% with this work, and both players and facilities have been placed to enhance the experience for the kids. This is a key point of difference between supporting Wrexham. The young United fan will never meet Rooney, but the young Wrexham fan will meet his heroes. It's a huge advantage in this respect.

We hope that you will agree that this programme will go a long way to encourage today's young Wrexham fans to turn their back on the dreary Sky Premiership nonsense and stand by their club. However, all of this costs money, and we have, for the first time, had to introduce a membership charge of £5, but we guarantee that the Junior Dragons will receive every penny of this, and more, back during the course of the season in the form of goodies

The board of the WST has agreed to under write the cost of this years programme, but we are looking for sponsors to help us enhance the overall package. If you, or your company can help with this, then please get in touch. We are also looking for volunteers, particularly fans who are CRB certificated to help with the work of the committee or just with specific events. However, don't worry if you are not CRB certificated, as the WST will reimburse you for this service.

If you would like to get involved, or interested in sponsorship of the JD's, then please contact us. Lets make this a great year for the Junior Dragons, one that they will always remember.

Junior Dragons Package

MEMBERSHIP PACK
10% DISCOUNT ON PURCHASES OVER £20 @ CLUB SHOP
REGULAR NEWSLETTER WITH MEMBERS EXCLUSIVE CONTENT
REGULAR MEMBERS MEETINGS WITH OPPORTUNITIES TO MEET THE PLAYERS
REGULAR EVENTS BASED AROUND SCHOOL HOLIDAYS
THE EVER POPULAR CHRISTMAS PARTY
AN ELECTED PRESIDENT FROM THE CURRENT SQUAD
DESIGNATED JUNIOR DRAGONS MATCHES WITH EXCLUSIVE AREA OF THE STADIUM

Section 5:
Season Review 2007/08

A Review of the 2007/08 Season

In the end we went out with a whimper, unable for the umpteenth time over the season to muster anything more substantial. Consigned to the non-leagues away from home on a mid-week night in April, this was the tin hat on a season that should be best forgotten but which, for the future of this football club and how it is administered, cannot be allowed to be written off without thorough investigation and serious de-briefing.

To state the obvious, 2007/08 was a season of few genuine highlights and a volume of new lows, and trawling back over match reports and clippings from the year makes for horrific reading. But our systems have become immune to this kind of carry-on over the last four or five years, and to this supporter at least, the writing's been on the wall since way back. By the time Hereford rolled in their second at Edgar Street and we'd signed off our own death certificate, we'd already been numbed into submission by recent history. The stomachs had long-since given up on the battle; - players and fans alike.

And of course it hurt, but the inevitability of our decline made the whole end-of-season experience seem very matter of fact, and even the anger on the terraces over the season's final furlongs seemed half-hearted and muted.

At Wrexham we've grown accustomed to bringing up the rear, routinely reminded that we're just lucky to have a club. To an entire generation of young supporters, our last promotion and that glorious day out at The Millennium are freak exceptions to the rule. We're used to losing, simple as; used to throwing away leads; giving the ball away; gifting goals; mailing it in; and simply going through the motions. We regularly

The season starts off well with a 2-1 home win over Morecambe.

fetch up for games with a sense that results don't matter because the really important thing is that the club still exists.

I routinely travel to games more in hope than in expectation, forever fearful of the worst and rarely confident that we can ever really endure; kick on; take home points. These days, seeing a decent Wrexham display is actually a bonus and we're consistently living off of scraps, both on the pitch and off of it. But because of what we've been through over the last five or six years – and because, I guess, we're genuine and senseless with our support - we continue to live for the big day, for when the dice rolls like we've hoped it would, for when our luck turns.

In one way, our relegation into the Blue Square Premier completes the work started here in earnest by Mark Guterman and Alex Hamilton who, knowing that we'd been run long-term like a pub-side for years, saw their opportunity and went for it in style. Having asset-stripped and humiliated our club in the most calculated, under-hand and devious manner imaginable, relegation out of league football - and eventually out of existence - was their vision for Wrexham AFC. Our utter lack of any kind of optimism or self-belief, our lack of stomach for battle and that sense that we're still blithely making it up as we go along is their legacy. This is the inheritance.

When I was asked by the editors to write a review of last season, I had a particular kind of factual piece in mind, something that maybe made a few general observances, with even a small bit of insight and even a fair and constructive account of our worst season in decades. But apart from highlighting a handful of key performances and a change of manager (and the arrival of a brand new team half way through the season), I can't actually find the stomach to wade through the wreckage in any great detail. But although we've been battered and broken this season, and we may find it difficult to summon the gut for another season of toil and turmoil, I do know that, come August, we'll be there, like we're always there. Wrexham fans together; - cautious and wary as ever but with a hint of optimism bubbling away, ready to spurt.

Having survived famously against Boston United on the last day of the 2006/2007 season – and remember, no matter how bad you felt after Hereford away, you could have been a Boston fan at Wrexham on that fateful Saturday – we fetched up for 2007/08 with no little hope in our hearts.

Brian Carey had been rewarded - and rightly so - for keeping the club up and started the season having been formally installed as manager, assisted by Steve Weaver. The signings of the likes of Richard Hope, Eifion Williams, Michael Proctor and Silvio Spann fuelled much of the optimism; with a squad based around a core of local lads like Danny Williams, Neil Roberts, Matty Done and the emerging Neil Taylor, enhanced by the new arrivals, the pre-season talk was more about play-offs than pay-offs. And as we set off for Darlington on the first day, our expectations were largely positive; - last time around we'd gone to the wire, and now it was payback time.

The often-quoted 'law of averages' suggested that we'd suffered our fair share of misfortune and bad luck and that we'd done enough to, for once, earn a decent break. The absence of both an out-and-out six-yard box merchant and a creative midfielder in the Darren Ferguson mode, didn't seem to matter. Loose talk in the punters' parlours fancied us to be involved at the business end. And then we kicked off.

In hindsight, we were at a distinct disadvantage even before we broke up for the summer. Unable to make fundamental personnel and staffing decisions until after our safety in the Football League had been assured, we were late into the transfer market and had already surrendered the staffing momentum to similar teams at our level who were safe and at home base four or five weeks earlier.

Wrexham fans at Accrington at last have something to cheer about with the first away win.

But with a youthful, committed and intelligent management; and a squad comprised of a seemingly good mix of experience, local extraction and one or two interesting new players, it was little wonder that we were routinely name-checked by neutrals as a sly bet capable of doing the business. While Brian Carey downplayed the hype and loose-talk, we couldn't help but feel that the club was certainly better prepared this time to take on all-comers. Anyone who saw us in pre-season in Northern Ireland couldn't but have been impressed by the approach; - we looked very much at home in the luxury of the Slieve Donard Hotel in County Down, and the core group seemed like a happy and fit bunch.

One week earlier, a pair of fine finishes from the recently arrived Eifion Williams against Liverpool's combination of squad players, reserves and youths, only whetted the appetite further. Even if we'd been thoroughly out-gunned early doors and defended poorly throughout, the fact that we were still in a pre-season honeymoon phase and that we'd scored goals masked the obvious deficiencies. In another of our pre-season games, against Blackburn Rovers, the long-anticipated graduation of Neil Taylor – and his splendid first senior performance on David Bentley, no less - suggested that the pot was on the boil.

And then it all went horribly, horribly wrong.

With the gift of hindsight – and at the risk, yet again, of stating the obvious - it was our inability to score goals and to defend with any sense of collective purpose that was to consistently un-do us. While it's easy to point the finger of blame at players, management, staff and owners, the fact is that teams who get relegated do so with the same attributes as teams who win championships; - only in reverse.

Ironically, Brian Carey and Steve Weaver's last game in charge was against their former team mate's Darren Ferguson and Kevin Russell's Peterborough United side in a 4-1 FA Cup defeat at London Road.

Over the course of a season, the best and the worst teams always get what they deserve, no debate. Teams who defend like we attempted to defend all season invariably get their just desserts and, when the going got tough, players from whom we expected much more – leadership, nous, guile and raw ability – disappeared. And while a handful of our boys manfully gave there all every time they pulled on the shirt, the shapelessness and sloppiness of our entire set-up rendered their best efforts pointless from the off. It's not our place in a forum like this to name and shame, but those players who were happy all season to mail it in while picking up the cheque, know well who they are. They'll also know, I'm sure, why they'll never amount to anything of consequence within the professional game.

And so last season's highlights – and there were two or three - don't take up too much band -width. But although drained of confidence from the moment in October when Macclesfield came from behind to beat us in injury time, we still managed the odd moment.

Michael Proctor and team mates celebrate the second of his two goals against rivals Chester City in Brian Little's first match in charge.

So with a parochial sneer, its worth remembering that in an appalling season, we still took four points from Chester and that we also beat the eventual champions, MK Dons, fairly and squarely at home.

We also went up to Accrington on a Friday night, reversed the recent pattern and helped to lay a few ghosts with a well-deserved 2-0 win. There was a hope-engendering home victory over Darlington and, immediately following Brian Little's arrival, a rare unbeaten run that stretched to three games, comprising of a 1-0 away win and a couple of draws. Which kind of says it all, really.

The season also saw the emergence of two new homegrown talents, the aforementioned Neil Taylor, and Wes Baynes. But given how, for most of the season we couldn't pass properly or defend our lines with any degree of conviction, our eventual tally of forty points – seven points off safety - tells the real story. We never established any real momentum and always looked vulnerable and, until last day away at Lincoln, never scored more than two goals in the one game.

And yet even though that same, last-day game was a dead-rubber for both sides, it still captured the very best and very worst of us over the course of the ninety minutes. For all of the good and the positive – Baynes' free-kicks, the youthful (and almost journeyman-free) line-up and the three points, basically – the game will be remembered more by neutrals for yet another appalling Steve Evans own-goal. One step up, one-step back.

Now, Brian Carey has been dignified enough to own up to some of his own inadequacies and brave enough to point to his own naiveté during his spell as manager. It's worth mentioning here that, an entire world away from life in football's basement, another Corkonian who's relocated to Manchester, Roy Keane, pointedly took his Sunderland squad to task for its lack of consistent performance during last season's Premier League. In a press briefing shortly before the close of the season, Keane pointedly referred to the lack of basic football intelligence in some of his own players. This is a trait characterised traditionally within the game by a player's inability to take basic instruction and to follow pre-agreed orders once he heads out and takes his place on the field of play. But if Keane has been aggrieved by the difficulty of some of the highest paid professionals in domestic football to heed basic advice, then imagine the frustrations experienced by solid, old-school pros like Carey – and latterly Brian Little – whose players routinely left their brains behind them in the changing rooms last season?

Writing in Cork's Evening Echo newspaper towards the end of last season, Carey claimed that one of his key mistakes as manager – and a very fundamental one at that – was that he had too much belief in his players from the off, treating them at all times like thorough professionals when in reality all that many of them deserved was a routine rollicking and a primal, cave-art approach to their trade. So whatever about the well-documented frustrations routinely felt on the terraces and in the stands, imagine the bewilderment endured on the sidelines watching a basic inability to defend, pass or finish easy goal chances?

Its no over-dramatization to say that last season some of our performances were so inept that they defied belief and, in what was for the most part a humdrum and mundane league, it was the teams with pace, spirit, flair and a distinct lack of fear who all went up directly. So no real surprises there, then. Its no co-incidence either that MK Dons, Peterborough and Hereford were also defensively sound throughout and could also find their own men with simple passing to feet. One of the many enduring clichés strewn all around football philosophy is that the game, in essence, is a very simple one. And it is.

But merely four weeks into the season it was clear, no matter how optimistic we were, that we just weren't functioning like we should have been. We'd rode our luck to hang on for a first home league win against Morecambe and played well against a poor Port Vale side to advance in The Carling Cup. But while we were tight at the back, we weren't threatening in the final third either.

Winning and Losing Streaks

Double Wins:	2	Bury & Lincoln City.
Double Defeats:	7	Barnet, Brentford, Chesterfield, Hereford United, Rotherham United, Stockport County & Shrewsbury Town.
Won from behind:	0	
Lost from in front:	3	Brentford (h), Macclesfield Town (a), Stockport County (a).

It shows how much it means to Neil Roberts as he scores the winner against league leaders MK Dons to start a six match unbeaten run, which gave fans hope of the Great Escape Part Two.

A 5-0 tonking at home to Aston Villa in the next round flattered to deceive the victors; - half an hour in and we were still very much in the game and, on the sidelines, we had them worried. But it was the same failings that put an unfair veneer on the final score and that, in retrospect, began the process of draining confidence from a team that had yet to achieve a settled look.

Another of those hoary old one-liners trotted out regularly by football's alickadoos is that luck evens itself out across the course of a season. Brian Carey, one suspects, wouldn't entirely agree with that premise and his brief tenure as Wrexham manager will be pock-marked in history by a flurry of last minute concessions, dubious refereeing awards and own-goals. By the time that Shrewsbury came to The Racecourse in November, set out their stall to defend from the front, deny us the time and space in the middle and made off with a 1-0 victory, it was obvious that it had all gone irretrievably flat.

With the team struggling for form, the one-time Aston Villa and Leicester City manager, Brian Little, arrived to take the reins and this, you thought, was a tender mercy. Brian Carey moved sideways and became Assistant Manager, while the former Port Vale striker and manager, Martin Foyle, later arrived to assist with coaching.

Brian Little is among football's more interesting characters and, in many ways, is entirely out of synch with much of the hoopla that surrounds the modern game. A deep-thinking, measured, motorcycling, conservative family man, God knows what he

Brian Little signed Drewe Broughton on loan to bring more of a physical presence to the Wrexham attack. Here he out jumps the Chester defence in Wrexham's 2-0 win at the Deva Stadium.

really makes of the set-up he's inherited here? What we do know, though, is that his teams tend to be physically big and play directly – defending from the front, always mean spirited at the back.

Little's tenure at Wrexham pre sented him with an interesting early challenge; - a home derby with Chester, who brought to the Racecourse one of their best sides in years. We came from behind twice and played with determination in part to nick a point and, on the following Saturday, went to Rochdale and held out for a scoreless draw.

Little extended his unbeaten run up at Bury on a cold Tuesday night (for the record, all Tuesday night away games are played in the cold!) and also earned his first victory as Wrexham manager. The goal – against the run of play – came courtesy of an appalling goalkeeping error and, when the ball was finally ushered into the net by Eifion Williams, the striker limped away in celebration, was substituted immediately and was never again seen in a Wrexham first-team shirt.

So here we were, unbeaten in three and on our longest run in ages without a defeat. But this was about as heady as it got, the most telling statistic being that, in three games unbeaten, we scored three goals and conceded two. And invariably - and in keeping with recent Wrexham tradition - we came unstuck appallingly away at a previously awful Dagenham and Redbridge and, days after the false-dawn at Gigg Lane, were turned over 0-3 when it could have been six or seven.

Shortly after the initial rush of blood to the head caused by Little's arrival, the new manager splurged into the loans-market and procured an entire team of new players who, momentarily, breathed life into a season that was now, formally, all about survival. As a battalion of has-beens, wannabes and never-were's descended on Colliers Park like snuff at a wake, it was obvious that Little had taken an informed look around the club and just didn't like what he saw.

His intelligent observations to the media referred constantly to 'players lacking confidence' and to 'losing mentalities';- in essence, he was saying that the players just weren't up to it and that even a 36 year-old biker in semi-retirement was a better bet than some battered and bruised local 22 year-old who'd spent all of his professional life in the bargain basement at a club in perennial crisis and run like a pub side.

But for a couple of optimism-heavy weeks, the arrival of the likes of Carl Tremarco,

Danny Sonner, Sam Aiston, Paul Hall and Drewe Broughton seemed to validate the manager's view. In hindsight though, all we were doing was thumbing the damn and postponing the inevitable, throwing enough journeymen at a wall in the hope that some of them were bound to stick. Or at least help us score goals.

As with Brian Carey's tenure, we routinely changed formation and personnel, and our team-sheets from game-to-game show no consistency. As anoraks everywhere will remind you, a dominant feature of teams struggling at the bottom of all leagues is the extent of squad numbers on display that are in the high twenties and early thirties. This feature is linked to desperate activity in the loan-market and the pre-mature blooding of raw and inexperienced local youths. Sound familiar?

In hindsight, those multiple formations and ever-changing line-ups did little to stem the tide and, in fairness, how could they have? Because In terms of on-field performances, last season simply concluded a consistently downward dip in results terms that started three seasons ago during the second half of the home game against Chester. Then, with us two up at half time and coasting, we switched off totally in the second half and were lucky to escape with the points.

We now face our first season out of league football in living memory, and if last season tells us anything, it's that pre-season loose talk and bookmakers' odds count for nothing once the hard stuff starts. It's a season in the deep unknown for us, but what we are certain of is that the management trio of Little, Foyle and Carey won't shirk the work-load, and are used to the long shifts.

As I write, Brian Little has wiped the slate clean and is taking a fresh approach. He's performed a savage cull on a core group who have consistently failed to perform over the course of several campaigns now and the implications are obvious; - if we succeed and come up at the first attempt, we'll have done so with a team built by Brian Little. His record in management speaks for itself, but nothing is certain in football. Should he get the requisite support from the club's owners, and should we start to finally run our club off the field like we aspire to on it, then who knows where he can take us?

The only certainty for now is that failure in the Blue Square Premier – to whatever degree – just isn't an option.

Players show there dejection at the final whistle.

2007/08 Player of the Season & Young Player of the Season

Simon Spender, Neil Roberts and Neil Taylor scooped the prizes at the Player of the Season Awards Dinner.
Neil Roberts won the Supporters Association award, and Neil Taylor the young player award.
Simon Spender snapped up the Buckley & District Reds, Kings Mills, Shropshire Reds and Supporters Trust awards, while Neil Taylor won the Mold & District award. Neil Roberts also won the Holywell & District Reds trophy.
Further awards presented were the Supporters Trust Extra Mile award which this year went to the matchday Programme team,

who this year celebrate 25 years of compling the programme, since taking it over in 1983. Well done to Geraint Parry, Phil Jones, Dave Roberts and the team.
Finally, groundsman John Edwards was presented with the Evening Leader's Dave Lovett Lifetime Achievement award for his efforts in maintaining a top class pitch.

Player of the Year Previous Winners

1975/76 Brian Lloyd	1987/88 Kevin Russell	1999/00 Darren Ferguson
1976/77 Graham Whittle	1988/89 Kevin Russell	2000/01 Mark McGregor
1977/78 Gareth Davies	1989/90 Nigel Beaumont	2001/02 Jim Whitley
1978/79 John Roberts	1990/91 Mark Morris	2002/03 Andy Morrell
1979/80 Dixie McNeil	1991/92 Andy Thackeray	2003/04 Dennis Lawrence
1980/81 Steve Fox	1992/93 Tony Humes	2004/05 Andy Holt
1981/82 Eddie Niedzwiecki	1993/94 Gary Bennett	2005/06 Danny Williams
1982/83 Robbie Savage	1994/95 Gary Bennett	2006/07 Steve Evans
1983/84 David Gregory	1995/96 Waynne Phillips	2007/08 Neil Roberts
1984/85 Jack Keay	1996/97 Andy Marriott	
1985/86 Mike Williams	1997/98 Brian Carey	
1986/87 Mike Williams	1998/99 Dean Spink	

Young Player of the Year Previous Winners

1983/84 Shaun Cunnington	1992/93 Jonathan Cross	2001/02 Shaun Pejic
1984/85 Andy Edwards	1993/94 David Brammer	2002/03 Craig Morgan
1985/86 Shaun Cunnington	1994/95 Bryan Hughes	2003/04 Craig Morgan
1986/87 Roger Preece	1995/96 Mark McGregor	2004/05 Mark Jones
1987/88 Darren Wright	1996/97 Mark McGregor	2005/06 Mark Jones
1988/89 Darren Wright	1997/98 Neil Roberts	2006/07 Matty Done
1989/90 Gareth Owen	1998/99 Robin Gibson	2007/08 Neil Taylor
1990/91 Gareth Owen	1999/00 Robin Gibson	
1991/92 Phil Hardy	2000/01 Lee Roche	

Coca Cola League 2 2007/08

FINAL TABLE

		P	Home W	D	L	F	A	Away W	D	L	F	A	Pts	
1	MK Dons	46	11	7	5	39	17	18	3	2	43	20	97	C
2	Peterborough	46	14	4	5	46	20	14	4	4	38	23	92	P
3	Hereford	46	11	6	6	34	19	15	4	4	38	22	88	P
4	Stockport	46	11	5	7	40	30	13	5	5	32	24	82	
5	Rochdale	46	11	4	8	37	28	12	7	4	40	26	80	
6	Darlington	46	11	7	5	36	22	11	5	7	31	18	78	P
7	Wycombe	46	13	6	4	29	15	9	6	8	27	27	78	
8	Chesterfield	46	9	8	6	42	29	10	4	9	34	27	69	
9	Rotherham*	46	12	4	7	37	29	9	7	7	25	29	64	
10	Bradford	46	10	4	9	30	30	7	7	9	33	31	62	
11	Morecambe	46	9	6	8	33	32	7	6	10	26	31	60	
12	Barnet	46	10	6	7	37	30	6	5	11	19	33	60	
13	Bury	46	8	6	9	30	30	8	5	10	28	31	59	
14	Brentford	46	7	5	11	25	35	10	3	10	27	35	59	
15	Lincoln	46	9	3	11	33	38	9	1	13	28	39	58	
16	Grimsby	46	7	5	11	26	34	8	5	10	29	32	55	
17	Accrington	46	7	1	15	20	39	9	2	12	29	44	51	
18	Shrewsbury	46	9	6	8	31	22	6	3	8	25	43	50	
19	Macclesfield	46	6	8	9	27	31	9	5	9	20	33	50	
20	Dagenham	46	6	7	10	27	32	7	3	13	22	38	49	
21	Notts County	46	8	5	10	19	23	6	2	9	18	30	48	
22	Chester	46	5	6	13	21	30	7	6	10	30	38	47	
23	Mansfield	46	6	3	14	30	39	6	4	17	16	29	42	R
24	Wrexham	46	6	7	10	16	28	4	3	16	22	42	40	R

* Rotherham United deducted 10 points for entering administration.

BLUE SQUARE PREMIER League 2007/08

FINAL TABLE

		P	Home W	D	L	F	A	Away W	D	L	F	A	Pts	
1	Aldershot	46	18	2	3	44	21	13	6	4	38	27	101	C
2	Cambridge	46	14	6	3	36	17	11	5	7	32	24	86	
3	Torquay	46	15	3	5	39	21	11	5	7	44	36	85	
4	Exeter	46	13	9	1	44	26	9	8	6	39	32	83	P
5	Burton	46	15	3	5	48	31	8	9	6	31	25	81	
6	Stevenage	46	13	5	5	47	25	11	2	10	35	30	79	
7	Histon	46	10	7	6	42	36	10	5	8	34	31	72	
8	Forest Green	46	11	6	6	45	34	8	8	7	31	25	71	
9	Oxford	46	10	8	5	32	21	10	3	10	24	27	71	
10	Grays	46	11	6	6	35	23	8	7	8	23	24	70	
11	Ebbsfleet	46	14	3	6	40	29	5	9	9	25	32	69	
12	Salisbury	46	12	7	4	35	22	6	7	10	35	38	68	
13	Kidderminster	46	12	5	6	38	23	7	5	11	36	34	67	
14	York	46	8	5	10	33	34	9	6	8	38	40	62	
15	Crawley*	46	12	5	6	47	31	7	4	12	26	36	60	
16	Rushden	46	7	10	6	26	22	8	4	11	29	33	59	
17	Woking	46	7	9	7	28	27	5	8	10	25	34	53	
18	Weymouth	46	7	5	11	24	34	4	8	11	29	39	46	
19	Northwich	46	7	7	10	30	36	5	4	14	22	42	44	
20	Halifax*	46	8	10	5	30	29	4	6	13	31	41	42	
21	Altrincham	46	6	6	11	32	44	3	8	12	24	38	41	
22	Farsley Celtic	46	6	5	12	27	38	4	4	15	21	48	39	R
23	Stafford	46	2	4	17	16	48	3	6	14	26	51	25	R
24	Droylsden	46	4	5	14	27	45	1	4	18	19	58	24	R

* Halifax & Crawley both deducted points for entering administration.

Ryan Valentine (right) shows his displeasure that a penalty wasn't given in the 62nd minute.

Coca Cola League 2: 11th August, 2007

Darlington 2 Wrexham 0

Ian Miller 42
Julian Joachim 72

Referee: Karl Evans (Manchester)
Attendance (Away): 4,408 (678)

There was the usual sense of anticipation amongst the large Wrexham following that made the long trek to the North East for this opening game of the new season at the cavernous Darlington Arena.

But most will also have made the journey unsure quite what to expect. Pre-season performances had generally been encouraging, but alarm bells had started ringing after the dismal defeat at Hednesford Town in the final warm-up game a week earlier.

Unfortunately, the Dragons produced another somewhat lacklustre display that did little to inspire the travelling faithful. In all truth Darlington were little better in a disappointing encounter, and a draw would probably have been a fair result. Two moments of indecision in the Dragons' back line proved crucial as the Quakers benefited on both occasions to clinch victory.

And despite boss Brian Carey finding room in his starting eleven for new signings Eifion Williams and Michael Proctor; alongside Chris Llewellyn and Neil Roberts, enough chances were squandered to give cause for concern!

A cagey opening period produced few clear cut chances with the Dragons' best moment being a Mark Jones 25-yard volley that Eifion Williams helped goalwards, but saved by Andy Oakes. However, the home side grabbed the all-important opening goal when £100,000 signing Pawel Abbott centred from the right and Kevin McBride, not picked up well enough by the Dragons' defence, glanced a header past Anthony Williams. Back came Wrexham immediately, and strong appeals for a penalty were waved away by the referee Karl Evans after Eifion Williams looked to have been nudged in the back by a defender when baring down on Oakes.

Proctor headed over at the start of the second half before Wrexham's hopes were boosted on 62 minutes when the striker lifted the ball past Oakes only to be floored by the 'keeper on the edge of the area. Oakes was duly sent off, but the ensuing free kick failed to appease both Dragons' players and fans that thought that it should have been a penalty kick!

Oakes' replacement David Stockdale immediately turned Proctor's free kick around the post, and the Dragons suddenly looked capable of salvaging something from the game. However, those hopes were finally dashed when debutant Richard Hope misjudged a bouncing ball and Julian Joachim pounced to emphatically beat Williams with a rising drive from just outside the area.

Stockdale somehow turned away a late Shaun Pejic header and a couple of late Proctor half-chances also went begging as the Dragons were left to reflect on a need for improvement at both ends of the pitch during the long coach journey home.

Darlington:
1 Andy Oakes ■, 2 Neil Ashton, 3 Tim Ryan, 5 Stephen Foster, 6 Ian Miller,9 Pawel Abbott (67), 12 Julian Joachim, 14 Ricky Ravenhill, 18 Kevin McBride ■, 20 Tommy Wright (78) ■, 27 Chris Palmer (66).

Subs: 4 Alan White, 11 Robert Purdie (67),13 David Stockdale (GK) (66), 16 Greg Blundell (78), Ian Harty.

Wrexham:
1 Anthony Williams, 2 Simon Spender, 3 Ryan Valentine ■, 4 Shaun Pejic ■, 6 Richard Hope, 7 Mark Jones (75), 8 Danny Williams ■, 9 Neil Roberts (85), 10 Michael Proctor, 11 Chris Llewellyn, 14 Eifion Williams (71).

Subs: 13 Michael Jones (GK), 15 Mike Williams, 16 Levi Mackin (75), 20 Matty Done (71), 21 Marc Williams (85).

Both Mark Jones and Danny Williams attempt to win the ball from Quakers striker Julian Joachim.		
Shots on Goal:	6	6
Shots on Target:	2	3
Shots off Target	4	3
Possession:	50%	50%
Fouls Conceded:	11	10
Corners:	9	2
Yellow Cards:	3	2
Red Cards:	0	1

Dragons striker Michael Proctor fires Wrexham into an early lead at Vale Park.

Coca Cola Cup Round One: 14th August, 2007

Port Vale 1 Wrexham 1

Luke Rodgers 33p Michael Proctor 10

Referee: Carl Boyeson (East Yorkshire)
Attendance: 2,916 (493)

(Wrexham Win 5-3 on penalty's)

Chris Llewellyn fired home the decisive penalty in the shoot-out as the Dragons knocked League One side Port Vale out of the Carling Cup. With the sides locked at 1-1 after an entertaining and often end-to-end 120 minutes' play the Welsh International slotted the ball past Vale keeper Joe Anyon to complete a nap-hand of successful Wrexham penalty kicks after Danny Whitaker had missed with the home side's fourth kick.

Wrexham, with three changes from the side beaten at the weekend, had opened the scoring when Danny Williams' superb pass from halfway found Michael Proctor who controlled the ball well and held off a defender before slotting the ball past Anyon and into the far corner of the net.

The goal came somewhat against the run of play as Vale had already gone close on several occasions, notably when Luke Rodgers' early shot struck the chest of

Michael Jones and the striker fired the rebound against the post!

After Chris Llewellyn was fortunate to only receive a yellow card for what appeared to be an elbow into the face of Jason Talbot on 16 minutes, Vale continued to dominate. George Pilkington had a header cleared off the line by Levi Mackin and Shane Tudor saw an effort clip the top of the crossbar.

Wrexham relieved the pressure briefly with efforts from Proctor and Llewellyn but there was still no surprise when Vale pulled themselves level, albeit from the penalty spot. Richard Hope clearly climbed all over Callum Willock and Rodgers confidently converted from the spot.

The home side continued to look the more lively side in the early stages of the second half with both Tudor and Rogers again going close, but gradually the Dragons started to gain the ascendancy and the longer the game went on they looked the fitter, and the side most likely to earn a second round place.

Anyon gathered a Proctor drive and Llewellyn forced a fine save from the keeper with an unmarked far post header in the 75th minute after a pinpoint centre

from substitute Josh Johnson. The rebound fell to the Welsh international whose follow-up effort appeared to strike the hand of a defender but penalty appeals were controversially waved away.

Jones denied Rodgers again in added-on time and so the tie went into an extra thirty minutes, but neither side could break the deadlock in an entertaining half-hour and so it went to the dreaded penalty shoot-out. Ryan Valentine, Simon Spender, Conall Murtagh and Matty Done all converted before Whitaker's miss proved crucial and Llewellyn sent the travelling fans home happy.

Wrexham:
13 Michael Jones, 2 Simon Spender, 3 Ryan Valentive, 4 Shaun Pejic, 6 Richard Hope, 8 Danny Williams (90), 9 Neil Roberts (84), 10 Michael Proctor (74), 11 Chris Llewellyn ■, 18 Levi Mackin, 20 Matty Done.

Subs: 1 Anthony Williams (GK), 15 Mike Williams, 17 Josh Johnson (74), 21 Marc Williams (84), 22 Connall Murtagh (90).

Port Vale:
12 Joe Anyon, 2 George Pilkington, 3 Jason Talbot (106), 4 Robert Hulbert (85), 5 Keith Lowe, 7 Shane Tudor, 10 Luke Rodgers, 14 Danny Whitaker, 16 Mark McGregor, 17 Craig Rocastle, 24 Callum Willock (76)

Subs: 1 Mark Goodlad (GK), 8 Paul Harsley, 9 Marc Richards (76), 11 Paul Edwards (85), 18 Colin Miles (106)

Neil Roberts chases for the ball with Vale's George Pilkington.

Shots on Goal:	12	9
Shots on Target:	3	3
Shots off Target	9	6
Possession:	48%	52%
Fouls Conceded:	4	10
Corners:	3	5
Yellow Cards:	0	1
Red Cards:	0	0

Michael Proctor is congratulated by his team mates as Wrexham record their first home win.

Coca Cola League 2: 18th August, 2007

Wrexham 2 Morecambe 1

Michael Proctor 6, 22   Newby 56

Referee: Graham Horwood (Bedfordshire)
Attendance: 5,504 (545)

A Michael Proctor double meant that newcomers Morecambe tasted defeat on their first League visit to the Racecourse after a game that could best be described using that well-worn footballing cliché of a 'game of two halves'.

So dominant were the Dragons in the opening forty-five minutes that it was surprising how they only had Proctor's two goals – both scored inside the opening 22 minutes – to show for their almost total domination at the break. The second half was a different proposition however, and

Morecambe did enough after the break to feel unlucky not to travel back up the M6 with a point for their efforts.

Wrexham started the game in scintillating fashion and opened the scoring when Chris Llewellyn crossed from the right and Michael Proctor's glancing header flew past keeper Joe Lewis. The duo then combined again a few minutes later, but Proctor this time thumped a more difficult chance just wide of the right-hand upright.

Apart from an Anthony Williams save from a Garry Thompson shot it was pretty much one-way traffic towards the Shrimps' goal, and it was no surprise when the second goal arrived. Ryan Valentine's perfect pass dissected the Morecambe back line and Proctor ran through unchecked and lobbed the ball perfectly over the advancing Lewis and into the unguarded net. It was no more than Wrexham deserved for a spell of enterprising and fluent football.

The onslaught continued and Llewellyn forced Michael Twiss to head off his own goal line on 27 minutes, Neil Roberts went close with a rasping 25-yarder that only just cleared the crossbar, and Llewellyn headed across the face of goal just too far ahead for the predatory Proctor to convert.

But the expected continued onslaught after the break never materialised and the visitors quickly began to show that they weren't prepared to just sit back and take what looked to be the inevitable defeat. Jim Bentley flashed a header just wide of the post and ex-Red Jon Newby, a half-time substitute, had a goal ruled out for offside.

But, almost inevitably, Newby did get his name on the score sheet when he was

found by Carl Baker's low cross and slotted home from close range. This galvanised the visitors, and Thompson and Bentley both failed to hit the target with headed opportunities.

Eifion Williams' low drive was saved by Lewis and fellow substitute Josh Johnson went close with a miscued cross, but generally it was Morecambe that finished the game stronger. And they were left to rue several missed chances. Anthony Williams denied Wayne Curtis, and Craig Stanley somehow blasted over the bar from close range in injury time, but Wrexham held on.....just!

Wrexham:
1 Anthony Williams, 2 Simon Spender, 3 Ryan Valentine, 4 Shaun Pejic, 6 Richard Hope, 8 Danny Williams, 9 Neil Roberts, 10 Michael Proctor ■, 11 Chris Llewellyn (76) ■, 18 Levi Mackin (78), 20 Matty Done (55).

Subs: 7 Mark Jones (78), 13 Michael Jones (GK), 14 Eifion Williams (55), 15 Mike Williams, 17 Josh Johnson (76).

Morecambe:
32 Joe Lewis, 2 Adam Yates ■, 4 David Artell, 5 Jim Bentley, 6 Craig Stanley, 7 Michael Twiss (88), 10 Carl Baker, 11 Garry Thompson (78), 14 Neil Sorvel, 17 Jamie Burns (46), 25 Danny Adams.

Subs: 1 Steven French (GK), 3 Michael Howard, 8 Gary Hunter (88), 9 Wayne Curtis (78), 20 Jon Newby (46).

Captain Neil Roberts leads the way with an attack down the touch line against the Shrimps.

Shots on Goal:	10	6
Shots on Target:	2	1
Shots off Target:	8	5
Possession:	44%	56%
Fouls Conceded:	15	10
Corners:	3	2
Yellow Cards:	2	1
Red Cards:	0	0

Midfielder Levi Mackin sweves his way around the Bradford defence.

Coca Cola League 2: 25th August, 2007

Bradford City 2

Eddie Johnson 49
Luke Medley 78

Wrexham 1

Neil Roberts 54

Referee: Michael Oliver (Northumberland)
Attendance (Away): 13,546 (507)

A wonder goal from debutant **Luke Medley within two minutes of coming on as a substitute** condemned Wrexham to an undeserved defeat in front of over 13,000 fans at Valley Parade.

Bradford's decision to sell cheap season tickets at around £130 certainly made for a superb atmosphere, helped in no small way by a good 500 or so travelling Dragons' followers. And those that did make the journey over the Pennines were rewarded with a display that deserved at least a point and possibly all three!

"You could probably say I'm gutted with the result, but I thought we played very well", were Brian Carey's sentiments after the game. "I don't think we deserved to go behind and we did enough to have won the game and that's what was really, really disappointing". His disappointment was understandable as the Dragons produced a promising performance that certainly didn't deserve a defeat.

However, it was the home side that began the game on the front foot with Anthony Williams twice being forced into saves within the opening ten minutes. But having weathered the early storm the Dragons gradually began to get a foothold in the game. Bradford's 'keeper Donovan Ricketts made a smart save from Matty Done on 22 minutes and then kept out a Chris Llewellyn header as Wrexham continued to threaten. And at the other end Kyle Nix wasted a cracking opportunity of giving the home side a 33rd minute lead, but miscued with a close-range header.

Goalless at the break, the large crowd didn't have long to wait for the contest to spring to life again after the restart, with two goals inside the opening nine minutes. Bradford grabbed the lead when Omar Daley set up Eddie Johnson who found the net with a crisp low drive from about 20 yards out. But back came Wrexham to level things; Danny Williams' goal-bound header was deflected wide, and the resultant corner was only partially cleared, and Danny clipped the ball back across for Neil Roberts to beat Ricketts with a well-timed header.

Wrexham now looked the more likely side to go on and win the game although, dis-

appointingly, clear-cut openings never really materialised. And the away fans were left stunned when Medley fired his amazing winner. Nix picked out the youngster with a ball down the left hand side, and as the ball dropped over his shoulder Medley let fly with a vicious dipping left-foot volley that flew over Williams' head and into the top corner of the net. Unstoppable!

The Dragons rallied again after this setback, and had appeals for a penalty for hands against Nix waved away, but time ran out and the home side held on.

Bradford City:
1 Donovan Ricketts, 2 Darren Williams (22), 3 Paul Heckingbottom, 4 Paul Evans, 5 David Wetherall, 6 Mark Bower, 7 Omar Daley, 8 Eddie Johnson, 9 Barry Conlon (76), 22 Kyle Nix ■, 24 Guylain Ndumnu-Nsungu (82) ■.

Subs: 15 Joe Colbeck (GK), 16 Simon Ainge (22) ■, 20 Scott Phelan (82), 21 Nathan Joynes, 25 Luke Medley (76).

Wrexham:
1 Anthony Williams, 2 Simon Spender, 3 Ryan Valentine, 4 Shaun Pejic, 6 Richard Hope, 8 Danny Williams (75), 9 Neil Roberts (86), 10 Michael Proctor ■, 11 Chris Llewellyn, 18 Levi Mackin ■, Matty Done (86).

Subs: 5 Steve Evans, 7 Mark Jones (86) ■, 13 Michael Jones (GK), 14 Eifion Williams (75), 17 Josh Johnson (86).

Neil Roberts turns away to show his delight after scoring the equalising goal with his head

Shots on Goal:	14	12
Shots on Target:	9	8
Shots off Target	5	4
Possession:	50%	50%
Fouls Conceded:	9	16
Corners:	6	6
Yellow Cards:	2	3
Red Cards:	0	0

The look on 'Carrots', Steve Evans and Shaun Pejic's faces says it all as Villa extend the lead.

Coca Cola League Cup Round Two: 28th August, 2007

Wrexham 0

Aston Villa 5

Shaun Maloney 32, 72
Stefan Moore 52
Nigel Reo-Coker 62
Marlon Harewood 78

Referee: Graham Laws (Whitley Bay)
Attendance (Away): 8,221 (2,129)

How often this day and age does a lower League club, play a Premier League side, and not put out its best side against their more illustrious opponents? Hardly ever: if at all: is probably the answer – especially in the early rounds of a competition.

Yet that's the impression most Wrexham fans will have taken away with them from this mauling by Martin O'Neill's side. To say that the Dragons weren't at the races – apart from a brief opening spell – is something of an understatement as once Villa had grabbed the lead through Shaun Maloney it really was a matter of how many! It certainly wasn't what the majority of the healthy crowd had in mind when the draw was made. It's doubtful that it did much to encourage the 'floating' fans to return at the weekend either!

Manager Brian Carey made five changes from the side that drew at Bradford at the weekend with Conall Murtagh, handed a central midfield role alongside Levi Mackin against the likes of England U21 captain Nigel Reo-Coker, being given his full debut. Okay, so O'Neill made six changes from the weekend, but the sixteen selected still boasted a superb array of talent!

But despite being forced onto the back foot for much of the game Wrexham made an encouraging start with Eifion Williams looking as if he had the beating of right back Craig Gardner. But it all proved to be false hope as Reo-Coker and midfield partner Isaiah Osborne took a grip on the middle of the park that they never relinquished.

The final margin of defeat was still somewhat tough on a Wrexham side that battled hard for the entire 90 minutes and were still in the game until Luke More doubled Villa's advantage seven minutes into the second half. And had Chris Llewellyn's deflected 28th minute free kick not just evaded Steve Evans then this could have been an entirely different report to write. But just two minutes later the unchallenged Maloney curled the ball beyond Michael Jones and the writing was very much on the wall.

Villa 'keeper Stuart Taylor denied Eifion Williams in the opening minute of the second period as hopes of a comeback were briefly raised, but then Moore headed in Gareth Barry's free kick, and normal service was resumed. Reo-Coker charged down a Shaun Pejic clearance and drilled the ball past Jones for number three and Maloney netted his second of the evening ten minutes later. Marlon Harewood rounded off the scoring with a near-post flick from a Maloney corner .

"I just think we showed them too much respect in the end," said Carey. Hmm, maybe not enough!

Wrexham:
13 Michael Jones, 2 Simon Spender, 3 Ryan Valentine ■, 4 Shaun Pejic, 5 Steve Evans, 7 Mark Jones, 10 Michael Proctor (61), 11 Chris Llewellyn, 14 Eifion Williams (79), 18 Levi Mackin, 22 Connall Murtagh (55).

Subs: 1 Anthony Williams (GK), 15 Mike Williams, 17 Josh Johnson (61), 21 Marc Williams (55), 26 Neil Taylor (79).

Aston Villa:
13 Stuart Taylor, 4 Olof Melberg, 6 Gareth Barry, 8 Luke Moore, 9 Marlon Harewood, 11 Gabriel Agbonlahor, 20 Nigel Reo-Coker (67), 21 Gary Cahill, 26 Craig Gardner, 27 Isaiah Osbourne, 28 Shaun Maloney.

Subs: 5 Martin Laursen, 7 Ashley Young, 10 John Carew, 19 Stillyan Petrov (67), 22 Scott Carson (GK).

Olof Melberg (4) and Nigel Reo-Coker both attempt to block Michael Proctor' cross.

	Wrexham	AVFC
Shots on Goal:	6	18
Shots on Target:	2	8
Shots off Target:	4	10
Possession:	41%	59%
Fouls Conceded:	13	12
Corners:	4	7
Yellow Cards:	1	0
Red Cards:	0	0

Danny Williams heads for goal, but ex-Chester 'keeper Wayne Brown is well placed to save.

Coca Cola Football League 2: 1st September, 2007

Wrexham 0

Hereford United 2

Kris Taylor 53
Trevor Benjamin 73

Referee: Phil Dowd (Stoke-on-Trent)
Attendance (Away): 4,004 (408)

The Dragons were booed off the pitch after a lacklustre ninety minutes that saw them well beaten by Hereford United at the Racecourse.

Hereford, in all truth, were no great shakes either, and their manager Graham Turner almost admitted as much after the game. "There wasn't much to choose between the teams today, but we made a break to get the first goal and we grew in confidence after that," he said. He may

have had a point, but he may also have been showing a little diplomacy as he'd started his playing career at the Racecourse back in the 1960s. For the Bulls were the better organised and more lively side, though surprisingly they carved out little in the way of genuine goal scoring chances themselves, yet ultimately capitalised on the only two real chances they created!

As expected there was numerous changes from the side comprehensively

---

beaten by Aston Villa in midweek, though Steve Evans did retain his place for a first League start of the season. Unfortunately, the big defenders contribution was a short-lived one as he limped off with a recurrence of the ankle ligament injury he sustained at Newtown in pre-season.

Wrexham were the first to show, and Neil Roberts was a bit unlucky with a shot that was blocked allowing former Chester 'keeper Wayne Brown to gather comfortably. But a Richard Hope shot that was also blocked late in the first half apart, Roberts' early effort was about as good as it got – for either side – in an instantly forgettable first half!

Michael Proctor couldn't quite reach a Mark Jones free kick that fizzed across the six-yard box immediately after the restart, but hopes of the Dragons taking the game by the scruff of the neck were quickly dissipated when the Bulls took the lead. Hope appeared to block the ball on the line with his hand after on-loan Theo Robinson had rounded Anthony Williams, but he was powerless to prevent Kris Taylor from latching onto the rebound to hammer the ball home. The defender received a yellow card when it would almost certainly have been red had the

ball not eventually ended up in the net.

Brown's first save came three minutes later when he gathered a 20-yard Proctor strike, before substitutes Eifion Williams and Mike Carvill combined almost instantly after entering the fray to create the Dragons' best chance of the afternoon. Carvill broke down the right and his cross was met cleanly by Williams, but Brown instinctively saved at close range.

Hereford made the game safe when substitute Trevor Benjamin neatly controlled a Clint Easton cross and smashed an unstoppable shot past Williams.

Wrexham:
1 Anthony Williams, 2 Simon Spender, 3 Ryan Valentine, 5 Steve Evans (16), 6 Richard Hope ■, 7 Mark Jones, 8 Danny Williams ■, 9 Neil Roberts, 10 Michael Proctor, 11 Chris Llewellyn (62), 20 Matty Done.

Subs: 4 Shaun Pejic (15), 13 Michael Jones (GK), 14 Eifion Williams (62), 18 Levi Mackin, 23 Michael Carvill (62).

Hereford United:
1 Wayne Brown, 2 Trent McClenahan, 4 Richard Rose ■, 6 Karl Broadhurst ■, 7 Lionel Ainsworth (85), 9 Stephen Guinan (67), 10 Kris Taylor (67), 11 Clint Easton, 20 Toumani Diagouraga ■, 22 Theo Robinson, 28 Dean Beckwith.

Subs: 5 John McCombe, 8 Ben Smith (67), 12 Trevor Benjamin (68), 14 Michael Ingham (GK), 15 Sam Gwynne (85).

Mark Jones attempts to run through the 'Bulls' defence.

	Wrexham	Hereford
Shots on Goal:	8	5
Shots on Target:	7	3
Shots off Target	1	2
Possession:	43%	57%
Fouls Conceded:	11	15
Corners:	7	4
Yellow Cards:	2	3
Red Cards:	0	0

Substitute Silvio Spann rises above the Millers defence to head for goal.

Coca Cola League 2: 15th September, 2007

Wrexham 0

Rotherham United 1

Chris O'Grady 78

Referee: Steve Bratt (West Midlands)
Attendance (Away): 3,711 (424)

A two-week break due to international call-ups failed to spark Wrexham into life as a Chris O'Grady (or was it Simon Spender?) goal 13 minutes from time maintained the doom and gloom in the stands following a third successive home defeat – and all without even scoring a goal! The defeat also saw the Dragons slip to bottom place in League Two!

It definitely wasn't a happy afternoon then – and the sight of police and stewards having to separate disgruntled home fans in the closing stages of the game was evi-

dence enough that patience in the stands was already starting to wear thin.

Brian Carey once again rang the changes with Levi Mackin and Eifion Williams returning to the starting eleven and Chris Llewellyn dropping down for a rare substitute's role.

But the re-shuffling obviously didn't have the desired effect as once again Wrexham failed to deliver; failed to muster together any decent spells of possession; resorted to the long ball forward far too often; and generally let the visitors dictate the game.

Marcus Bean had an early chance for the Millers, but fired over the bar and only a timely intervention by Spender denied Derek Holmes what would have been a simple opportunity to open the scoring.

Wrexham's main (only?) threat was coming from Matty Done, whose 23rd minute centre was miscued by Michael Proctor with Eifion Williams' follow-up effort being blocked.

But the main threat was always at the other end and Millers' striker Derek Holmes first headed straight at Anthony Williams and then, just before the break, headed a Bruce Dyer cross against the post with Williams beaten.

Matty Crowell replaced the ineffective Mark Jones for the restart, his first appearance since a knee injury back in January, and his 49th minute corner was headed back by Steve Evans, but Neil Roberts' header drifted wide.

Danny Harrison and Peter Holmes both wasted opportunities as the visitors began to exert some control on proceedings, and Stephen Brogan's 20-yard shot brought a fingertip save out of Williams.

A rare Wrexham threat then saw substitute

Llewellyn have Andy Warrington at full stretch to tip his drive behind for a corner, and from the resulting flag kick Silvio Spann's downward header was deflected wide.

But any hopes of grabbing a late winner were dashed when Peter Holmes' defence-splitting pass found Andy Todd who ran through before sliding the ball across for a combination of O'Grady and Spender to slot the ball into the empty net.

Wrexham did mount a late rally that saw a Spann free kick turned behind by Warrington, and Roberts' header cleared off the line by O'Grady, but it was never going to be enough.

Wrexham:
1 Anthony Williams, 2 Simon Spender, 3 Ryan Valentine ■, 5 Steve Evans, 6 Richard Hope, 7 Mark Jones (46), 9 Neil Roberts, 10 Michael Proctor ■, 14 Eifion Williams, 18 Levi Mackin (67), 20 Matty Done (67) ■.

Subs: 4 Shaun Pejic, 11 Chris Llewellyn (67), 12 Matt Crowell (46), 13 Michael Jones (GK), 16 Silvio Spann (67).

Rotherham United:
1 Andy Warrington, 2 Dale Tonge, 4 Danny Harrison, 6 Graham Coughlan, 7 Andy Todd, 8 Peter Holmes, 9 Derek Holmes (67), 11 Stephen Brogan, 12 Marc Joseph, 14 Marcus Blean ■, 28 Bruce Dyer (80).

Subs: 15 Chris O'Grady (67), 17 Marc Newsham (80), 19 Liam King, 22 Natt Kerr, 27 Jamie Annerson (GK).

Neil Roberts manoeuvres himself awkwardly to head at goal		
Shots on Goal:	7	12
Shots on Target:	4	7
Shots off Target	3	5
Possession:	50%	50%
Fouls Conceded:	13	19
Corners:	11	7
Yellow Cards:	3	1
Red Cards:	0	0

A Michael Carvill's run for goal comes to an end with a solid challenge by Jim McNulty.

Johnstone's Paint Trophy Round One: 18th September, 2007

Wrexham 0   Macclesfield Town 1

Michael Husbands 67p

Referee: Darren Drysdale (Lincolnshire)

Attendance (Away): 1,503 (89)

Chris Llewellyn and Michael Proctor both saw red as Wrexham crashed out of the Johnstone's Paint Trophy in controversial circumstances at the Racecourse, despite battering the visitors for virtually the entire game!

Following Saturday's third successive home defeat – all without scoring – boss Brian Carey made five changes in the starting eleven and the early signs looked encouraging as the Dragons quickly gained the upper hand.

Chris Llewellyn had a third minute shot blocked and a couple of minutes later

Eifion Williams turned well before testing Jon Brain.

Former Red Jimmy McNulty almost caught Anthony Williams off guard with a glancing header in a rare Macclesfield raid, but normal service was quickly resumed when Mike Carvill was extremely unlucky with a fine curling effort that had Brain beaten, but drifted just wide via an upright.

Matty Done then seized on a poor pass to find Llewellyn, but the Welsh International, who only had Brian to beat, directed his shot straight at the advancing keeper. The football on display was a huge improvement on what had been evident in recent Racecourse outings, and so it was unfortunate that the flow of the game was disrupted late on in the half to injuries to full backs Ryan Valentine and Mike Williams, leaving Carey having to shuffle his pack around somewhat.

But the reshuffling didn't seem to deter the Dragons too much, and both Steve Evans and Llewellyn had efforts blocked in the opening exchanges of the second half. Substitute Marc Williams smashed another effort across the face of the six-yard box and Done, after outpacing two defenders, hammered a shot against the crossbar.

However, Wrexham's world was once again to start falling in only four minutes later when referee Darren Drysdale somehow spotted a handball by Marc Williams inside the penalty area and Michael Husbands neatly converted from the spot kick. It looked an extremely harsh decision, as the ball seemed to just ricochet against him!

Five minutes later Llewellyn was booked for a foul, and then received a second yellow almost immediately, followed by a red, for dissent towards the official.

Wrexham still continued to press though,

and an Evans header from Matty Crowell's corner was cleared off the line, while Carvill's 25-yard shot flew inches wide.

Proctor could possibly have had a late penalty after being pulled back inside the area, but his frustrations got the better of him moments later when he was shown the red card for stamping on James Jennings near the touchline, though feelings after the game seemed to be about 50/50 on whether there was any intent in the challenge.

"His performance is what most people will be talking about after this," was Carey's assessment of Mr Drysdale. It was too!

Wrexham:
1 Anthony Williams, 3 Ryan Valentine (43), 5 Steve Evans, 6 Richard Hope, 11 Chris Llewellyn ■■, 12 Matt Crowell ■, 14 Eifion Williams (59), Mike Williams (37), 16 Silvio Spann ■, 20 Matty Done, 23 Michael Carvill.

Subs: 4 Shaun Pejic (37), 10 Michael Proctor (59) ■, 13 Michael Jones (GK), 17 Josh Johnson, 21 Marc Williams (43).

Macclesfield Town:
30 Jonny Brain, 3 Carl Regan ■, 4 David Morley, 7 Simon Wiles, 9 Martin Gritton (57), 10 Michael Husbands ■, 12 Danny Thomas (64), 13 Levi Reid, 17 Jordan Hadfield, 19 James Jennings (90) ■, 21 James McNulty.

Subs: 16 Izak Reid (64), 22 Matthew Flynn (90), 26 Gareth Evans (57), 27 Christian Miller, 28 Matthew Lowe.

Chris Llewellyn avoids a challenge in his run for goal watched by Matty Crowell.

	Wrexham	Macclesfield
Shots on Goal:	9	9
Shots on Target:	4	4
Shots off Target	5	5
Possession:	46%	54%
Fouls Conceded:	10	10
Corners:	2	4
Yellow Cards:	3	3
Red Cards:	2	0

Marc Williams rises high to beat Conrad Logan to head in Neil Taylor's deep cross.

Coca Cola League 2: 22nd September, 2007

Stockport County 2

Anthony Elding 29
Dominic Blizzard 65

Wrexham 1

Marc Williams 26

Referee: Colin Webster (Tyne & Wear)
Attendance (Away): 5,513 (500ish)

Agame almost completely lacking in entertainment and quality went the home side's way by the odd goal in three after Wrexham's defensive frailties once again surfaced prominently.

This was an instantly forgettable game with only two abiding memories to take away from the game – the assured debut of defender Neil Taylor and a rare appearance (as a late substitute) of a certain Juan Ugarte. Little did we know at the

time, but this would be his last appearance in a Wrexham shirt!

County should have opened the scoring on 12 minutes when an unmarked Adam Proudlock failed to connect properly with a header, Richard Hope failed to clear, and the striker somehow blazed high over the bar from the loose ball.

But Wrexham gradually got into the game and their reward came with the opening goal when Matty Done released Taylor down the left, and the young defender's deep cross was met by Marc Williams who sent a looping header over 'keeper Conrad Logan into the net.

Given the dismal nature of the majority of the game with neither side really looking like carving out a decent goal scoring opportunity themselves, this one goal should have been enough to earn all three points, or a share of the spoils at the very least!

Unfortunately the lead wasn't to last for long – four minutes in fact – as a hopeful punt forward by Logan was flicked on by Matty McNeil and Anthony Elding capitalised on some hesitation between Steve Evans and Anthony Williams to fire home from 25 yards out.

Elding could have added a second on 35 minutes but headed over. Generally the game looked to be drifting nowhere, and a stalemate the most likely outcome. Marc Williams had a couple of half chances, but it ddn't look as if either side would conjure up a winning goal.

However, it's Wrexham we're talking about, and when Paul Tierney whipped in a corner that found the Dragons' defence

AWOL, and the ball found its way to Dominic Blizzard who gratefully headed easily into the net from six yards out.

Ugarte was soon brought on in an attempt to bring some fresh impetus into the Dragons' attack and, despite efforts from Evans and Mike Carvill narrowly missing the target, the home side held on without any genuine alarm to leave the Dragons rooted to the bottom of League Two.

"This club does not deserve to be bottom of the League," said boss Brian Carey after the game. "The pressure has to be applied and that's fine. If that's what it takes to get the job done then that's fine. We have got two home games and they are now must-win games!"

Stockport County:
26 Conrad Logan, 4 Jason Taylor, 5 Gareth Owen, 6 Ashley Williams, 9 Anthony Elding, 10 Matty McNeil, 11 Adam Griffin (90), 19 Paul Tierney, 30 Dominic Blizzard, 31 Adam Proudlock (75), 32 James Smith.

Subs: 7 David Poole (75), 8 Gary Dicker, 18 Greg Tansley, 21 Tommy Rowe (90), 22 Zac Jones (GK).

Wrexham:
1 Anthony Williams, 2 Simon Spender, 5 Steve Evans, 6 Richard Hope ■, 7 Mark Jones ■, 8 Danny Williams, 16 Silvio Spann (46), 20 Matt Done (69), 21 Marc Williams, 23 Michael Carvill, 25 Neil Taylor (63).

Subs: 4 Shaun Pejic (63), 9 Neil Roberts, 12 Matt Crowell (46), 13 Michael Jones (GK), 30 Juan Ugarte (69).

Debutante Neil Taylor is chased by former Wolves striker Adam Proudlock.

Shots on Goal:	9	7
Shots on Target:	4	2
Shots off Target	5	5
Possession:	51%	49%
Fouls Conceded:	8	10
Corners:	5	6
Yellow Cards:	0	2
Red Cards:	0	0

Marc Williams under challenge from two Lincoln defenders plays the ball out wide.

Coca Cola League 2: 29th September, 2007

Wrexham 1   Lincoln City 0

Marc Williams 51

Referee: Roger East (Salisbury)
Attendance (Away): 3,614 (179)

The first of two home games that Brian Carey had described a week earlier as being "must-win games" saw the Dragons move up to 21st place and bring a six-game losing streak to an end with a deserved victory over fellow strugglers Lincoln City at the Racecourse.

Marc Williams' second goal in successive games, a fine curling effort from the left-hand corner of the penalty area, was enough to clinch the three points though there were the inevitable nervy moments late on.

Carey responded to the recent bad run by opting for a 3-5-2 system that saw Danny Williams deployed as an extra central defender and Robbie Garrett, beginning a second spell at the club on loan from Stoke City, in the middle of the park.

Wrexham seized the initiative almost immediately, but frustratingly again failed to turn the amount of quality possession they enjoyed into genuine chances.

They did get the perfect opportunity to grab the lead on 18 minutes when Nat Brown tripped Marc Williams inside the penalty area, but Imps' 'keeper Alan Marriott dived to his right to turn Neil Roberts' spot kick behind for a corner.

To their credit though the Dragons didn't dwell on this setback for long and quickly got back into their stride, but once again didn't cause too much concern for Marriott.

Despite being very much second best in the first half it was the visitors that created the first chance after the restart when Mark Stallard found his way through the defence far too easily, but Mark Jones was on hand to make a vital interception just in the nick of time.

The importance of Jonah's contribution became more significant soon afterwards when Wrexham grabbed the all-important goal. Williams turned his marker at the edge of the box before sending a sweet right-foot curler over Marriott and into the far corner of the net.

Ten minutes later the visitors' task became even harder when Gary Croft, not long after receiving his first yellow card, lunged rashly at Mike Carvill and duly picked up his second caution and the inevitable walk for an early bath.

It seemed a certainty that the Dragons would add to their lead as they enjoyed the benefit of having the extra man. Mark Jones saw an effort just clear the crossbar and Marc Williams twice failed to find the finish to match that of his earlier strike.

As the minutes rapidly counted down to the final whistle and a massive three points, thought's inevitably turned to holding onto the lead rather than extending it, and the Dragons were forced to soak up some pressure in the closing moments, but they thankfully held on!

Wrexham:
1 Anthony Williams, 5 Steve Evans, 6 Richard Hope, 7 Mark Jones, 8 Danny Williams, 9 Neil Roberts (88), 12 Matt Crowell, 21 Marc Williams, 23 Michael Carvill, 25, Neil Taylor (82), 26 Robbie Garrett ■.

Subs: 2 Simon Spender, 4 Shaun Pejic, 13 Michael Jones (GK), 17 Josh Johnson (88), 20 Matty Done (82).

Lincoln City:
1 Alan Marriott, 2 Paul Green, 3 Gary Croft ■ ■, 4 Adie Moses (80), 5 Lee Beevers, 6 Nat Brown, 8 Jamie Forrester (71), 9 Mark Stallard ■, 11 Scott Kerr, 19 Louis Dodd (38) ■, 26 Jamie Hand.

Subs: 7 Lee Frecklington (38), 10 Steve Torpey, 15 Ben Wright, 17 Danny N'Guessan (80), 18 Oliver Ryan (71).

Neil Roberts holds his head indisbelief after /Imps 'keeper Alan Marriott saves his penalty.

	Wrexham	Lincoln City
Shots on Goal:	15	4
Shots on Target:	5	2
Shots off Target:	10	2
Possession:	55%	45%
Fouls Conceded:	18	18
Corners:	6	8
Yellow Cards:	1	3
Red Cards:	0	1

The Spireites Peter Leven gets the better of Robbie Garrett watched by Matty Crowell.

Coca Cola League 2: 2nd October, 2007

Wrexham 0

Chesterfield 4

Jack Lester 6, 15
Adam Rooney 14
Peter Leven 60

Referee: David Foster (Tyne & Wear)
Attendance (Away): 3,058 (151)

Oh dear! What can you say? Wrexham were simply swept away by an impressive Chesterfield side, and got away lightly with a 4-0 defeat!

Looking to build on the weekend win against Lincoln, Brian Carey understandably went with an unchanged side, but any hopes of recording a second successive home win were soon blown away.

Had Robbie Garrett not wasted a good chance of giving the Dragons the lead inside the opening 90 seconds, the mid-

fielder blasting wide after being played in by Marc Williams, then maybe the evening would have panned out differently. Of course, we'll never know!

But Chesterfield capitalised on their early let-off and began their onslaught when Felix Bastians, on loan from Nottingham Forest, sent over a teasing cross from the left that Anthony Williams failed to collect and Jack Lester hammered home the loose ball.

Wrexham nearly equalised when 'keeper Barry Roche reacted superbly to palm the ball away after Aaron Downes had deflected Mike Carvill's cross goalwards.

Any hopes of mounting a comeback were quickly quashed as the visitors doubled their lead. Bastians was again the provider, weaving his way to the by-line again and crossing for Adam Rooney to net from close range.

A minute later and further gloom and despondency befell the Racecourse faithful as Rooney nodded down Jamie Lowry's cross and the unmarked Lester calmly slotted the ball past Williams.

The Dragons did keep plugging away though and a Neil Roberts effort was deflected wide. Roche saved a 20-yard drive by Garrett, and tipped a teasing Neil Taylor cross over the bar, before substitute Chris Llewellyn, on for the injured Marc Williams, fired just wide.

There was always more of a threat when the visitors attacked, and Phil Picken crashed a 25-yard effort against the post and a Lester shot clipped the crossbar.

Any possibility of a second half revival needed an early goal after the restart and Llewellyn led the way with a shot that drifted narrowly wide and a header that

Roche had to tip over for a corner.

But that's about as good as it got really and it was no surprise when Chesterfield added a fourth goal on the hour when Peter Leven's rocket shot flew into the top corner of the net to cap fine build-up play. Rooney should have added a fifth in the closing seconds but blazed over the bar before the referee's final whistle finally put the home crowd out of their misery.

"I take the flak that goes with it and I can understand people's frustrations," declared Carey after the game. "I would not want to sit there and support a team that is getting beat three or four nil at home." Who would?

Wrexham:
1 Anthony Williams, 5 Steve Evans, 6 Richard Hope, 7 Mark Jones, 8 Danny Williams ■, 9 Neil Roberts ■, 12 Matt Crowell (62) ■, 21 Marc Williams (16), 23 Michael Carvill (62), 25 Neil Taylor, 26 Robbie Garrett.

Subs: 2 Simon Spender (62), 4 Shaun Pejic, 11 Chris Llewellyn (16), 13 Michael Jones (GK), 20 Matty Done (62).

Chesterfield:
1 Barry Roche, 2 Janos Kovacs (71) ■, 4 Jamie Lowry, 5 Phil Picken ■, 8 Derek Niven, 11 Gregor Robertson, 13 Felix Bastians (75), 14 Jack Lester (81), 15 Aaron Downes ■, 19 Peter Leven, 20 Adam Rooney.

Subs: 6 Kevin Gray (71), 16 Jamie Winter, 18 Alan O'Hare, 22 Wayne Allison (81), 23 Nicky Travis (75).

Brian Carey and his assistant Steve Weaver can only watch in dismay as there team crumble in front of them.

Shots on Goal:	12	12
Shots on Target:	3	6
Shots off Target	9	6
Possession:	40%	60%
Fouls Conceded:	9	10
Corners:	6	5
Yellow Cards:	3	3
Red Cards:	0	0

Mark Jones bursts through Accrington's defence in yet another Wrexham attack,

Coca Cola League 2: 5th October, 2007

Accrington Stanley 0

Wrexham 2

Neil Roberts 37, 66

Referee: Stuart Attwell (Warwickshire)
Attendance (Away): 1,822 (500+)

The Dragons returned to the scene of probably their worst performance of last season with this Friday night visit to the Fraser Eagle Stadium. And as well as banishing the memories of the 5-0 mauling by Stanley just over a year ago there was also the small matter of bouncing back from the embarrassing home defeat by Chesterfield just three days earlier.

Thankfully the players delivered on both counts and produced a performance probably deserving of more than the final 2-0 margin of victory.

There was no surprise that Brian Carey made four changes from Tuesday's humiliation, with Michael Proctor returning after suspension, Chris Llewellyn back in the starting eleven, and call-ups also for defenders Shaun Pejic and Simon Spender.

And the changes obviously worked, as the Dragons were dominant throughout and restricted the home side to only a few openings.

Danny Williams came close to giving the Dragons a 12th minute lead, but his header from Mark Jones' corner struck a post before Peter Cavanagh was able to hack the loose ball off the goal line.

Proctor couldn't quite force the ball over the line after 'keeper Ian Dunbavin failed to gather a Richard Hope free kick when under pressure from the returning striker, and Llewellyn went close with a header.

This adventurous approach finally paid off when Proctor's flick on found Llewellyn whose shot was blocked, but the ball cannoned into the path of Roberts who picked his spot and gleefully side-footed the ball into the bottom corner of the net from about 20-yards out.

Wrexham deserved their lead at the break and came close to extending it on 57 minutes when Neil Taylor delivered the perfect cross, but Proctor's point-blank header was directed straight at Dunbavin who blocked the ball with his legs.

Anthony Williams was called into action at the other end to keep out a David Brown shot before the goal that made it a comfortable closing quarter of the game for the Dragons arrived when Mark Jones' superb looping cross was just asking to be put away and Roberts duly delivered with an unerring finish.

Former Red Lee McEvilly was introduced to try and beef up the home attack – much to the amusement of the travelling fans – and twice came close to pulling a goal back, firstly with a snapshot that Williams saved and secondly with a header that went wide.

Jones tested Dunbavin, Roberts had strong shouts for a penalty turned down after he appeared to be pulled back inside the area, and Robbie Garrett had a 25-yard drive turned away by the 'keeper, but Wrexham, and their fans, were happy to settle for the two goals and three much-needed points.

.**Accrington Stanley:**
25 Ian Dunbavin, 2 Peter Cavanagh, Liam Richardson (70), 4 Robbie Williams, 5 Mark Roberts, 6 Andrew Proctor, 9 Roscie D'Sane (72), 10 Paul Mullin, 16 Paul Carden, 18 David Brown (72), 21 Sean Webb ■.

Subs: 7 Shaun Whalley (70), 11 John Miles (72), 14 Romuald Boco, 15 Lee McEvilly (72), 26 Martin Fearon (GK).

Wrexham:
1 Anthony Williams, 2 Simon Spender, 4 Shaun Pejic, 6 Richard Hope, 7 Mark Jones (90), 8 Danny Williams (46), 9 Neil Roberts (86), 10 Michael Proctor, 11 Chris Llewellyn, 25 Neil Taylor, 26 Robbie Garrett.

Subs: 5 Steve Evans (46), 12 Matt Crowell (90), 13 Michael Jones (GK), 14 Eifion Williams (86), 20 Matty Done.

Neil Roberts is congratulated having scored both goals in the 2-0 win at the Fraser Eagle Stadium.

Shots on Goal:	11	10
Shots on Target:	6	8
Shots off Target	5	2
Possession:	43%	57%
Fouls Conceded:	10	16
Corners:	3	7
Yellow Cards:	1	2
Red Cards:	0	0

Michael Proctor is brought down by the Silkmen's former Dragon Jim McNulty.

Coca Cola League 2: 13th October, 2007

Macclesfield Town 3   Wrexham 2

Martin Gritton 36   Michael Proctor 6p,
Dave Morley 90   Chris Llewellyn 22
Danny Thomas 90

Referee: Lee Probert (Gloucestershire)
Attendance (Away): 2,256 (701)

Well, how do you explain this one then? Leading 2-1 with only a couple of minutes remaining you'd have been disappointed to have left Moss Rose with only a point – despite the controversial 82nd minute dismissal of midfielder Robbie Garrett.

So to concede twice in the brief time remaining and travel home with no points whatsoever left the travelling away support simply flabbergasted.

All had looked so different in the opening stages of the contest as the Dragons roared into a two-goal lead inside the opening quarter of the game thanks to a Michael Proctor penalty and Chris Llewellyn.

But the sending off of Garrett was to prove a pivotal moment in the game. "That decision has turned the game," raged a clearly upset Brian Carey. "Absolutely it has. The lad's clashed with the goalkeeper, but he's just trying to get away and the keeper is all over him." It looked a harsh decision, as the aggressor in the incident was clearly Macclesfield 'keeper Tommy Lee. But the referee saw it (or did he?) differently and showed both players a yellow card that meant that Robbie, booked earlier in the game for a rash challenge on Adam Murray, had to go.

David Morley should have given the home side a third minute lead, but somehow blazed over the bar, but Wrexham were soon on the offensive and took the lead when former Racecourse youngster Jimmy McNulty brought a Proctor run into the box to a premature end, and the striker dusted himself down to make no mistake from the spot.

Several more opportunities came the Dragons' way before they finally extended the lead. Neil Roberts flicked on Anthony Williams' long clearance for Mark Jones to chase before sliding the ball back into the stride of Llewellyn who curled the ball past Jones for his first goal of the campaign.

In truth Wrexham had struggled under high balls from the home side all afternoon and succumbed to such a move when a Danny Thomas cross wasn't dealt

with and Levi Reid nodded the ball on for Martin Gritton to head past Williams from close range.

The home side enjoyed the better of the second period without really looking like finding an equaliser, until the late intervention by referee Lee Probert gave them fresh impetus in the closing minutes.

Two minutes into added-on time the home side equalised when Morley headed Kevin McIntyre's cross past Williams and then, barely a minute later, Thomas' deep centre from the left somehow found its way over Williams and into the net.

Unbelievable!

Macclesfield Town:
1 Tommy Lee ■, 2 Richard Edghill, 4 David Morley ■, 8 Francis Green (62), 9 Martin Gritton, 12 Danny Thomas, 13 Levi Reid (67), 14 Kevin McIntyre, 15 Adam Murray, 21 James McNulty, 25 Terry Dunfield.

Subs: 3 Carl Regan, 7 Simon Wiles (67), 16 Izak Reid, 26 Gareth Evans (62), 30 Jonny Brain (GK).

Wrexham:
1 Anthony Williams, 2 Simon Spender, 4 Shaun Pejic, 6 Richard Hope, 7 Mark Jones ■, 8 Danny Williams (46), 9 Neil Roberts, 10 Michael Proctor (63), 11 Chris Llewellyn, 25 Neil Taylor, 26 Robbie Garrett ■ ■.

Subs: 13 Michael Jones (GK), 14 Eifion Williams (63),15 Mike Williams (46), 16 Silvio Spann, 21 Marc Williams.

Michael Proctor dusts himself down to take the penalty to give Wrexham an early lead.

Shots on Goal:	11	4
Shots on Target:	6	2
Shots off Target	5	2
Possession:	46%	54%
Fouls Conceded:	8	16
Corners:	8	1
Yellow Cards:	2	2
Red Cards:	0	1

Eifion Williams is thwarted by a packed Barnet defence in his attempt for goal.

Coca Cola League 2: 20th October, 2007

Wrexham 0

Barnet 2

Liam Hatch 59, 69

Referee: Ray Lee (Essex)
Attendance (Away): 3,591 (107)

Boss Brian Carey admitted that his job was on the line after this non-performance by his side. "If performances and results carry on like that I probably won't be here myself," he admitted. "You have to be realistic about these things and I'm sorry we are not giving the fans what we are capable of."

Just what the Dragons are capable of exactly hasn't been evident too much to date, especially at the Racecourse where this defeat against an in-form Barnet side

made it six defeats in eight home outings! And just three goals in those eight outings also clearly demonstrate why the inevitable boos greeted the final whistle once again.

In response to the calamitous events in the closing stages at Macclesfield a week earlier Carey made four changes to the starting eleven, including a surprise return for Michael Jones in goal.

The first forty-five minutes was a forgettable affair as both sides cancelled each other out and defences were easily on top. Barnet had the best chance of the half in the 10th minute when Liam Hatch latched onto a poor clearance and clipped the crossbar with a looping shot.

Michael Proctor had a 'goal' correctly ruled out for offside and Wrexham's best chance of the half came in injury time when Silvio Spann stung the hands of Bees' 'keeper Lee Harrison with a well-struck free kick from fully 35 yards out.

The Dragons were the better side in the opening exchanges after the break with Simon Spender a prominent figure, even forcing a comfortable save from Harrison with an attempted chip. The 'keeper also turned a Mark Jones drive around the post for a corner, but the threat from the home side quickly petered out and Barnet thought they'd opened the scoring in the 57th minute when Hatch headed home an Ashley Carew cross but the referee blew for a foul by the striker.

Two minutes later though they did take the lead when Spender slipped at the most inopportune time and Jason Puncheon crossed low and hard for Hatch to convert at the far post.

This seemed to visibly knock the stuffing out of the Dragons and a second goal ten minutes later simply compounded matters. A hopeful punt forward by Sagi Burton forced Jones to come off his line to head clear, but the ball cannoned back off Hatch and the striker had the simple task of driving the ball into the empty net.

In a desperate late attempt to salvaging something from a disappointing afternoon the Dragons suddenly forced a few opportunities, but Harrison denied both Mark Jones and Marc Williams and substitute Eifion Williams twice failed to convert in the closing stages.

Wrexham:
1 Michael Jones, 2 Simon Spender ▨, 6 Richard Hope, 7 Mark Jones, 9 Neil Roberts (64), 10 Michael Proctor (46), 11 Chris Llewellyn, 15 Mike Williams (67), 16 Silvio Spann, 24 Gareth Evans, 25 Neil Taylor.

Subs: 1 Anthony Williams (GK), 5 Steve Evans, 14 Eifion Williams (46), 20 Matty Done (67), 21 Marc Williams (64).

Barnet:
1 Lee Harrison, 2 Joe Devera, 3 Nicky Nicolau, 4 Neal Bishop, 7 Liam Hatch (90), 10 Adam Birchill (87), 11 Jason Puncheon, 16 Ashley Carew, 19 Sagi Burton, 22 Joe O'Cearuill, 24 Josh Wright.

Subs: 9 Giuliano Grazioli (87), 14 Max Porter, 15 Stephane Seanla (90), 18 Rob Beckwith (GK), 20 Ian Hendon.

 Neil Roberts closes in on Barnet's Nicky Nicolau.

Shots on Goal:	12	3
Shots on Target:	8	1
Shots off Target	4	2
Possession:	63%	37%
Fouls Conceded:	11	20
Corners:	6	3
Yellow Cards:	0	1
Red Cards:	0	0

Eifion Williams keeps possession from the 'Magpies' defenders.

Coca Cola League 2: 27th October, 2007

Notts County 2   Wrexham 1

Spencer Weir-Daley 17   Silvio Spann 70
Neil MacKenzie 90

Referee: Andy Haines (Newcastle)
Attendance (Away): 4,359 (286)

Amistake by Steve Evans in the first half and an injury time free kick condemned Wrexham to a ninth League defeat of the season to leave them firmly in the relegation zone.

Changes were once again afoot after the Barnet defeat a week earlier with Anthony Williams, Steve Evans, Robbie Garrett (from suspension) and Eifion Williams all returning.

But these changes didn't have the desired effect in the opening stages as County made all the early running before taking the lead, thanks to further evidence of Wrexham's defensive frailty. After cutting out an attempted pass Steve Evans' lazy attempt to pass the ball back to Anthony Williams was seized upon by Spencer Weir-Daley who rounded the advancing Williams to roll the ball into the empty net.

Williams then kept his side in the hunt with a superb save to turn Myles Weston's 25-yard shot for a corner, and two minutes later Chris Llewellyn came close to equalising, but he steered his header wide from close range after Neil Roberts had nodded down a Simon Spender cross.

County continued to enjoy the better of the first half, but the Dragons again came close to equalising in the dying seconds when substitute Silvio Spann's free kick was volleyed goalwards by Richard Hope only for 'keeper Kevin Pilkington's finger tips to keep the ball out.

Although easily second best for much of the first half, the second was a different story and suddenly more questions were beginning to be asked of the home defence. Hope and Eifion Williams both came close; Pilkington got firmly behind a 20-yard Garrett volley; and Spann's well-struck effort from the edge of the area took an unfortunate deflection wide off Eifion Williams.

County twice came close to extending their lead, firstly through Matt Somner and then Weston.

But the equaliser the Dragons' second half display deserved arrived when Spender found Spann in space down the

right, and the Trinidadian international let fly with a powerful right-foot shot from just outside the penalty area that fizzed past Pilkington and into the net.

But, alas, a first League draw of the season wasn't to be. Former Red Hector Sam, who'd only been on the field a couple of minutes, burst clear in the last minute only to be up-ended by his fellow Trinidadian near the edge of the area. Spann was duly red carded, but worse was still to come, as Neil Mackenzie stepped up to take the free kick and precisely curled the ball past Williams into the top right-hand corner of the net.

Notts County
1 Kevin Pilkington, 2 Lee Canoville, 5 Adam Tann, 6 Matthew Somner ■, 8 Neil MacKenzie, 10 Lawrie Dudfield, 15 Paul Mayo, 18 Stephen Hunt, 21 Spencer Weir-Daley (86), 23 Richard Butcher, 30 Myles Weston (71).

Subs: 3 Austin McCann, 11 Andy Parkinson (71), 12 Gary Silk, 13 Hector Sam (86), 20 Tim Sandercombe (GK).

Wrexham:
1 Anthony Williams, 2 Simon Spender (79), 5 Steve Evans (64), 6 Richard Hope, 7 Mark Jones (28), 9 Neil Roberts, 11 Chris Llewellyn, 14 Eifion Williams, 24 Gareth Evans, 25 Neil Taylor, 26 Robbie Garrett.

Subs: 10 Michael Proctor (79), 15 Mike Williams, 16 Silvio Spann (28) ■, 20 Matty Done (64), 21 Marc Williams.

The Dragons Trinidadian midfielder Silvio Spann fires in Wrexham's equaliser.

	Notts County	Wrexham
Shots on Goal:	9	6
Shots on Target:	5	3
Shots off Target	4	3
Possession:	62%	38%
Fouls Conceded:	13	12
Corners:	4	2
Yellow Cards:	1	0
Red Cards:	0	1

Welsh under-21 international Marc Williams shoots at goal

Coca Cola League 2: 4th November, 2007

Wrexham 0

Shrewsbury Town 1

Michael Symes 59

Referee: Neil Swarbrick (Lancashire)
Attendance (Away): 4,305 (1,276)

The Dragons fired blanks in front of their own fans once again as Shrewsbury maintained their excellent recent record at the Racecourse with a deserved victory in this local derby.

It really is a sobering statistic that despite this being the ninth game of the season at the Racecourse, Wrexham are actually only the third top scorers at the famous old ground behind Aston Villa (5) and Chesterfield (4)!

With new signing Matty Collins beginning a month-long loan spell from Swansea

City the Dragons had slightly the better of the first half, but sadly failed to kick on in the second period. Shrewsbury on the other hand, even though on a 7-game win-less run, grew stronger after the break to just about deserve their narrow victory.

It was Collins that had the first effort at goal after just four minutes. but his volleyed effort drifted wide.

And sixty seconds later the visitors very nearly grabbed the lead themselves when former Wrexham favourite Neil 'Wally' Wainwright, making his first start since joining on loan from Darlington, crossed from the right, but David Hibbert somehow headed wide from close range when it looked easier to score!

Welsh international Glyn Garner was at full stretch to deny Eifion Williams, Steve Evans headed over and Neil Roberts turned a Chris Llewellyn shot over as Wrexham maintained some pressure during the opening period.

Strong appeals for a penalty were waved away by the overly fussy Neil Swarbrick after Mike Carvill's surging run was brought to an end by a clumsy challenge by Marc Tierney.

The first half display had given the Racecourse faithful some anticipation of better things after the break but unfortunately the opposite proved to be the case – especially after the Shrews snatched the lead.

Anthony Williams had already spared ex-Shrew Richard Hopes' blushes with a fine finger tip save to keep out a miscued header, but he was powerless when Evans' hurried clearance was charged down by Hibbert and rebounded into the path of Michael Symes who drilled the ball home.

There was still over a third of the game remaining, but the feeling quickly spread throughout the stands that the Dragons didn't really have enough about them to get themselves back on level terms.

Garner made a double save on 71 minutes to keep out efforts from Marc Williams and Robbie Garrett, but generally the visitors saw the game out fairly comfortably. The defeat leaves the Dragons sitting very precariously in 23rd place with just three wins and nine points to show from ten games, making Wednesday's home clash with Wycombe Wanderers something of a must-win game – for everyone concerned!

Wrexham:
1 Anthony Williams, 2 Simon Spender, 3 Ryan Valentine, 4 Shaun Pejic, 6 Richard Hope, 9 Neil Roberts (63), 11 Chris Llewellyn (75), 14 Eifion Williams, 23 Michael Carvill (45), 26 Robbie Garrett ■, 28 Matty Collins.

Subs: 10 Michael Proctor (75), 20 Matty Done (45) ■, 21 Marc Williams (63), 24 Gareth Evans, 25 Neil Taylor.

Shrewsbury Town:
1 Glyn Garner, 2 Darren Moss 46 ■, 4 Stuart Drummond, 6 David Hunt, 7 Marc Pugh (82), 8 Kevin Langmead, 9 David Hibbert (62), 11 Michael Symes ■, 19 Neil Wainwright, 22 Colin Murdock, 23 Marc Tierney.

Subs: 3 Neil Ashton (62), 10 Stuart Nicholson, 12 Ben Herd (46), 16 Daniel Hall (84), 31 Ryan Esson (GK),

Former Shrewsbury old boy Richard Hope shows his war wounds from the battle against his former club.

Shots on Goal:	11	3
Shots on Target:	4	2
Shots off Target	7	1
Possession:	47%	53%
Fouls Conceded:	14	15
Corners:	2	3
Yellow Cards:	2	2
Red Cards:	0	0

Robbie Garrett races away from Wycombe's Reuben Reid.

Coca Cola League 2: 7th November, 2007

Wrexham 0   Wycombe Wanderers 0

Referee: Jonathan Moss (West Yorkshire)
Attendance (Away): 2,805 (102)

The statement from co-owners Geoff Moss and Neville Dickens 24 hours earlier saying that the club were looking for an "experienced, senior manager" to oversee team affairs certainly had the rumour mill turning before, during and after this improved display against play-off hopefuls Wycombe Wanderers.

Speculation about who had turned up and was watching from the sidelines was rife throughout the game and, in truth, deflected somewhat from a fighting display by Brian Carey's side.

The crowd were treated to a spirited performance and it was refreshing that the booing that has greeted the final whistle in most home games this season was replaced by appreciative applause for a change.

Unfortunately the Dragons couldn't turn their efforts into a much-needed three points and were left ruing what might have been had Ryan Valentine converted a penalty after Matty Done had been upended by defender Russell Martin.

But nevertheless this was a performance that finally gave optimism that better things might lie ahead – providing that chances can be turned into goals!

There was a surprise in the starting line-up with Neil Roberts relegated to the sub-stitute's bench, which meant that Chris Llewellyn switched to a more forward role to that he'd been deployed in of late.

Wycombe perhaps understandably enjoyed the better of the opening exchanges, but gradually the Dragons managed to get on top and dominate the remainder of the game.

A timely intervention by Martin denied Done a clear shot on goal after 18 min-utes and the returning Silvio Spann forced a good block from defender Tom Williams. Then came the penalty incident, but Chairboys' keeper Frank Fielding guessed right and saved Valentine's spot kick.

It was the Dragons' second failed penalty attempt of the season, but whereas Roberts' miss against Lincoln back in September didn't ultimately prove costly this one unfortunately did!

Despite having dominated the half, Fielding, the penalty apart, was never seriously called into action. But that changed three minutes into the second period when he was forced to hold a fiercely struck drive from Eifion Williams.

Llewellyn charged down a Fielding clear-ance, but couldn't get the ball under con-trol quick enough to take advantage of the open goal that had presented itself.

Substitute Michael Proctor also failed to cash in on a poor clearance by Fielding on 78 minutes, his long range effort drift-ing wide, and he also sent a late free kick just over the bar from 20 yards out.

Anthony Williams then twice denied Reuben Reid in added-on time as Wycombe chased what would have been an undeserved late winner, but in the end the Dragons had to settle for a point from a first draw of the season.

Wrexham:
1 Anthony Williams, 2 Simon Spender, 3 Ryan Valentine, 6 Richard Hope, 11 Chris Llewellyn, 14 Eifion Williams (69), 16 Silvio Spann (75) ■, 20 Matty Done (81), 24 Gareth Evans, 26 Robbie Garrett, 28 Matty Collins ■.

Subs: 4 Shaun Pejic, 9 Neil Roberts, 10 Michael Proc-tor (75), 21 Marc Williams (69), 25 Neil Taylor (81).

Wycombe Wanderers:
34 Frank Fielding, 4 Russell Martin (87) ■, 5 Will Antwi (46), 7 David McCracken, 8 Stefan Oakes, 10 Matt Bloomfield, 11 Martin Bullock, 12 Tom Williams, 17 Scott McGleish (85), 22 Sergio Torres, 32 Reuben Reid.

Subs: 15 Gary Holt, 16 John Sutton (85), 20 Leon Johnson (46), 25 Sam Stockley (87), 36 Robert Douglas (GK).

Ryan Valentine's 26th minute penalty is saved by Chairboys 'keeper Frank Fielding.r

Shots on Goal:	4	5
Shots on Target:	0	0
Shots off Target	4	5
Possession:	47%	53%
Fouls Conceded:	14	11
Corners:	2	6
Yellow Cards:	2	1
Red Cards:	0	0

Wrexham captain Richard Hope denies former 'Dragon' and Welsh international Craig Morgan.

FA Cup Round One: 10th November, 2007

Peterborough United 4   Wrexham 1

Craig Mackail-Smith 2, 41, 53
Aaron McLean 88

Neil Roberts 66

Referee: Mike Thorpe (Suffolk)
Attendance (Away): 4,266 (293)

In what was almost certainly Brian Carey's last game in charge of team affairs as the Dragons delivered the type of display that emphasised why things have to change. Yes they battled to the end, but the manner in which they conceded possession and goals just about summed up the predicament the club is in.

You can imagine Carey's final words before the players emerged from the dressing room to be something along the lines of keeping things tight at the back early on to try to frustrate Fergie's expen-

sively-assembled front line. So to concede within the opening ninety seconds certainly didn't help!

There was a stroke of luck about it as far as the home side were concerned as George Boyd looked to have clearly handled the ball in the build-up – right in front of the Wrexham fans as well! But he was allowed to centre from the left and Craig Mackail-Smith was unmarked to head home from close range.

Chris Llewellyn responded with a shot that was deflected just wide, but at the other end Boyd, Mackail-Smith and Aaron McLean all could have doubled the home side's lead.

But the Dragons briefly began to create a few decent openings of their own as the half wore on, and only an excellent challenge by Claude Gnapka denied Matty Done a shot at goal. Eifion Williams then found himself in a one-on-one with Posh 'keeper Mark Tyler, but saw his effort blocked by the experienced keeper.

The Posh then knocked the stuffing out of the Dragons – and the travelling fans – with a second goal on 41 minutes. And it came in truly farcical circumstances!

An innocuous-looking long ball shouldn't have caused any problems at all, but Anthony Williams and Richard Hope calamitously collided with each other outside the area and Mackail-Smith walked the ball into the empty net. At least it got us on Match Of The Day in the evening!

The game was effectively up, and McLean should have added a third before the break but again cleared the bar. On 53 minutes Garrett's misplaced pass was quickly seized upon by Boyd, who immediately released Mackail-Smith and the striker completed his hat trick with a confident finish.

Neil Roberts pulled a goal back by beating Tyler to a long ball through and managing to poke the ball into an empty net from just outside the area.

This was the catalyst for the Dragons to enjoy their best spell of the game. Llewellyn stung Tyler's hands after a long run, Roberts had an effort deflected over, and Simon Spender headed wide.

But inevitably it was the home side that had the final word when McLean had plenty of time and space to make it 4-1.

Peterborough United:
1 Mark Tyler, 4 Craig Morgan, 5 Chris Westwood, 8 Micah Hyde, 9 Aaron McLean, 10 George Boyd, 11 Dean Keates (84), 12 Craig Mackail-Smith (83), 17 Jamie Day, 18 Chris Whelpdale (80), 27 Claude Gnakpa.

Subs: 2 Josh Low (80), 6 Charlie Lee (84), 7 Adam Newton, 13 Shwan Jalal (GK), 23 Rene Howe (83).

Wrexham:
1 Anthony Williams, 2 Simon Spender, 3 Ryan Valentine, 6 Richard Hope (46), 11 Chris Llewellyn, 14 Eifion Williams (60), 16 Silvio Spann, 20 Matty Done, 24 Gareth Evans, 26 Robbie Garrett, 28 Matty Collins (46).

Subs: 4 Shaun Pejic (46), 9 Neil Roberts (46), 10 Michael Proctor, 21 Marc Williams (60), 25 Neil Taylor.

Neil Roberts scores a consolation for the Dragons.

Shots on Goal:	19	13
Shots on Target:	6	2
Shots off Target:	13	11
Possession:	51%	49%
Fouls Conceded:	6	9
Corners:	3	6
Yellow Cards:	0	0
Red Cards:	0	0

Michael Proctor fires home, despite an attempt by former Dragon Paul Linwood to deny him.

Coca Cola League 2: 25th November, 2007

Wrexham 2
Michael Proctor 37, 75

Chester City 2
Kevin Roberts 27
Paul Linwood 45

Referee: Andy Woolmer (Northampton)
Attendance (Away): 7,687 (1,977)

Brian Little couldn't have picked a much bigger occasion to mark his first game in charge than a derby clash in front of over 7,500 on the Racecourse.

The form of the respective sides going into the game couldn't have been much different, Wrexham being desperately out of form (and dropping to the bottom of the League 24 hours earlier) and Chester dropping a mere five points on their travels! Dragons' fans were therefore apprehensive that our rivals would end their near 30-year wait for League success on

the 'Course.

Happily we needn't have worried as a brace from Michael Proctor - restored to the starting line-up by Little - twice brought the Dragons level and heaped more frustration on the travelling hordes. There was also a debut for new loan signing Sam Aiston, the shock inclusion of teenager Wes Baynes for the first time, and club captain Neil Roberts lining up in an unfamiliar midfield role.

After the dismal goalless draw between the sides in the corresponding fixture last season, thankfully this clash lived up to its pre-match hype and billing with an entertaining end-to-end 90 minutes that kept both sets of supporters fully enthralled. Both sides had early openings, but it was Chester that opened the scoring when Kevin Roberts latched onto a flick on by Nathan Lowndes and beat Anthony Williams with a looping effort from 20 yards out.

This setback rocked the Dragons for a short time, and Paul Butler could have increased the visitors' advantage five minutes later, but Baynes cleared his goal bound header off the line.

It was to prove a decisive moment as the Dragons equalised against the run of play when Proctor raced onto Roberts' through ball and held off the challenge of Paul Linwood before firing the ball past John Danby.

This galvanised the Dragons and Linwood knew little of a deflection off another Proctor effort that drifted just wide. But the visitors were back in front five minutes into added-on time when Linwood rose unmarked to head a Richie Partridge corner past Williams.

Steve Evans and Chris Llewellyn both went close as Wrexham upped the tempo at the start of the second period, before the visitors gradually began to again take a modicum of control on proceedings. But they failed to grab a killer third goal and paid the price when substitute Matty Done crossed from the left and Proctor was on hand to volley home the equaliser from 10 yards out.

It took a block by Linwood to deny Aiston a debut goal and Paul McManus headed narrowly over at the other end but a thrilling encounter finally ended with both sides having to settle for a point.

Wrexham:
1 Anthony Williams, 4 Shaun Pejic (66), 5 Steve Evans, 6 Richard Hope, 9 Neil Roberts (78) ■, 10 Michael Proctor ■, 11 Chris Llewellyn, 14 Eifion Williams, 25 Neil Taylor, 29 Sam Aiston (83), 31 Wes Baines ■.

Subs: 2 Simon Spender (83), 13 Michael Jones (GK), 20 Matty Done (66), 24 Gareth Evans, 26 Robbie Garrett (78).

Chester City:
12 John Danby, 2 Simon Marples, 4 Tony Dinning (26), 6 Paul Butler, 7 Richie Partridge, 10 Nathan Lowndes (52) ■, 11 Kevin Ellison, 14 Mark Hughes ■, 17 Laurence Wilson, 19 Paul Linwood, 25 Kevin Roberts.

Subs: 1 Gavin Ward (GK), 8 Simon Yeo (67), 20 Chris Holroyd, 30 Tony Grant (26) (67), 32 Paul McManus (52)

Wrexham's new manager, Brian Little, in his first game in charge tells his team to 'use their heads'.

Shots on Goal:	10	13
Shots on Target:	8	9
Shots off Target	2	4
Possession:	49%	51%
Fouls Conceded:	13	14
Corners:	5	4
Yellow Cards:	3	2
Red Cards:	0	0

Despite being grounded, Neil Roberts is still attempting to force his way through the Dale defence.

Coca Cola League 2: 1st December, 2007

Rochdale 0   Wrexham 0

Referee: Matt Haywood (Leeds)
Attendance (Away): 2,808 (400+)

Adour defensive display from Brian Little's side earned a valuable point at Spotland, but earned criticism from former Wrexham defender and current 'Dale manager Keith Hill.

"That's not football for me," he said after the game. "I can understand why Wrexham set up like they did because they needed a clean sheet and they came to frustrate us. We've got to come up with a plan to get round that, but it was very frustrating and I would not watch that. It's not surprising that the fans aren't turning up."

Okay, yes, it wasn't pretty, but maybe Keith should concentrate on his own

side's failings rather than criticise the opposition for making it a difficult afternoon for his side. Mind you, he did then add that we played very well!

Little on the other hand understandably made no apologies for setting his side with points rather than performances in mind.

"It's not over-expansive football, I have to say," he admitted. "But initially what I have got to do is look at the players and find a system that suits us."

That system included three central defenders with two wing-backs offering additional protection when necessary. And whilst it understandably conceded ground to the home side for much of the game it clearly provided a solid display that, thankfully, was also devoid of the calamitous mistakes of recent away trips!

Rochdale began in a confident fashion with Adam Le Fondre going close in the first minute and forced a succession of early corners.

But the Dragons stood firm and Matty Done possibly should have done better with a 10th minute opening after neat build-up play involving Sam Aiston and Neil Roberts, but fired over from the edge of the box.

David Perkins forced a save from Anthony Williams, Le Fondre shot wide and a Gary Jones effort deflected off ex-Red Lee McEvilly to force another Williams save as the home side continued to press.

But they couldn't make the all-important breakthrough, even after the break, the nearest they came was on 64 minutes when Le Fondre's curling effort beat Williams, but cannoned back off the inside of the post before being cleared.

Almost immediately after this somewhat lucky escape came Wrexham's best

chance, when Done's well struck 25-yard shot was parried away by a surprised-looking Sam Russell in the 'Dale goal.

Done's pace was starting to cause the home defence a few problems and his teasing centre only just evaded the out-stretched boot of Michael Proctor.

The closing minutes were virtually all Rochdale with Williams turning Rory Prendergast's header round the post, and holding on to another header from Glenn Murray at the resulting corner. Then Le Fondre put a diving header wide a couple of minutes from time. But Wrexham held on!

Rochdale:
21 Sam Russell, 2 Simon Ramsden, 3 Thomas Kennedy, 4 Nathan Stanton, 8 Gary Jones, 10 Adam Le Fondre, 11 Adam Rundle (59), 16 David Perkins (63), 18 Kallum Higginbotham ■, 19 Lee McEvilly (71), 31 Marcus Holness.

Subs: 1 James Spencer (GK), 5 John Doolan (63), 17 Glen Murray (59) ■, 23 Rory McArdle, 27 Rory Prendergast (71).

Wrexham:
1 Anthony Williams, 4 Shaun Pejic, 5 Steve Evans, 6 Richard Hope, 9 Neil Roberts, 10 Michael Proctor (70), 11 Chris Llewellyn, 20 Matty Done (81), 25 Neil Taylor ■, 29 Sam Aiston, 31 Wes Baines ■.

Subs: 13 Michael Jones (GK), 14 Eifion Williams, 17 Josh Johnson (81), 21 Marc Williams (70), 26 Robbie Garrett.

Neil Taylor shows his determination in trying to make a break-through.

	Rochdale	Wrexham
Shots on Goal:	14	8
Shots on Target:	8	4
Shots off Target	6	4
Possession:	53%	47%
Fouls Conceded:	11	12
Corners:	13	3
Yellow Cards:	2	2
Red Cards:	0	0

Eifion Williams capitalises on Jim Provett's mistake to head in the only goal.

Coca Cola League 2: 4th December, 2007

Bury 0

Wrexham 1

Eifion Williams 31

Referee: Scott Mathieson (Stockport)
Attendance (Away): 2,248 (539)

Wrexham moved out of the relegation zone with victory at Gigg Lane. As with the weekend encounter at Spotland, the performance was centred on a solid defensive display - especially after the calamitous error by Shakers' keeper Jim Provett that gifted Eifion Williams his first goal for the club.

There were three changes to the side that drew at Spotland with Matty Done and Sam Aiston unavailable through illness, and Neil Taylor rested. In came Eifion,

Robbie Garrett and Ryan Valentine.

The decisive goal came when Anthony Williams launched a long punt forward. There appeared to be little danger, but Provett misjudged the bounce of the ball and Eifion nipped round him to head the ball into the empty net in front of the travelling fans.

Unfortunately for the striker it proved to be his last involvement in the game as he pulled a hamstring in the process of scoring and had to be replaced by Marc

Williams. And as events panned out it also proved to be his last touch in League football before announcing his retirement later in the season!

It was a lead that the Dragons deserved for their first half efforts against a side boasting a four-game winning run. Michael Proctor almost doubled the lead early in the second period, but his 20-yard drive was saved by Provett, before Bury finally started to pose a threat themselves with Andy Bishop heading over from close range under pressure from Wes Baynes.

Baynes then showed his attacking worth with a pinpoint cross that Marc Williams headed straight at Provett.

There was the inevitable spell of late pressure from the home side that forced the Dragons to defend in numbers, but they dealt with everything the Shakers could throw at them to earn an important, and very welcome, three points.

After the victory, which maintained his unbeaten record since taking over the reigns, manager Brian Little refused to get too carried away. "Psychologically it is good," he said. "But we go to Dagenham and if we don't get anything there, we are certainly going to come backwards pretty quickly again.

"To come here and get a result is great for us. In the end Bury were having to be direct and throw big fellows in there to try and win the game, and credit to them for that.

"But I thought we held out well and limited their chances. They had a couple of little scrambles around the box, which again I thought we dealt with great in terms of wanting to defend. To have hung on is great!"

Bury:
1 Jim Provett, 2 Paul Scott, 3 Colin Woodthorpe (74), 4 Ben Futcher, 6 Paul Morgan, 7 Steve Haslam (61), 10 Andy Bishop, 12 David Buchanan, 14 Andy Parrish (86), 16 Nicky Adams, 25 Lee Bullock.

Subs: 8 Richie Baker, 9 Glyn Hurst (86), 11 Brian Barry-Murphy, 19 Andrew Mangan (74), 28 Liam Hughes (61).

Wrexham:
1 Anthony Williams, 3 Ryan Valentine, 4 Shaun Pejic, 5 Steve Evans, 6 Richard Hope, 9 Neil Roberts, 10 Michael Proctor (79), 11 Chris Llewellyn, 14 Eifion Williams (33), 26 Robie Garrett ▨, Wes Baines.

Subs: 2 Simon Spender, 13 Michael Jones (GK), 17 Josh Johnson (79), 21 Marc Williams (33) ▨, 24 Gareth Evans.

Michael Proctor is denied by the Bury defence on this occasion.

Shots on Goal:	9	10
Shots on Target:	4	7
Shots off Target	5	3
Possession:	47%	53%
Fouls Conceded:	8	9
Corners:	4	6
Yellow Cards:	0	2
Red Cards:	0	0

Neil Roberts is denied by the 'Daggers' defence as Anwar Uddin (15) heads clear

Coca Cola League 2: 8th December, 2007

Dagenham & Redbridge 3   Wrexham 0

Steve Evans 24 (og)
Ben Strevens 86
Jamie Taylor 90

Referee: Patrick Miller (Bedfordshire)
Attendance (Away): 1,520 (358)

With four points from two away games in the week leading up to this first ever visit to Victoria Road, hopes were high that another three points would lift the Dragons further up the table. How wrong those hopes were!

On a wet and miserable afternoon - with no cover on the away terrace - the home side rarely looked like world-beaters, but still had too much for Brian Little's side. From the moment Steve Evans turned a Jon Nurse cross into his own net the writing was very much on the wall.

Two further goals in the closing four minutes (albeit giving the final score a flattering look as far as the home side is concerned) simply compounded the misery.

The level of the Dragons' performance was nowhere near where it had been at both Rochdale and Bury in the first two legs of their travels, but to be beaten so emphatically by a side that had lost its previous five home League game is simply unacceptable.

With the exception of Marc Williams replacing the injured Eifion Williams manager Brian Little elected to go with the side victorious at Bury in midweek, a policy he later admitted had been a mistake. "I genuinely believe I picked the wrong team today because we won at Bury," he said.

"In this business you have to be honest enough to admit a mistake and that applies to me. On another day with this sort of experience it has taught me a lesson and that is sometimes you have to change a winning side to deal with a particular system."

Whatever the reasoning behind the Dragons' display the home side totally dominated the opening 45 minutes. However, their opening goal came immediately after the Dragons almost grabbed the lead themselves when Robbie Garrett's low cross just evaded Michael Proctor. From the resulting breakaway the ball found its way to Nurse down the right and the rest is history.

Dominic Green, on his League debut, almost doubled the Daggers' lead moments later, but his chip curled just wide of Anthony Williams' goal.

Brian Little shuffled his pack for the second period and Neil Roberts almost levelled things up on 66 minutes, but former Wales international Tony Roberts somehow smothered the ball on the goal line. That's about as good as it got for the visitors - despite an improvement after the break - and they were caught twice on the break in the closing minutes.

Substitute Ben Strevens dispossessed Chris Llewellyn before hammering the ball past Williams from 30 yards out on 86 minutes and fellow sub Jamie Taylor fired home the third in added-on time.

Dagenham & Redbridge:
1 Tony Roberts, 2 Magnus Okuonghae, 3 Sam Sloma, 5 Jon Boardman, 6 Shane Huke, 8 Glen Southam, 9 Jon Nurse (89), 14 Paul Benson, 15 Anwar Uddin, 21 Dominic Green (75), 22 Marlon Patterson.

Subs: 16 Jame Taylor (89), 18 Ben Strevens (75), 24 Soloman Taiwo, 25 Tony Cook, 30 Ed Thompson (GK).

Wrexham:
1 Anthony Williams, 3 Ryan Valentine ■, 4 Shaun Pejic, 5 Steve Evans, 6 Richard Hope, 9 Neil Roberts (77), 10 Michael Proctor, 11 Chris Llewellyn, 21 Marc Williams (84), 26 Robbie Garrett, 31 Wes Baynes (46).

Subs: 13 Michael Jones (GK), 17 Josh Johnson (84), 20 Matty Done (77), 25 Neil Taylor, 29 Sam Aiston (46).

The Dragons' Marc Williams rises above Paul Benson to head for goal.

Shots on Goal:	10	4
Shots on Target:	5	2
Shots off Target:	5	2
Possession:	52%	48%
Fouls Conceded:	8	13
Corners:	9	12
Yellow Cards:	0	1
Red Cards:	0	0

Neil Roberts races towards the Bees goal watched by Chris Llewellyn.

Coca Cola League 2: 15th December, 2007

Wrexham 1   Brentford 3

Chris Llewellyn 41

Alan Connell 66, 77
Steve Evans 72 (og)

Referee: A Taylor (Somerset)
Attendance (Away): 3,811 (122)

Things continue to go from bad to worse as the Dragons slumped to another embarrassing defeat. Brentford arrived at the Racecourse having just parted company with manager Terry Butcher, on a five-game losing streak, and having not found the back of the net in over 500 minutes!

But ninety minutes of football later and they headed home with three well-deserved points thanks to what can only be described as a 'horror show' from Brian Little's side.

Even the benefit of taking a 41st minute lead - albeit against the run of play - did little to inject any encouragement into Wrexham's display. Quite simply, they were awful!

Starved of quality possession due to an inability to retain the ball for any length of time the Dragons gifted the initiative to the Bees pretty much from the outset. Alan Connell curled a free kick just wide, Ryan Dickson headed straight at Anthony Williams, and Lee Thorpe saw a header crash against the post as the visitors dominated.

So it was certainly unexpected when Sam Aiston's cross from the left was nodded back across goal by Neil Roberts and Chris Llewellyn was on hand to head past Simon Brown from close range.

But Brentford responded immediately and were awarded a penalty when Shaun Pejic caught Dickson's ankle. Thorpe stepped forward, but Williams showed just why he's made a name for himself saving penalties by guessing correctly to push the ball away.

Llewellyn should then have doubled Wrexham's advantage just before the break, but he screwed his shot wide. Had that gone in then it may have proved to be a different scenario after the break, but instead the Bees were still firmly in the game and upped the ante in the second forty-five minutes.

The equaliser came when substitute Ricky Shakes won possession on the edge of the box and crossed for Connell to head into the roof of the net.

Six minutes later the visitors went ahead in comical fashion when Gary Smith's mis-hit cross was missed by Thorpe, but Steve Evans stuck a foot out and diverted the ball past a stranded Williams. It was his second own-goal in successive games!

The misery was completed when Connell's shot rebounded back off a post, Thorpe's follow-up was cleared off the line, and Connell was still able to hook the loose ball home amid a motionless defence.

"I haven't got an answer to what happened, but it showed me the size of the task ahead," admitted Brian Little after the game. "All three goals were shocking!"

Wrexham:
1 Anthony Williams, 4 Shaun Pejic (76) ■, 5 Steve Evans, 6 Richard Hope, 7 Mark Jones (54), 9 Neil Roberts, 11 Chris Llewellyn, 16 Silvio Spann (32), 25 Neil Taylor ■, 29 Sam Aiston, 31 Wes Baynes ■.

Subs: 3 Ryan Valentine, 10 Michael Proctor (76), 13 Michael Jones (GK), 20 Matty Done (54) 26 Robbie Garrett (32).

Brentford:
1 Simon Brown, 2 Kevin O'Connor, 7 Gary Smith (79), 9 Lee Thorpe, 10 Alan Connell (88) ■, 15 Matt Heywood, 16 Charlie Ide (60), 18 Darius Charles ■, 19 Ryan Dickson, 22 Karleigh Osbourne ■, 25 Ben Starosta.

Subs: 4 Sammy Moore, Glenn Poole (79), 21 Clark Masters (GK), 26 Emile Sinclair (88), 29 Ricky Shakes (60).

Wrexham's Chris Llewellyn celebrates his opening goal, but it was all in vain.

Shots on Goal:	9	11
Shots on Target:	4	5
Shots off Target	5	6
Possession:	42%	58%
Fouls Conceded:	20	21
Corners:	2	3
Yellow Cards:	3	3
Red Cards:	0	0

Wrexham's Sam Aiston shoots at the Millers goal as Michael Proctor follows up.

Coca Cola League 2: 22nd December, 2007

Rotherham United 3　　　Wrexham 0

Derek Holmes 40, 72
Marc Newsham 82

Referee: Gavin Ward (Surrey)
Attendance (Away): 3,773 (185)

A **moment of madness from Matty Crowell - in his first outing since October - gave Wrexham an early mountain to climb at Millmoor. His 13th minute lunge on Ian Ross looked more clumsy than vicious, but referee Gavin Ward showed no hesitation in brandishing a red card to the midfielder.**

Wrexham had started promisingly as well, but being reduced to ten men so early on in the proceedings ultimately proved too big an obstacle to overcome. But the ten men showed tremendous spirit and still

took the game to their full-strength hosts as much as possible and carved out several openings that kept the Millers on their toes throughout.

Chris Llewellyn twice beat the offside trap in the opening moments, but couldn't quite pick out either Neil Roberts or Michael Proctor on each occasion and, soon after Crowell's dismissal, Steve Evans headed a Mark Jones free kick wide.

Despite their numerical advantage the home side's efforts were repeatedly thwarted by a resilient defensive display from the Dragons until five minutes before the break. Stephen Brogan found Danny Harrison on the edge of the penalty area. His shot was blocked, but the ball dropped kindly for Derek Holmes to clinically beat Anthony Williams.

Having dropped Roberts back into midfield as a result of Crowell's misdemeanour Brian Little moved him further forward again after the break. And the tactical reshuffle seemed to have the desired effect as the Dragons enjoyed their best spell of the game in the period immediately after the restart.

Jones snatched at a chance after good play by Proctor and Sam Aiston should have done better after running through from the halfway line, but his shot was blocked at the last by keeper Andy Warrington.

It proved to be a costly miss as the Millers began to compose themselves again and made the game safe when Wrexham's stubborn resistance was again broken. Brogan made headway down the left and crossed for Holmes to head home unmarked at the far post.

Chasing the game, the Dragons inevitably left space in behind and the home side capitalised to add a third goal when substitute Marc Newsham beat Williams with a powerful first-time shot.

So a disappointing afternoon for Brian Little and his side, but at least some pride was restored after the recent debacles against Dagenham & Redbridge and Brentford by a battling and spirited performance by the ten men.

"We're struggling to win games with 11 men, so being down to 10 against a team as strong as them then you have got a problem," said Little afterwards.

Rotherham United:
1 Andy Warrington, 4 Danny Harrison (44), 5 Ian Sharps ■, 6 Graham Coughlan, 9 Derek Holmes (86), 11 Stephen Brogan, 12 Marc Joseph, 15 Chris O'Grady, 20 Ryan Taylor (70), 25 Pablo Mills, 29 Ian Ross.

Subs: 2 Dale Tonge (44), 7 Andy Todd, 16 Jamie Yates (86), 17 Marc Newsham (70), 27 Mark Oxley.

Wrexham:
1 Anthony Williams, 3 Ryan Valentine, 5 Steve Evans ■, 6 Richard Hope, 7 Mark Jones (79), 9 Neil Roberts, 10 Michael Proctor, 11 Chris Llewellyn ■, 12 Matt Crowell ■, 29 Sam Aiston, 31 Wes Baynes.

Subs: 4 Shaun Pejic, 13 Michael Jones (GK), 15 Mike Williams, 17 Josh Johnson (79), 24 Gareth Evans.

It's all over for Matty Crowell as he is sent off in what was his last appearance in a Wrexham shirt.

Shots on Goal:	19	6
Shots on Target:	11	3
Shots off Target	8	3
Possession:	53%	47%
Fouls Conceded:	10	11
Corners:	6	3
Yellow Cards:	1	2
Red Cards:	0	1

The Wrexham attack are denied by the Rochdale defence in a frantic attempt to score.

Coca Cola League 2: 26th December, 2007

Wrexham 0

Rochdale 2

Glenn Murray 7
Lee McEvilly 60

Referee: Karl Evans (Manchester)
Attendance (Away): 4,302 (686)

Wrexham slumped to the foot of the table after a Rochdale's comfortable victory at the Racecourse condemned Brian Little's side to a fourth straight defeat, and still looking for a first home victory since Lincoln City were beaten in late September!

Only 6 goals in 13 games in all competitions at the Racecourse this season is also a telling statistic and one that clearly shows why the Dragons are occupying such a perilous position.

Silvio Spann came in for the suspended Matty Crowell and youngster Wes Baynes was left out for the first time since Brian Little took charge, with fellow youngster Neil Taylor returning to the side.

The 4-3-3 formation was intended to provide a more attacking threat, but it was the visitors - who arrived boasting an impressive record on their travels - who were quickest out of the blocks and took the lead after just seven minutes!

Kallum Higginbotham made progress

down the left and his cross was flicked on by Glen Murray to Adam Le Fondre at the far post. The striker once scored four goals in a game against Wrexham in his Stockport County days, but this time his shot was parried by Anthony Williams. Unfortunately for him the ball fell kindly for Murray to score from close range.

Steve Evans almost provided an immediate reply, but hooked the ball narrowly wide from about 12 yards out, before the visitors showed their mettle once again with Murray twice going close to doubling his tally.

Neil Roberts, stretching to reach a scuffed shot from Chris Llewellyn, diverted the ball narrowly wide on 31 minutes, but generally it was 'Dale that enjoyed the upper hand throughout the opening half. Desperate times call for desperate measures and the Dragons came out after the break with centre-back Gareth Evans on in place of Spann, Steve Evans moved up front, and Roberts dropping back into midfield.

But the changes had little effect and 'Dale doubled their lead on the hour mark through a certain Lee McEvilly! The former-Red had received a good deal of

barracking from the Racecourse faithful as he took the field, but quickly left his mark on the game.

Higginbotham was again the creator down the left, his centre reaching Adam Rundle beyond the far post he sent the ball back in for 'Evil' to slot home from close range.

Llewellyn saw an effort cleared from the goal line and, at last, Sam Russell was forced into a save from the Welsh international on 67 minutes, but in truth the Dragons never looked like salvaging something from another disappointing afternoon.

Wrexham:
1 Anthony Williams, 3 Ryan Valentine, 5 Steve Evans, 6 Richard Hope, 7 Mark Jones, 9 Neil Roberts, 10 Michael Proctor, 11 Chris Llewellyn, 16 Silvio Spann (46) ■, 29 Sam Aiston, 31 Wes Baynes.

Subs: 4 Shaun Pejic, 13 Michael Jones (GK), 15 Mike Williams, 17 Josh Johnson, 24 Gareth Evans (46).

Rochdale:
21 Sam Russell, 2 Simon Ramsden, 3 Tom Kennedy, 4 Nathan Stanton, 6 Lee Crooks, 8 Gary Jones, 10 Adam Le Fondre (57), 11 Adam Rundle (88), 17 Glenn Murray ■, 18 Kallum Higginbotham (90), 23 Rory McArdle.

Subs: 1 James Spencer (GK), 15 Joe Thompson (90), 19 Lee McEvilly (57), 27 Rory Prendergast (88), 31 Marcus Holness.

Chris Llewellyn fires at the 'Dale' goal as Rory McArdle attempts to block him.

Shots on Goal:	8	8
Shots on Target:	0	3
Shots off Target:	8	5
Possession:	46%	54%
Fouls Conceded:	12	20
Corners:	4	8
Yellow Cards:	1	1
Red Cards:	0	0

Marc Williams' challenge is deemed unfair, and thus denies Wrexham a goal.

Coca Cola League 2: 29th December, 2007

Wrexham 0   Stockport County 1

Anthony Elding 59

Referee: Richard Beeby (Northamptonshire)
Attendance (Away): 4,287 (995)

Another home defeat and another blank in front of goal brought down the curtain on an extremely disappointing 2007 for Wrexham followers.

Home victories - and goals - have been a rare commodity at the Racecourse in the past 12 months and there have been few occasions when you could say in the pub after the game that the Dragons had been unfortunate not to get something out of the game. This, however, was one of those occasions when you most definitely could

argue that the effort put into a game played in difficult conditions was deserving of far more than yet another defeat!

Brian Little once again sprang a couple of surprises. Firstly, he switched dressing rooms with the Dragons changing in the 'away' dressing room because "it's logistically the best thing for me to do. I have an office down there and we have got a treatment room there."

And secondly he switched Ryan Valentine into midfield to provide some desperately needed "bite" in the middle of the park.

The decision seemed to have the desired effect in the opening exchanges as Wrexham started well, with Chris Llewellyn heading a Wes Baynes corner over the bar on 12 minutes, and then unleashing a 25-yarder that flew inches over the bar.

Anthony Pilkington could have given County the lead just before the break, but he scuffed his shot when well placed, and at the other end the Dragons were denied a couple of times in a frantic goalmouth scramble.

Goalless at the break but the Dragons could feel satisfied with their first half efforts, and they continued to press upon the resumption.

Within 30 seconds of the restart Neil Roberts met Baynes' cross from the right, but County keeper Conrad Logan somehow kept out his close-range header.

It proved to be a costly miss, as on 59 minutes the visitors grabbed the lead, when substitute Adam Griffin's shot was steered over the line by the slightest of touches from fellow substitute Anthony Elding.

Steve Evans went close to an equaliser but

headed wide, before Wrexham were awarded a penalty on 76 minutes after Michael Raynes was adjudged to have handled. But just to sum up the season to date Valentine had the confidence to step forward despite his miss against Wycombe earlier in the season only to see his poorly struck attempt easily saved by Logan.

Substitute Marc Williams almost capitalised on some hesitation from Logan in the closing moments, but the final whistle brought a familiar scenario - a defeat - for the long-suffering Racecourse faithful, albeit an undeserved one!

Wrexham:
1 Anthony Williams, 3 Ryan Valentine, 4 Shaun Pejic, 5 Steve Evans, 9 Neil Roberts (71), 10 Michael Proctor (64), 11 Chris Llewellyn ■, 15 Mike Williams, 25 Neil Taylor ■, 29 Sam Aiston, Wes Baynes.

Subs: 7 Mark Jones, 13 Michael Jones (GK), 21 Marc Williams (71), Michael Carvill (64), 24 Gareth Evans.

Stockport County:
26 Conrad Logan, 3 Michael Rose, 4 Jason Taylor, 5 Gareth Owen, 7 David Poole (46), 8 Gary Dicker, 15 Michael Raynes, 17 Anthony Pilkington, 20 Liam Dickenson, 28 Paul Turnbull, 31 Adam Proudlock (46).

Subs: 9 Anthony Elding (46), 11 Adam Griffin 46 ■, 16 James Tunnicliffe, 18 Greg Tansey, 19 Paul Tierney.

Ryan Valentine misses from the penalty spot following a hand ball on the edge of the box.		
Shots on Goal:	4	4
Shots on Target:	1	2
Shots off Target	3	2
Possession:	51%	49%
Fouls Conceded:	13	9
Corners:	5	8
Yellow Cards:	2	1
Red Cards:	0	0

The 'Spireites' Barry Roche grips the ball to deny Steve Evans heading for goal.

Coca Cola League 2: 1st January, 2008

Chesterfield 2   Wrexham 1

Peter Leven 7   Steve Evans 68
Jack Lester 41

Referee: Darren Deadman (Cambridgeshire)
Attendance (Away): 4,293 (239)

New year, but the same old story as Wrexham slumped to a sixth straight defeat to leave them firmly rooted to the bottom of the table.

Saltergate's never the easiest of places to get to - especially on a New Year's Day - and following a 4-0 mauling by the Spireites at the Racecourse three months earlier those Dragons' fans that journeyed over to Derbyshire surely didn't travel in anticipation of witnessing a much-needed victory.

Such pessimism was soon founded on fact as the home side put the Wrexham defence under early pressure and it was no surprise that it cracked in the 7th minute, albeit in calamitous circumstances once again!

This time Anthony Williams was the culprit, as his poor clearance landed straight at the feet of Peter Leven 35 yards out, and the midfielder wasted no time in lobbing the ball over Williams and into the net, although the keeper's efforts did appear more to help the ball over the line rather than try to keep it out!

Chesterfield were rampant at this stage and both Adam Rooney and Derek Niven should have added to Wrexham's woes with a second goal.

Neil Roberts was brought crashing down by keeper Barry Roche, with referee Darren Deadman not even giving a free kick never mind brandishing a red card.

And when Conall Murtagh, given a surprise League debut in midfield alongside Levi Mackin, saw his afternoon brought to a premature end after a clash of heads with Janos Kovacs - an incident that again went unpunished - things just weren't going Wrexham's way!

Jamie Ward fired wide of the target, and was then denied by a superb save from Williams - no doubt anxious to make up for his earlier mistake.

But there was nothing the keeper could do when the defence failed to deal with an innocuous-looking ball into the box and Jack Lester confidently steered the ball into the bottom right-hand corner of the net.
Wrexham were lucky to be only two goals

down at the break but dug deep to give a much-improved display after the break. The catalyst for this came when Steve Evans pulled a goal back, heading home Mackin's corner from close range after a flick on at the near post by Chris Llewellyn.

Kovacs then denied Llewellyn an equaliser with a last-ditch tackle, substitute Michael Proctor was twice denied by Roche - once when clear on goal with only the keeper to beat - and a late Roberts back heel was cleared off the line with the home side suddenly hanging on. But hang on they did, to condemn the Dragons to yet another defeat.

Chesterfield:
1 Barry Roche, 2 Janos Kovacs, 4 Jamie Lowry, 7 Jamie Ward, 8 Derek Niven (78), 11 Gregor Robertson, 14 Jack Lester, 15 Aaron Downes, 16 Jamie Winter, 19 Peter Leven, 20 Adam Rooney (78).

Sub: 9 Adam Smith, 12 Michael Jordan (GK), 17 Gareth Davies (78), 18 Alan O'Hare (78), 22 Wayne Allison.

Wrexham:
1 Anthony Williams, 2 Simon Spender, 3 Ryan Valentine, 4 Shaun Pejic, 5 Steve Evans, 9 Neil Roberts, 11 Chris Llewellyn, 15 Mike Williams, 18 Levi Mackin, 22 Connall Murtagh (29), 29 Sam Aiston (46).

Subs: 10 Michael Proctor (29), 13 Michael Jones (GK), 21 Marc Williams, 25 Neil Taylor (46) ■, 31 Wes Baynes.

Steve Evans finally heads Wrexham back into the game. Here he collects the ball from the back of the net

Shots on Goal:	12	10
Shots on Target:	8	9
Shots off Target	4	1
Possession:	55%	45%
Fouls Conceded:	7	4
Corners:	8	9
Yellow Cards:	0	1
Red Cards:	0	0

Chris Llewellyn rounds ex-Dragons 'keeper, Ryan Harrison to give Wrexham an early lead.

FAW Premier Cup Quarter-Final: 9th January, 2008

Llanelli 4   Wrexham 2

(After extra-time)

Rhys Griffiths 23, 88p   Chris Llewellyn 12, 22
Chris Holloway 94, 95

Referee: Mark Whitby (Swansea)
Attendance (Away): 473 (40+)

The corresponding report for this stage of the competition in last year's Yearbook started with the question "Does it come much worse than this?" following the dismal defeat at Newport County.

Well, on the evidence of this embarrassment at Stebonheath Park is clearly does! Okay so Llanelli, to be fair, are no mugs. And even the most optimistic fan would have made the long trek down to south Wales with some trepidation about the Dragons' chances of overcoming the

Welsh Premier League leaders.

But having taken a two-goal lead inside the opening 23 minutes of the game this should have presented Brian Little's revamped side with a comfortable passage into the semi-finals of this lucrative competition. And if it hadn't been for more errant defending then a comfortable passage it surely would have been.

New signings Gavin Ward and Phil Bolland were brought in to bring some much-needed solidity to the Dragons' defence but, nevertheless, and despite Michal Proctor almost finding the net inside 15 seconds, it was the home side that dominated early on and they could have taken the lead on no less than four occasions inside the opening ten minutes!

Add the fact that Bolland was lucky to only see yellow for clumsily hauling down Craig Jones on nine minutes and it was a torrid start for the Dragons.

But against the run of play Wrexham took the lead when Chris Llewellyn capitalised on a poor back-pass by Antonio Corbisiero to round former Wrexham keeper Ryan Harrison and roll the ball into the empty net.

It was 2-0 when Llewellyn netted his second of the evening after more sloppy defensive play from the home side.

That should have been game over, but inexplicably within a minute Mike Williams was caught in possession and Craig Jones squared for Rhys Griffiths to accept the easy opportunity to score.

Wes Baynes nearly restored Wrexham's two-goal advantage on 51 minutes, but Harrison saved well and, despite not

looking completely assured at the back, you never sensed that the home side would take the game into extra time.

But with the seconds ticking away, Steve Evans grabbed at Griffiths' ankle inside the area, and the in-form striker hammered in the penalty after the defender had made the long walk to an early bath.

Two quick-fire goals from Chris Holloway gave 10-man Wrexham a mountain to climb in the extra-time period, a mountain that they never looked like climbing. "I'm so very disappointed over this," remarked Brian Little afterwards.......He wasn't the only one!

Llanelli:
1 Ryan Harrison, 3 Gary Lloyd, 4 Andrew Mumford, 6 Wyn Thomas, 8 Antonio Corbisiero, 9 Rhys Griffiths, 10 Chris Holloway, 11 Craig Williams (71), 14 Craig Jones, 15 Mark Jones (77), 21 Andy Legg. ■,

Subs: 12 Mark Pritchard (71), 16 Sam Small, 18 Duncan Roberts (GK), 19 Nick Holland, 20 Jordan Follows (77).

Wrexham:
1 Gavin Ward, 3 Ryan Valentine, 5 Steve Evans ■, 9 Neil Roberts, 10 Michael Proctor (63), 11 Chris Llewellyn, 15 Mike Williams, 18 Levi Mackin, 25 Neil Taylor (91) ■, 28 Phil Bolland ■, 31 Wes Baynes (82).

Subs: 1 Anthony Williams (GK), 2 Simon Spender, (82) 5 Shaun Pejic (91), 7 Mark Jones (63), 21 Marc Williams.

Wes Baynes run at goal is denied by Llanelli's ex-Swansea defender Andrew Mumford.

Shots on Goal:	n/a	n/a
Shots on Target:	n/a	n/a
Shots off Target:	n/a	n/a
Possession:	n/a	n/a
Fouls Conceded:	n/a	n/a
Corners:	n/a	n/a
Yellow Cards:	0	2
Red Cards:	0	1

Steve Evans attempts to show his wizardry skills against the 'Mariners' Peter Till.

Coca Cola League 2: 12th January, 2008

Grimsby Town 1   Wrexham 0

Danny North 68

Referee: Graham Salisbury (Lancashire)
Attendance (Away): 4,084 (172)

The encouraging debuts of new signings Paul Hall and Danny Sonner raised hopes that the Dragons could turn things around before the end of the season, but they couldn't prevent a seventh straight League defeat. It did show a significant improvement on the dismal showing at Llanelli in midweek though!

The home side went into the game on a good run that had lifted them clear of the relegation zone into a mid-table position, something the Dragons have to do very soon to avoid the dreaded drop.

Gary Jones squandered a good chance for the home side early on, and only a goal line header from Steve Evans after a fumble by Gavin Ward denied Nick Hegarty soon afterwards.

Hall, providing a much-needed presence in attack, then almost gave the Dragons a 12th minute lead with a snap shot that looked destined for the top the corner until Phil Barnes somehow clawed the ball out with a save that almost defied gravity before defender Rob Atkinson finally cleared the danger with a clearance from near the goal line. Had that gone in then who knows what the final outcome might have been?

Mark Jones' teasing cross only just evaded the alert Hall, and the latter was played in by Marc Williams soon afterwards only to see his shot blocked by Atkinson. From the resulting corner Barnes saved Williams' effort and Richard Hope couldn't quite force the follow up over the line.

The closest either side came to breaking the deadlock before the break came on 40 minutes when both Evans and Jones failed to clear their lines, but Paul Bolland's shot struck the angle of post and bar.

Danny North fired into the side-netting in the 53rd minute as Grimsby again posed the greater danger, before a rare moment saw referee Graham Salisbury have to be replaced by his assistant Mark Brown because of an injury on the hour mark.

Barnes again denied Hall as the new striker continued to look dangerous, but it was the home side that grabbed the all-important goal when Tom Newey sent an

innocuous-looking ball over the Wrexham back line, but livewire striker North was quickest to react and easily lobbed the ball over the advancing Ward from the edge of the box.

A torn hamstring saw Mark Jones stretchered off the field four minutes later, and Brian Little changed things around with Evans moved up front in an attempt to create some havoc.

The makeshift striker and substitute Michael Proctor both had half-chances of grabbing an equaliser, but it was the Mariners that came closing to scoring again when Justin Whittle's close-range shot struck the foot of a post late on.

Grimsby Town:
1 Phil Barnes, 2 Jamie Clarke (62), 3 Tom Newey, 4 James Hunt ■, 6 Nick Fenton (81), 8 Paul Bolland, 9 Danny North, 14 Sam Hird (46), 17 Nick Hegarty, 19 Gary Jones, 25 Rob Atkinson.

Subs: 7 Peter Till (46), 10 Ciaran Toner (62), 13 Gary Montgomery (GK), 15 Justin Whittle (81), 20 Andy Taylor.

Wrexham:
12 Gavin Ward, 2 Simon Spender, 3 Ryan Valentine, 5 Steve Evans 6 Richard Hope, 7 Mark Jones (72), 9 Neil Roberts (82), 11 Chris Llewellyn, 21 Marc Williams (82), 28 Phil Bolland, 34 Danny Somner.

Subs: 1 Anthony Williams (GK), 4 Shaun Pejic, 10 Michael Proctor (82), 19 Andy Fleming (72), 20 Matty Done (82).

An early opportunity for Paul Hall on his debut for the Dragons.

Shots on Goal:	14	9
Shots on Target:	8	5
Shots off Target	6	4
Possession:	46%	54%
Fouls Conceded:	9	13
Corners:	12	5
Yellow Cards:	1	0
Red Cards:	0	0

The 'Dons' Lloyd Dyer arrives too late as Neil Roberts exquisitely chips home the Dragons winner.

Coca Cola League 2: 19th January, 2008

Wrexham 1   MK Dons 0

Neil Roberts 71

Referee: Clive Oliver (Northumberland)
Attendance (Away): 4,319 (321)

At last something for the Wrexham faithful to sing about after Neil Robert's sublime finish on a heavy pitch shocked League leaders MK Dons at the Racecourse.

It was a deserved success too, with Brian Little's new look side proving more than a match for the high-flying visitors, and bringing the long losing run to an unexpected end.

Such a shame then that Dons' boss Paul Ince couldn't be more gracious in defeat, firstly blaming the pitch and then complaining about a foul in the build up to the decisive goal. It was also a tad unfair to apportion some blame on the referee, especially after several contentious decisions had gone the visitors' way earlier in the proceedings.

Two more new arrivals - Carl Tremarco from Tranmere Rovers and Stuart Nicholson from West Brom - plus a late substitute appearance for the returning Jeff Whitley all brought fresh optimism that the Dragons could beat the drop, a feeling no doubt borne out by the fantastic backing from the home crowd. The only down side to the afternoon was the hamstring injury suffered by Paul Hall in the first half.

Conditions were the dominant factor in an

evenly contested first half in which no quarter was given by either side. Chances were therefore at a premium, the best falling to Steve Evans just a couple of minutes before the break, but the Welsh international headed Danny Sonner's free kick wide.

With referee Clive Oliver giving most decisions the visitors' way in the opening exchanges, after the break it was proving difficult for the Dragons to get anything going.

Mind you the League leaders found it just as difficult against a well-drilled Wrexham defensive unit, and it was hard to see where a goal might come from - until Roberts pounced.

Dons' keeper Willy Gueret punched away an Evans header from Sonner's corner, but only as far as Roberts lurking just outside the penalty area. With time to compose himself he declined the obvious option of driving the ball goal wards at pace, and instead elected to deliver the perfect chip from 25-yards that sailed over Gueret and into the net.

Pandemonium instantly broke out in the stands and terraces, before the inevitable nervy moments followed in what remained of the game.

Mark Wright was denied by a superb block by Evans, and Drissa Diallo headed Dean Lewington's corner wide as the Dragons were in danger of sitting back too much in the closing stages.

However, the best chance fell once again to Roberts in the closing minutes, but the former Welsh international's diving header from Chris Llewellyn's centre fell just wide.

It didn't matter in the end though! Happy days!

Wrexham:
12 Gavin Ward, 2 Simon Spender ▪, 5 Steve Evans ▪, 6 Richard Hope, 9 Neil Roberts, 11 Chris Llewellyn, 28 Paul Bolland, 33 Paul Hall, 34 Danny Somner, 35 Stuart Nicholson (90) ▪, 36 Carl Tremarco.

Subs: 1 Anthony Williamss (GK), 4 Shaun Pejic, 10 Michael Proctor (34), 20 Matty Done, 37 Jeff Whitley (90).

MK Dons:
12 Willy Gueret ▪, 3 Dean Lewington, 4 Keith Andrews, 5 Drissa Diallo, 6 Sean O'Hanlon, 10 Colin Cameron (61), 14 Mark Wright, 16 Aaron Wilbraham ▪, 20 Alan Navarro, 21 Luke Howell, 23 Jemal Johnson (87) ▪.

Subs: 8 Kevin Gallen (75), 11 Lloyd Dyer (61), 24 Matt Carbon (87), 29 Nathan Abbey (GK), 32 Jordan Hadfield.

Carl Tremarco's run is brought to a halt by a 'Dons' defender.

Shots on Goal:	3	7
Shots on Target:	1	1
Shots off Target:	2	6
Possession:	50%	50%
Fouls Conceded:	16	10
Corners:	5	3
Yellow Cards:	3	3
Red Cards:	0	0

Neil Roberts fires the Dragons in front at home to the 'Bantams'

Coca Cola League 2: 26th January, 2008

Wrexham 1   Bradford City 1

Neil Roberts 38   Kyle Nix 49

Referee: Andy Woolmer (Northampton)
Attendance (Away): 4,341 (535)

Following the impressive victory over high-flying MK Dons seven days earlier, there was always the danger that expectations might prove a little unrealistic when the Bantams visited the Racecourse.

Fans probably predicted another much-needed three points towards safety, especially after Neil Roberts' opener. But football's not that predictable and maybe it should be looked at as taking a few steps towards walking rather than breaking out into a sprint almost immediately.

Yes, both fans and management alike will have been a little disappointed not to record a second successive win for the first time this season. But, remember, there's always two sides to every story and visiting manager Stuart McCall probably went home a bit disappointed as well.

Probably more galling for Brian Little and his players was the manner of Bradford's equaliser four minutes into the second half, Kyle Nix's scuffed shot from the edge of the area taking a cruel deflection off Steve Evans to divert the ball past Gavin Ward.

After the intensity of the MK Dons match the first half here slipped back into the ways of many previous Racecourse matches this campaign, with the scrappy nature of the football on offer doing little to excite the fans.

But at least it was the Dragons that looked the more likely side to break the deadlock and debutant Drewe Broughton - Brian Little's ninth signing since taking over the reins in November - being particularly unlucky with a shot that crashed against the bar after good work by Roberts.

In a rare Bradford attack Barry Conlon directed a free header straight at Ward before the Dragons broke the deadlock seven minutes before the break. Danny Sonner was the instigator with a long pass that found Roberts to the right of goal. The striker's shot was parried by 'keeper Donovan Ricketts, but the ball looped goal wards. Stuart Nicholson and defender Darren Williams were both in attendance as the ball dropped over the line with the latter possibly getting the final touch before the ball crossed the line. Nevertheless Roberts still claimed the goal - and why not?

City's early equaliser after the restart seemed to galvanise the game into life and they very nearly added a second soon afterwards following a rare slip by Sonner, but Phil Bolland was on hand to make a cracking last-ditch challenge on Omar Daley (who'd been lucky to stay on the pitch just before after a late tackle on Bolland!) to avert the danger.

Little's substitutions suggested a 'go for broke' mentality in the closing stages and Chris Llewellyn should have won it on 76 minutes when Ricketts got the ball stuck under his feet, but the Welsh international hesitated and a defender cleared.

Wrexham:
12 Gavin Ward, 2 Simon Spender, 5 Steve Evans, 6 Richard Hope, 9 Neil Roberts ■, 11 Chris Llewellyn, 28 Phil Bolland (64), 34 Danny Somner, 35 Stuart Nicholson (64), 36 Carl Tremarco, 39 Drewe Broughton.

Subs: 1 Anthony Williams (GK), 4 Shaun Pejic, 10 Michael Proctor (64), 37 Jeff Whitley (64), 38 Robert Duffy.

Bradford City:
1 Donovan Ricketts, 2 Darren Williams (46), 3 Paul Heckingbottom, 5 David Wetherall, 7 Omar Daley ■, 8 Eddie Johnson (66), 9 Barry Conlon, 12 Matthew Clarke, 15 Joe Colbeck, 22 Kyle Nix, 32 Lee Bullock.

Subs: 4 Paul Evans (66), 16 Simon Ainge, 23 Willy Topp, 30 Ben Saynor (GK), 33 Ben Starosta (46).

On-loan striker Stuart Nicholson claims a corner.

	Wrexham	Bradford City
Shots on Goal:	12	5
Shots on Target:	4	3
Shots off Target	8	2
Possession:	52%	48%
Fouls Conceded:	10	11
Corners:	3	7
Yellow Cards:	1	1
Red Cards:	0	0

Stuart Nicholson is denied by the Shrimps defence in the scramble for goal.

Coca Cola League 2: 29th January, 2008

Morecambe 2   Wrexham 2

Curtis 8   Danny Somner 30p
Neil Roberts 52 (og)   Michael Proctor 79p

Referee: Andy Hall (West Midlands)
Attendance (Away): 2,421 (619)

Things may just be starting to look up for the Dragons after a gritty performance grabbed an undeserved draw at Christie Park.

Morecambe will surely look back on the evening with bewilderment, and wonder just how they didn't take all three points after outclassing the Dragons for long periods.

But two controversial penalties gave the Dragons another vital point in their survival battle. It also extended the unbeaten run to three games, which is a remarkable transformation.

Brian Little made one change to the side that drew with Bradford City on the weekend with Shaun Pejic a surprise inclusion instead of Phil Bolland.

In stark contrast to what was to follow it was Wrexham that made the brighter start, but they were rocked after when the Shrimpers grabbed the lead in their first meaningful attack. Carl Baker beat two defenders far too easily before crossing low into the danger zone. The ball was only partially cleared and Baker drove the ball in a second time for the unmarked Wayne Curtis to tap the ball home from close range.

Morecambe then proceeded to lay siege almost to the Wrexham goal for a short spell, but failed to capitalise and were shocked on the half hour mark when they were pegged back level. Sonner was once again the creator with a neat pass to Drewe Broughton. The big target man flicked the ball neatly on to Nicholson who was bundled to the ground by Danny Adams as he surged into the box. Up stepped Sonner who coolly netted his first goal for the club from the resulting spot kick.

Incredibly the Dragons should have been ahead on 38 minutes, but Chris Llewellyn's shot struck a post and the keeper somehow kept out Broughton's follow up attempt.

With Sonner forced off at the break and Carl Tremarco limping off soon after the restart, Brian Little was forced to reshuffle his troops, but it made little difference as the hosts continued to impress and dominate the play.

They were rewarded when Baker's low cross from the left was unfortunately diverted past Ward by Roberts at the near post.

Having been under almost constant pressure since the second Morecambe goal, it was again against the run of play when the Dragons were awarded a second spot kick. The referee adjudged that Llewellyn was fouled in a goalmouth scramble and Proctor made no mistake from 12 yards.

Craig Stanley missed an open goal as Morecambe sought a deserved winner, but Wrexham held on - despite the sending off of Richard Hope in added-on time for a second yellow card.

Morecambe:
32 Shwan Jalal, 2 Adam Yates ■, 4 David Artell, 5 Jim Bentley, 6 Craif Stanley, 9 Wayne Curtis (77), 10 Carl Baker, 11 Garry Thompson, 16 Stuart Drummond, 21 Matthew Blinkhorn, 25 Danny Adams.

Subs: 7 Michael Twiss (77), 8 Gary Hunter, 17 Jamie Burns, 20 Jon Newby, 30 Scott Davies (GK).

Wrexham:
12 Gavin Ward, 2 Simon Spender (67), 4 Shaun Pejic, 5 Steve Evans, 6 Richard Hope ■■, 9 Neil Roberts, 11 Chris Llewellyn, 34 Danny Somner (46), 35 Stuart Nicholson, 36 Carl Tremarco (48) ■, 39 Drewe Broughton.

Subs: 1 Anthony Williams (GK), 10 Michael Proctor (67), 25 Neil Taylor (48), 28 Phil Bolland, 37 Jeff Whitley (46).

Drewe Broughton shows his frustration as he heads just wide.

	Morecambe	Wrexham
Shots on Goal:	17	12
Shots on Target:	8	4
Shots off Target	9	8
Possession:	51%	49%
Fouls Conceded:	10	13
Corners:	4	3
Yellow Cards:	1	3
Red Cards:	0	1

Steve Evans celebrates his headed goal against the Quakers.

Coca Cola League 2: 2nd February, 2008

Wrexham 2   Darlington 0

Steve Evans 20
Michael Proctor 86

Referee: Steven Cook (Essex)
Attendance (Away): 4,013 (204)

Wrexham moved off the bottom of the table for the first time since Boxing Day with a convincing performance against second-placed Darlington at the Racecourse.

And the standing ovation at the final whistle said it all about a display that left fans contemplating better times ahead.

Phil Bolland was restored to the starting line-up after the defensive frailties evident at Morecambe in midweek, and Under-21 international Mike Williams stepped in for the suspended Richard Hope.

Whatever the reasons behind the changes they certainly had the desired effect as a solid display at the back laid the foundations for a dominant performance further forward as well. Putting it simply, Darlington can have no complaints whatsoever about the result!

In a bright opening to the game Stuart Nicholson brought the first save of the game out of Quakers' keeper David Stockdale on 11 minutes, and Dragons' keeper Gavin Ward saved from Steve Foster. Former Welsh under-21 international Kevin Gall then cleared the crossbar after Steve Evans had misjudged a long clearance.

The opening goal arrived when Danny Sonner's perfectly-delivered corner kick was met by an unmarked Evans who powerfully headed the ball past Stockdale.

Nicholson almost netted his first goal for the club with a glancing header from another Sonner delivery and Drewe Broughton went close with a looping header that flew just too high. Chris Llewellyn was also just off target with a 25-yard free kick as Wrexham looked to increase their advantage before the break.

Darlington responded as you'd expect from a side in their position upon the restart, and Neil Taylor somehow managed to clear over his own bar from a dangerous position and Kevin Gall fired into the side netting as the Dragons were forced onto the back foot for a spell.

But Wrexham rode out the threat and began to reassert their authority on the game. Substitute Michael Proctor headed a Llewellyn cross wide soon after entering the fray, and could have made the points safe on 81 minutes after being put through by Broughton, but Stockdale saved.

Thankfully the striker made no mistake when he was put clear by Llewellyn's threaded through ball and slotted home his eighth goal of the season from the edge of the box.

"Today was pleasing because it was a solid performance and I thought we deserved to win the game," said boss Brian Little afterwards. "We won't get carried away, but it was a decent performance against a good team. In the situation we are in it's about winning games, and the performances are secondary in many respects."

Four games unbeaten - but can it continue at Peterborough?

Wrexham:
12 Gavin Ward, 2 Simon Spender, 5 Steve Evans, 9 Neil Roberts, 11 Chris Llewellyn, 15 Mike Williams, 24 Neil Taylor, 28 Phil Bolland, 34 Danny Somner (85), 35 Stuart Nicholson (76), 39 Drewe Broughton (88).

Subs: 4 Shaun Pejic, 10 Michael Proctor (76), 29 Sam Aiston, 37 Jeff Whitley (85), 38 Rob Duffy (88).

Darlington:
13 David Stockdale, 2 Neil Austin, 4 Alan White, 5 Stephen Foster (46), 8 Mickey Cummins ■, 12 Julian Joachim, 14 Richard Ravenhill (59) ■, 18 Paul Mayo (59), 20 Tommy Wright, 23 Ryan Valentine, 29 Kevin Gall.

Subs: 6 Ian Miller (46), 10 Clark Keltie (59), 11 Robert Purdie, 15 Przemyslaw Kazimierczak (GK), 16 Greg Blundell (59).

Michael Proctor fires in Wrexham's second goal of the match.

Shots on Goal:	11	4
Shots on Target:	4	2
Shots off Target	7	2
Possession:	54%	46%
Fouls Conceded:	14	19
Corners:	3	5
Yellow Cards:	0	2
Red Cards:	0	0

Claude Gnapka knocks out his own' keeper Joe Lewis in attempting to deny Chris Llewellyn.

Coca Cola League 2: 9th February, 2008

Peterborough United 0   Wrexham 0

Referee: Graham Horwood (Bedfordshire)
Attendance (Away): 5,505 (350)

The progress made in recent weeks was clearly evident as Wrexham returned to the scene of an FA Cup drubbing three months earlier and earned a point with a battling performance.

Shame then that the media focused more on Steve Evans' 69th minute challenge on Posh 'keeper Joe Lewis than on the Dragons' gutsy display.

What was even more disappointing was the comments from Posh manager and ex-Wrexham legend Darren Ferguson immediately after the game. "The disap-

pointing thing is that the referee gave us absolutely no protection whatsoever," he raged. "Basically their centre back just went and head-butted our goalkeeper, and then he's elbowed our forward."

Strong words indeed! And isn't it strange that he never mentioned the first half incident when Claude Gnapka struck Drewe Broughton in the face nor the fact that Chris Westwood could also have been sent off for his part in the melee that followed Evans' challenge?

Maybe Fergie's reaction should be taken as a compliment as he no doubt looked to deflect criticism for his expensively assembled side's inability to win the game as expected.

Typically though, Mansfield scored a 90th minute winner at Wycombe (goalscorer a certain Jefferson Louis!) so the point - unexpected as it was - couldn't prevent the Dragons from slipping to the foot of the table once again.

Wrexham had the better of the first half and came within inches of taking a 9th minute lead when Broughton's flick on was hammered by Gnapka against Chris Llewellyn and the ball was fortunately gathered on the goal line by Lewis.

Phil Bolland glanced a header on to the top of the net and Llewellyn tested Lewis with a well-struck volley. And Posh came close to conceding an own goal again when Charlie Lee diverted a Danny Sonner corner onto the post.

Peterborough predictably upped the tempo after the break and George Boyd missed a glaring chance to open the scoring on 52 minutes when he failed to find the target with Gavin Ward out of his goal. Lewis saved from Simon Spender and Ward denied Boyd as chances came

and went at both ends.

Then came the incident that this game will forever be remembered for. Gnapka headed behind for a corner, but flattened Lewis in the process. After receiving treatment the 'keeper then collided with Evans from the resulting flag kick and a mass brawl broke out.

Punishments were dished out and play restarted after a seven minute stoppage!

Both sides could have won it late on and Craig Mackail-Smith was denied a winner for the home side after ex-Red Craig Morgan fouled Neil Taylor.

Peterborough United:
32 Joe Lewis (76), 4 Craig Morgan ▪, 5 Chris Westwood ▪, 6 Charlie Lee ▪, 7 Adam Newton (68), 9 Aaron McLean, 10 George Boyd, 11 Dean Keates, 12 Craig Mackail-Smith, 17 Jamie Day, 27 Claude Gnakpa ▪.

Subs: 14 Scott Mitchell (68), 20 Alfie Potter, 26 Liam Hatch, 29 Tom Williams, 31 James McKeown (GK).

Wrexham:
12 Gavin Ward, 2 Simon Spender, 5 Steve Evans ▪, 9 Neil Roberts ▪, 11 Chris Llewellyn, 15 Mike Williams, 25 Neil Taylor, 28 Phil Bolland, 34 Danny Sonner (88), 35 Stuart Nicholson (68), 39 Drewe Broughton (90) ▪.

Subs: 1 Anthony Williams (GK), 10 Michael Proctor (68), 29 Sam Aiston, 37 Jeff Whitley (88), 38 Rob Duffy (90).

Danny Sonner takes control of the midfield to deny the high flying 'Posh' a home win.

Shots on Goal:	14	8
Shots on Target:	6	4
Shots off Target	8	4
Possession:	55%	45%
Fouls Conceded:	10	15
Corners:	4	7
Yellow Cards:	4	3
Red Cards:	0	0

On loan Stuart Nicholson shoots for goal in a disappointing stalemate with the 'Mariners'

Coca Cola League 2: 23rd February, 2008

Wrexham 0   Grimsby Town 0

Referee: Andy Haines (Tyne & Wear)
Attendance (Away): 4,217 (163)

There have been some awful games at the Racecourse in recent years, but this was arguably the worst of them all!

The state of the pitch - resembling a beach more than a football pitch - clearly hindered both sides, but even still the entertainment on offer did nothing to lift another impressive 4,000+ turnout.

Another clean sheet, and six games unbeaten, represents progress, and Brian Little has clearly organised the side up to be difficult to beat. But after this stalemate

it's obvious that more of an attacking threat is required if the Dragons are to accumulate the number of points necessary to avoid the drop.

Jeff Whitley was drafted into the starting eleven for the first time since his return from injury to replace Neil Roberts, and Carl Tremarco returned after missing two games in place of Neil Taylor.

Wrexham dominated the opening exchanges, but despite several glimpses of the Mariners' goal the nearest they came to taking the lead was on 24 minutes when Stuart Nicholson centred from the right and Tremarco headed over at the far post.

Grimsby gradually came more into the game and it was they who forced the first save of the game in the 38th minute when Gavin Ward held a 25-yard effort from Ciaran Toner.

Decent appeals for a penalty were turned down just before the interval when Rob Atkinson appeared to handle under pressure from Nicholson, but referee Andy Haines decided that the incident was fractionally outside the area and gave a free kick instead. This came to nothing and the game, predictably given the dearth of chances in the opening 45 minutes, was goalless at the break.

If the first half was bad, then the second half was probably worse! In fairness, both managers tried to inject a bit of life into the proceedings with a number of substitutions, but they only had a limited effect.

One of the replacements, Michael Proctor, twice almost won it for the Dragons late on. Firstly when he was denied by the arm of Ryan Bennett, but again Mr. Haines waved penalty claims away, and secondly in the dying moments when he latched

onto a long clearance by Ward, but his 20-yard shot arced just over the crossbar. It was to prove the last chance of an instantly forgettable game.

"We had a similar problem to this when we played them there," explained Brian Little after the game. "We felt both teams pretty much cancelled themselves out.

"Every point we get is a good one, and in the past at 0-0 we might have made mistakes, so that's one positive from today. One point is better than none - that's for sure!"

Wrexham:
12 Gavin Ward, 2 Simon Spender, 5 Steve Evans, 11 Chris Llewellyn, 15 Mike Williams, 28 Phil Bolland, 34 Danny Sonner, 35, Stuart Nicholson (66), 36 Carl Tremarco, 37 Jeff Whitley (63), 39 Drewe Broughton 66).

Subs: 1 Anthony Williams (GK), 6 Richard Hope, 10 Michael Proctor (66), 29 Sam Aiston (63), Rob Duffy (66)■.

Grimsby Town:
1 Phil Barnes, 2 Jamie Clark, 4 James Hunt, 5 Ryan Bennett, 6 Nick Fenton■, 7 Peter Till (68), 9 Danny North 80), 10 Ciaran Toner (46), 11 Danny Boshell, 17 Nick Hegarty, 25 Rob Atkinson■.

Subs: 8 Paul Bolland (46), 13 Gary Montgomery (GK), 15 Justin Whittle, 18 Peter Bore (80), 19 Gary Jones (68).

Jeff Whitley works hard to find a way through the 'Mariners' defence, but to no avail.

	Wrexham	Grimsby
Shots on Goal:	3	3
Shots on Target:	1	2
Shots off Target	2	1
Possession:	49%	51%
Fouls Conceded:	10	6
Corners:	2	1
Yellow Cards:	1	2
Red Cards:	0	0

Steve Evans attempts to outjump the out stretched arms of Posh's Joe Lewis.

Coca Cola League 2: 26th February, 2008

Wrexham 0   Peterborough United 2

Jamie Day 65, 81

Referee: Mike Thorpe (Suffolk)
Attendance (Away): 4,103 (179)

The eagerly awaited second meeting of the sides in a matter of weeks lived up to its billing with Wrexham matching high-flying Peterborough for most of the game, but finally being undone by two Jamie Day free kicks in the closing 25 minutes.

Annoyingly for the Racecourse faithful the opening goal came when the Dragons were enjoying their best spell of the game, and looking the more likely side to score.

With Danny Sonner failing to recover from the injury picked up at the weekend, Trinidadian Silvio Spann returned to the side for the first time since Boxing Day, and Drewe Broughton continued leading the front line despite playing (and scoring the winning penalty) for his parent club MK Dons just 24 hours earlier!

The striker could have given the Dragons a sensational start, but his shot was blocked by 'keeper Joe Lewis in the opening moments. Lewis then saved again, this time from Jeff Whitley, before the

Posh started to show why they're such a feared side in the Division.

Steve Evans blocked a strike from Aaron McLean, and Carl Tremarco had to react quickly to clear a dangerous ball in by Chris Welpdale after Gavin Ward had failed to collect.

It was no surprise that the visitors posed the greater threat and looked the more stylish side, but the Dragons refused to be overwhelmed and showed enough in the opening period to suggest that an away victory was anything but guaranteed.

This was emphasised by the opening exchanges after the restart; Broughton twice going close and Evans being denied by Lewis. After the fracas following the defender's challenge on the 'keeper at London Road in the reverse fixture, all eyes were on the pair again, but this time the game passed by without incident.

Evans volleyed just wide as Wrexham continued to press, but against the run of play the visitors snatched the lead. Chris Llewellyn handled on the edge of the area and Day's free kick was cruelly deflected to wrong-foot Ward, and leave the ball nestling in the bottom corner of the net.

Wrexham tried valiantly to get back on level terms, but Darren Ferguson's side made the game safe eight minutes from time. Whitley fouled Liam Hatch and this time Day needed no slice of luck with his dead ball delivery, and gave Ward no chance with a superb 25-yard strike.

The Dragons kept going, but it was always a forlorn hope once the second goal had gone in, but at least the players left the field with their heads held high following another battling display.

A repeat in the six-pointer against Mansfield at the weekend certainly wouldn't go amiss.

Wrexham:
12 Gavin Ward, 2 Simon Spender, 5 Steve Evans, 11 Chris Llewellyn, 15 Mike Williams (82), 16 Silvio Spann, 28 Phil Bolland, 35 Stuart Nicholson (76), 36 Carl Tremarco, 37 Jeff Whitley, 39 Drewe Broughton (76).

Subs: 6 Richard Hope, 10 Michael Proctor (76), 29 Sam Aiston, 33 Paul Hall (82), 38 Rob Duffy (76).

Peterborough:
32 Joe Lewis, 4 Craig Morgan, 5 Chris Westwood, 6 Charlie Lee (87), 9 Aaron McLean, 10 George Boyd, 11 Dean Keates■, 12 Craig Mackail-Smith (76), 17 Jamie Day, 18 Chris Whelpdale, 27 Claude Gnakpa.

Subs: 8 Micah Hyde (87), 15 Scott Rendell, 26 Liam Hatch (76)■, 31 James McKeown (GK), 33 Daniel Blanchett.

Ex-Dragon Craig Morgan goes in high for a challenge on Drewe Broughton.

Shots on Goal:	8	8
Shots on Target:	4	3
Shots off Target:	4	5
Possession:	48%	52%
Fouls Conceded:	5	15
Corners:	11	4
Yellow Cards:	0	2
Red Cards:	0	0

Michael Proctor attempts to break the deadlock as the Stags Johnny Mullins tries to block.

Coca Cola League 2: 1st March, 2008

Wrexham 0   Mansfield Town 0

Referee: Paul Taylor (London)
Attendance (Away): 4,865 (303)

This St David's Day battle between the League's two bottom sides failed to live up to its billing, and was ultimately a bit of a let down for all concerned.

Six points adrift of safety following this stalemate, a draw doesn't help the Dragons much, but could yet prove crucial in the final reckoning. Especially given the fact that if either side deserved to win this tense struggle then on the balance of the play it was Mansfield!

So taking into account the fact that

Wrexham didn't play well, then you have to take some consolation from not letting one of your rivals get further away from you.

"Today we didn't play well, but thankfully we've come out of it with something," said Brian Little afterwards." That's probably a fair reflection!

Wrexham struggled to find any rhythm, and as a result tended to rely on hitting long balls far too often. Too often passes went astray and consequently this led to a disjointed and lacklustre performance.

Little's decision to go with a 3-4-3 formation suggested an attacking intent, but sadly it was the visitors that generally looked the more lively.

It could have been different though had Silvio Spann's early shot not been deflected behind for a corner. A routine save by Carl Muggleton from Michael Proctor apart, Silvio's effort was about as good as it got for the Dragons in a disappointing first half.

It wasn't much different at the other end either, as Gavin Ward only had one save to make in the opening period as well!

The second half had to improve, and thankfully it did. Proctor brought the first real save out of Muggleton on 50 minutes with a volley on the turn before the visitors snatched the lead in somewhat fortuitous circumstances three minutes later.

Keith Briggs made progress far too easily and his shot from 25 yards took a deflection off leading scorer Michael Boulding to wrong foot Ward and find the net.

Chris Llewellyn responded with a rasping shot that Muggleton did well to turn over the bar and from a corner a Mike

Williams effort just cleared the bar.

Wrexham desperately needed something to happen and it did in the 70th minute when Chris Wood fouled Proctor just outside the penalty area. The striker dusted himself down and expertly found the bottom corner of the net with the resulting free kick.

John Mullins almost diverted a Spann free kick into his own net on 82 minutes as the Dragons strived for a winner, but it was Mansfield that finished the stronger and should have won it in the dying seconds, but Boulding scuffed his shot with only Ward to beat.

Wrexham:
12 Gavin Ward, 2 Simon Spender, 6 Richard Hope, 10 Michael Proctor, 11 Chris Llewellyn (61), 15 Mike Williams (61), 16 Silvio Spann, 28 Paul Bolland ■, 36 Carl Tremarco, 37 Jeff Whitley, 39 Drewe Broughton (71).

Subs: 1 Anthony Williams (GK), 29 Sam Aiston (61), 33 Paul Hall (61), 35 Stuart Nicholson, 38 Rob Duffy (71).

Mansfield Town:
19 Carl Muggleton, 2 Johnny Mullins, 3 Gareth Jelleyman, 4 Jonathan D'Laryea, 7 Matty Hamshaw (46), 11 Michael Boulding, 12 Jake Buxton, 20 Jefferson Louis, 22 Will Atkinson, 24 Chris Wood, 27 Keith Briggs.

Subs: 1 Jason White (GK), 10 Simon Brown, 14 Daniel Martin, 16 Nathan Arnold (46), 18 Ian Holmes.

Drewe Broughton wins a challenge for the ball watched by Phil Bolland.

Shots on Goal:	10	10
Shots on Target:	3	4
Shots off Target	7	6
Possession:	53%	47%
Fouls Conceded:	13	14
Corners:	8	6
Yellow Cards:	1	0
Red Cards:	0	0

The Dragons goalscoring hero Paul Hall fends off Laurence Wilson to shoot at the Chester goal.

Coca Cola League 2: 9th March, 2008

Chester City 0

Wrexham 2

Paul Hall 22
Michael Proctor 65

Referee: A D'Urso (Essex)
Attendance (Away): 3,849 (1,398)

A superb display from Gavin Ward and two fantastic breakaway goals gave Wrexham another stunning victory at the Deva Stadium.

The win, coupled with the previous day's results, leaves the Dragons just three points adrift of safety with three games in hand on third-bottom Macclesfield Town. So this victory was about far more than just local bragging rights.

But it was still nice to ram the "going down" chants from the home fans back down their throats as goals from Paul Hall and Michael Proctor gave the Dragons a real fighting chance of avoiding the drop.

Ward was called into action inside the first minute with a superb save to push a Chris Holroyd effort behind for a corner and the home side piled on the pressure in the opening moments of the game.

The pressure was finally released when James Vaughan fouled Chris Llewellyn, and Proctor tested 'keeper Jon Danby from the subsequent free kick.

Chester thought they'd taken the lead on 21 minutes when Ward fumbled Kevin Ellison's corner into the net, but referee Andy D'Urso saw an infringement and ruled it out. Chester's agony was confounded immediately when Ward took the free kick, Drewe Broughton flicked the ball on, and Hall held off a defender and drilled the ball past Danby from the edge of the box.

The home fans were stunned, as mass celebrations broke out amongst the 1,400 Dragons' fans in the disappointing crowd of less than 4,000.

Ward turned an Ellison shot round the post as Chester came forward once again, but Hall could have doubled the Dragons' lead just before the break, but steered his shot just wide.

Chester upped the tempo at the start of the second half, forcing Wrexham to defend resolutely. Mark Hughes, Laurence Wilson and Ellison all went close with long-range efforts before Ward pulled off an incredible save from point-blank range to deny Holroyd. The former Chester stopper then tipped over another effort from Ellison.

Then, remarkably, the Dragons grabbed a second in identical circumstances to the first. Again Chester thought they'd scored only for Holroyd to be adjudged offside, and almost immediately Wrexham broke away and Carl Tremarco's long throw into the box fell to Proctor who turned and hooked a superb right-foot volley over Danby and into the top right-hand corner of the net.

Ward then denied Ellison for the umpteenth time as the home side tried to salvage something from the game, but the Dragons showed the grit and determination that will be required in the closing couple of months of the season and held on.

Chester City:
12 John Danby, 3 Kevin Sandwith, 4 Tony Dinning, 9 John Murphy, 11 Kevin Ellison, 14 Mark Hughes■, 17 Laurence Wilson (62), 19 Paul Linwood■, 20 Chris Holroyd (77), 22 James Vaughan, 25 Kevin Roberts.

Subs: 21 Paul Rutherford (62), 23 Phil Palethorpe (GK), 27 Shaun Kelly, 32 Paul McManus (77) 33 Glenn Rule.

Wrexham:
12 Gavin Ward, 2 Simon Spender■, 6 Richard Hope■, 10 Michael Proctor (85), 11 Chris Llewellyn, 15 Mike Williams, 28 Phil Bolland, 33 Paul Hall■ (72), 36 Carl Tremarco■, 37 Jeff Whitley, 39 Drewe Broughton (80).

Subs: 1 Anthony Williams (GK), 16 Silvio Spann, 29 Sam Aiston (85), 35 Stuart Nicholson (72), 38 Robert Duffy (80).

Drewe Broughton outjumps the Chester defence to head for goal.

Shots on Goal:	4	6
Shots on Target:	2	3
Shots off Target:	2	3
Possession:	47%	53%
Fouls Conceded:	11	17
Corners:	14	1
Yellow Cards:	2	4
Red Cards:	0	0

Sam Aiston fires at goal as the Chairboy's Sam Stockley attempts to block the ball.

Coca Cola League 2: 11th March, 2008

Wycombe Wanderers 2   Wrexham 1

Leon Knight 14
Scott McGleish 21

Michael Proctor 53

Referee: Clive Penton (Sussex)
Attendance (Away): 4,002 (219)

A stirring second half performance saw Wrexham come up just short at a windswept Adams Park. This was the proverbial game of two halves with the Dragons woeful in the first half, and fortunate to be only 2-0 down at the break. Second half was a different story, with Wycombe hanging on at the end.

Play-off chasing Wycombe was always going to be a tough ask especially coming just two days after a hard-fought derby clash at Chester, but the manner in which the Dragons conceded two first half goals was farcical.

The opener came when, although there looked to be no danger after home striker Scott McGleish was flagged offside, Gavin Ward took the free kick into the wind and the ball fell straight to the feet of the dangerous Leon Knight who strode forward and comprehensively beat Ward with a low drive from 20 yards out.

Worse was to follow just seven minutes later! Again Ward's clearance lacked distance but at least this time it went straight to Carl Tremarco. However, the left back's poor backward header lacked pace and McGleish nipped in to round Ward and finish with ease.

Chris Llewellyn shot wide in a rare Wrexham excursion forward and the over-worked Dragons' defence had a let-off soon afterwards when McGleish rattled the crossbar when a third goal looked the more likely outcome.

A knee injury saw Jeff Whitley replaced by Sam Aiston just before the interval and during the break Brian Little decided to change things around with youngsters Neil Taylor and Gareth Evans coming on in place of the experienced duo of Phil Bolland and Richard Hope as Wrexham went with an attacking 4-2-4 formation.

This change, coupled with the strong wind now behind them, breathed new life into the Dragons and suddenly it was a totally different game.

Llewellyn forced a fine finger-tip save by keeper Frank Fielding with a 25-yard strike before the Dragons did register on the score sheet in the 53rd minute.

Tremarco made amends for his earlier error with a perfectly delivered free kick that Evans flicked on and Michael Proctor hammered the ball past Fielding from 12 yards out.

Proctor was denied an equaliser by a last-ditch tackle from Leon Johnson and Wrexham were given further hope eleven minutes from time when Chairboys' mid-fielder Tommy Doherty was sent off after collecting his second yellow card for a bad foul on Aiston.

Proctor's free kick was superbly kept out by Fielding and not even the keeper him-self will know how he kept a Paul Hall drive out with his feet in the last minute.

Proctor then had an injury time header saved before time finally ran out on Wrexham.

Wycombe Wanderers:
34 Frank Fielding, 4 Russell Martin, 7 David McCracken, 8 Stefan Oakes (66), 9 Leon Knight (81), 15 Gary Holt, 17 Scott McGleish (76)■, 18 Craig Woodman, 20 Leon Johnson, 25 Sam Stockley, 35 Tommy Doherty■■■.

Subs: 6 Mike Williamson (66), 11 Martin Bullock, 16 John Sutton (76), 19 Jamie Young (GK), 44 Neil Lennon (81).

Wrexham:
12 Gavin Ward, 2 Simon Spender, 6 Richard Hope (46)■, 10 Michael Proctor, 11 Chris Llewellyn, 15 Mike Williams, 28 Phil Bolland (46)■, 33 Paul Hall, 36 Carl Tremarco■, 37 Jeff Whitley (45), 39 Drewe Broughton.

Subs: 1 Anthony Williams (GK), 24 Gareth Evans (46), 25 Neil Taylor (46), 29 Sam Aiston (45)■, 35 Stuart Nicholson.

Michael Proctor on the ball sets up another Wrexham attack in search of an equaliser.

	Wycombe	Wrexham
Shots on Goal:	5	11
Shots on Target:	3	7
Shots off Target:	2	4
Possession:	56%	44%
Fouls Conceded:	9	13
Corners:	2	9
Yellow Cards:	2	4
Red Cards:	1	0

Sam Aiston is denied by Shakers 'keeper Darren Randolph, but Drewe Broughton follows up to score.

Coca Cola Legue 2: 15th March, 2008

Wrexham 2

Drewe Broughton 25
Michael Proctor 77

Bury 1

Glynn Hurst 45

Referee: Howard Webb (South Yorkshire)
Attendance (Away): 4,431 (634)

On a day when relegation rivals Mansfield and Macclesfield won, and Notts County drew, the importance of Michael Proctor's winner cannot be under-stated.

Even with a valuable three points in the bag the Dragons still sit four points behind safety - albeit with two games in hand on County - so anything other than victory here would have been disastrous to Wrexham's survival hopes.

With three changes from the midweek

defeat at Wycombe - Gareth Evans, Neil Taylor and Sam Aiston were given starting roles as reward for their second half displays at Adams Park - the Dragons delivered a gritty and battling display to earn three hard-fought points.

Wrexham started sluggishly though and Bury were the dominant force in the opening quarter of the game, forcing six corners during this period.

Gavin Ward made a smart save to deny Bury's leading scorer Andy Bishop on 23 minutes, and then from Glyn Hurst after a poor back header from Phil Bolland.

These saves proved crucial as Chris Llewellyn's clearance found Aiston who was allowed to run at the visiting defence. His shot was well parried by Shakers' Darren Randolph, but the ball dropped kindly to Drewe Broughton who netted his first goal for the club from close range.

Ward then kept Wrexham ahead with saves from both Bishop and Elliott Bennett. An ankle injury saw Carl Tremarco replaced by Mike Williams, whilst Neil Taylor was struggling after a strong tackle with Ben Futcher.

And the Dragons' problems mounted deep into first half injury time when Hurst met a Brian Barry-Murphy free kick to head past Ward for the equaliser.

Matty Done emerged for the second period instead of the struggling Taylor as a nerve-wracking forty-five minutes lay ahead.

Broughton was denied a second goal by Randolph on 49 minutes, and Efe Sodje wasted a good opening at the other end, but generally chances were at a premium.

The importance of a winning goal was not lost on the Dragons, and their reward for taking the game to the visitors in the final quarter of the game came with a crucial second goal.

Simon Spender ventured forward down the right and centred to the near post where substitute Stuart Nicholson missed his kick, but the ball went through to Proctor who gleefully slotted the ball past Randolph.

Ward again saved from Bishop, but it was the Dragons that looked the more likely side to score in the closing minutes, but Proctor, put clear by Done's pass, fired wide with just Randolph to beat.

Wrexham:
12 Gavin Ward, 2 Simon Spender, 10 Michael Proctor, 11 Chris Llewellyn■, 24 Gareth Evans■, 25 Neil Taylor (46), 28 Phil Bolland, 29 Sam Aiston, 33 Paul Hall (75), 36 Carl Tremarco (41), 39 Drewe Broughton■.

Subs: 1 Anthony Williams (GK), 15 Mike Williams (41) 20 Matty Done (46), 21 Marc Williams, 35 Stuart Nicholson (75).

Bury:
29 Darren Randolph, 2 Paul Scott, 4 Ben Futcher, 7 Steve Haslam, 9 Glynn Hurst (69), 10 Andy Bishop, 11 Brian Barry-Murphy, 12 David Buchanan, 16 Nicky Adams, 23 Elliott Bennett (85), 28 Efetobore Sodje.

Subs: 1 Jim Provett (GK), 8 Richie Parker, 14 Andy Parrish, 25 Adam Rooney (69), 34 Simon Yeo (85).

The Dragons Michael Proctor turns away to celebrate his winning goal.

	Wrexham	Bury
Shots on Goal:	9	9
Shots on Target:	3	8
Shots off Target	6	1
Possession:	53%	47%
Fouls Conceded:	14	6
Corners:	2	12
Yellow Cards:	3	0
Red Cards:	0	0

'The Bees' Karleigh Osborne looks on as Michael Proctor makes an attempt at goal.

Coca Cola League 2: 22nd March, 2008

Brentford 2   Wrexham 0

Ricky Shakes 31, 81

Referee: Grant Hegley (Hertfordshire)
Attendance (Away): 4,448 (465)

Wrexham moved significantly closer to the relegation trap door after a miserable defeat at a windswept and wintry Griffin Park.

A disappointing game - and a poor advert for League Two football - saw little to choose between the two sides, though you could argue that Wrexham probably had the better of what few opportunities there were.

But a failure to convert the few half-chances that came their way, coupled with two moments of defensive uncertainty that led to the two Brentford goals,

proved costly.

And the fact that Mansfield and Macclesfield both lost meant that the Dragons wasted a great chance of closing the gap on the sides immediately above them.

With Danny Sonner and Neil Roberts both returning to the side after spells on the sidelines there was a fair degree of optimism amongst the near-500 following from Wrexham that a successive victories could be recorded for the first time this season. Alas it wasn't to be!

Ricky Shakes volleyed over for the Bees early on and Michael Proctor also failed to hit the target with the Dragons' first decent chance on 26 minutes.

But the stalemate was broken when Gavin Ward saved from Alan Connell, but with ball still dangerously inside the penalty area and the Dragons' defence hesitant Shakes easily headed the loose ball past Ward.

Wrexham very nearly levelled things up just before the break when Simon Spender's free kick caught the wind and flew over the head of Bees' keeper Simon Brown and struck the crossbar. A melee followed inside the home penalty area, which ended when Gareth Evans' header was saved by Brown after both Chris Llewellyn and Neil Roberts had been unable to force the ball over the line.

And there was still time before the half time whistle for Phil Bolland to head a Sonner free kick just over, but the Bees held on.

The second half began in equally encouraging fashion for the Dragons and they very nearly netted an equaliser on 50 minutes when Roberts' effort was deflect-ed goal wards by a defender, but Brown clutched the ball right on the goal line despite claims by several Dragons' players that the ball had crossed the line.

Connell and Nathan Elder could both have added a second goal for the home side before their goal lead something of a charmed life again when Brown dropped substitute Matty Done's cross, but managed to get back in time to prevent Proctor's shot from crossing the line.

A point would still have been valuable, but any such hopes were dashed nine minutes from time when Elder's cross led to more hesitation and Connell headed the ball down for Shakes to finish.

Brentford:
1 Simon Brown, 2 Kevin O'Connor, 5 Alan Bennett, 7 Gary Smith (27), 8 Craig Pead, 10 Alan Connell, 11 Glenn Poole, 14 Nathan Elder, 19 Ryan Dickson, 22 Karleigh Osborne, 29 Ricky Shakes.

Subs: 6 Osei Sankofa, 12 John Mousinho (27), 17 Reuben Reid, 21 Wayne Brown, 27 Ben Hamer (GK).

Wrexham:
12 Gavin Ward, 2 Simon Spender, 9 Neil Roberts (66), 10 Michael Proctor, 11 Chris Llewellyn, 15 Mike Williams, 24 Gareth Evans, 28 Phil Bolland, 29 Sam Aiston, 34 Danny Sonner (66), 39 Drewe Broughton.

Subs: 1 Anthony Williams (GK), 6 Richard Hope, 20 Matty Done (66), 33 Paul Hall (66), 37 Jeff Whitley.

Danny Sonner tries for goal in a disappointing 2-0 defeat at Griffin Park.		
Shots on Goal:	10	6
Shots on Target:	6	3
Shots off Target	4	3
Possession:	53%	47%
Fouls Conceded:	13	11
Corners:	3	4
Yellow Cards:	0	0
Red Cards:	0	0

Michael Proctor looks agonisingly on as the ball frustratingly goes the wrong side of the post.

Coca Cola League 2: 24th March, 2008

Wrexham 0   Dagenham & Redbridge 0

Referee: Anthony Taylor (Manchester)
Attendance (Away): 4,692 (143)

Wrexham were left seven points away from safety with just nine games remaining after failing to convert any of the umpteen chances created against fellow-strugglers Dagenham & Redbridge at the Racecourse.

Surely there was never going to be a better opportunity for the Dragons to demonstrate their survival credentials such was the dominant nature of their performance, but the inability to take more than a point from the contest could mean the first nail being hammered into their coffin.

Understandably given the disappointing

display in west London two days earlier, manager Brian Little changed things round and went for a 3-5-2 formation with Richard Hope returning in place of Mike Williams (absent with Wales U21s) and Matty Done's inclusion seeing Neil Roberts dropped to the bench.

Michael Proctor had a third minute effort deflected behind for a corner from which Drewe Broughton's header brought a goal line save from former Wales international Tony Roberts.

Broughton shot wide and then had two headers saved by Roberts, the second a superb stop, as Wrexham continued to create chances.

Sam Aiston also steered a header wide and Proctor couldn't quite force a shot away after a good flick on by Broughton.

It wasn't all one-way traffic though. Gavin Ward was grateful to see Ben Strevens' effort fly straight at him and only a fine block by Phil Bolland inside the six-yard box denied Peter Gain.

Broughton, whose aerial power was a constant source of problems for the visiting defence, saw another header drift wide and Chris Llewellyn twice had shots blocked as the Dragons strove desperately for a breakthrough.

Roberts replaced Danny Sonner for the restart, but the pattern of play continued to be mainly towards the Daggers' goal, with Broughton setting up Aiston for a shot well saved by Roberts and Proctor's follow-up was blocked.

The visitors' goal led even more of a charmed life in the 54th minute when Roberts reacted quickly to keep out Broughton's effort, and Proctor's follow-up struck the foot of a post.

Three minutes later, Broughton, who was having a game to forget in front of goal, came agonisingly close with a clever flick, and then saw a 20-yard curler sail wide.

Strevens tested Ward in a rare Dagenham attack in the 65th minute, but normal service was quickly resumed, but strive as they might the Dragons just couldn't deliver the killer punch.

Llewellyn crossed for Broughton to once again fail to find the target with another header, and Roberts saw a downward header drop just wide of the target late on to leave the Racecourse faithful wondering just how damaging this result could be in the final reckoning.

Wrexham:
12 Gavin Ward, 2 Simon Spender (82), 6 Richard Hope, 10 Michael Proctor (76), 11 Chris Llewellyn■, 20 Matty Done, 24 Gareth Evans, 28 Phil Bolland, 29 Sam Aiston, 34 Danny Sonner (46), 39 Drewe Broughton■.

Subs: 9 Neil Roberts (46), 31 Wes Baynes (82), 33 Paul Hall, 35 Stuart Nicholson (76), 37 Jeff Whitley.

Dagenham & Redbridge:
1 Tony Roberts, 6 Shane Huke, 8 Glen Southam, 11 Dave Rainford■, 12 Scott Griffiths, 14 Paul Benson, 15 Anwar Uddin, 16 Mark Arber, 18 Ben Strevens (82), 20 Ross Smith, 33 Peter Gain,

Subs: 3 Sam Sloma, 5 Jon Boardman, 23 Chris Moore (82), 25 Soloman Taiwo, 27 Dave Hogan (GK),

Chris Llewellyn shoots at goal, but without success.

Shots on Goal:	15	6
Shots on Target:	5	2
Shots off Target:	10	4
Possession:	55%	45%
Fouls Conceded:	18	9
Corners:	6	6
Yellow Cards:	2	1
Red Cards:	0	0

On loan striker Drewe Broughton fires in a shot at the Barnet goal.

Coca Cola League 2: 29th March, 2008

Barnet 3

Ismail Yakubu 45
Anthony Thomas 51
Nicky Nicolau 62

Wrexham 2

Drewe Broughton 55
Simon Spender 66

Referee: Roger East (Wiltshire)
Attendance (Away): 2,286 (391)

Wrexham's relegation woes deepened after a defeat that was probably more convincing for the home side than the narrow one-goal margin might suggest.

Wrexham kicked off, but somehow contrived to lose possession to Anthony Thomas almost immediately, and the quick-fire front man surged forward and forced the first save of the game from Gavin Ward.

Not the best of starts then, but the

Dragons could have opened the scoring themselves on nine minutes, but after Paul Hall's quickly-taken free kick put Michael Proctor away, his pull back just evaded Drewe Broughton and Chris Llewellyn in the goalmouth.

Heavy rain made conditions difficult and chances were at a premium, though the home side were just about edging things. Thomas shot wide for Barnet; a Matty Done free kick was easily saved by Barnet keeper Lee Harrison; Simon Spender cleared off the line from Ismail

Yakubu; and Ward saved smartly from Thomas.

But just when you thought the Dragons would get to half time with their goal intact the Bees grabbed the lead in added-on time. A poor challenge by Llewellyn on Joe Devera out on the right touchline led to a Nicky Nicolau free kick from which Yakubu stole a yard on Broughton to glance a header past Ward.

Six minutes into the second half the Bees doubled their lead when Albert Adomah headed down and Thomas, unchallenged, hooked the ball with his back to goal over Ward and into the far corner of the net for a neat and clever finish.

Wrexham's hopes were briefly raised three minutes later though when Gareth Evans' free kick was met by the head of Broughton whose looping header beat Harrison via the inside of a post.

Such hopes were quickly dashed once again when Barnet restored their two-goal cushion. Thomas was again allowed to move forward unhampered and an unmarked Nicolau easily turned his cross-cum-shot home.

Four minutes later though and the Dragons clawed themselves back into the game again when Spender surged forward, continued running to collect Hall's clever back heel, and drilled the ball right-footed from the edge of the penalty area into the bottom left-hand corner of the net.

There was plenty of time remaining to salvage something from the game, and Done was denied by a fingertip save from Harrison.

But Barnet came closer to extending their lead when both Josh Wright and Sagi Burton exposed the inevitable gaps at the back but saw efforts strike the woodwork.

Barnet:
1 Lee Harrison, 2 Joe Devera, 3 Nicky Nicolau, 4 Neal Bishop, 5 Ismail Yakubu, 7 Albert Adomah, 8 Anthony Thomas (86), 10 Adam Birchall, 19 Sagi Burton, 21 Kenny Gillet (90), 24 Josh Wright.

Subs: 6 Michael Leary, 11 Jason Puncheon, 14 Max Porter (90), 16 Ashley Carew, 23 Kieron St Aimee (86).

Wrexham:
12 Gavin Ward, 2 Simon Spender, 6 Richard Hope (69), 10 Michael Proctor, 11 Chris Llewellyn, 20 Matty Done, 24 Gareth Evans, 28 Phil Bolland, 29 Sam Aiston (72), 34 Paul Hall, 39 Drewe Broughton.

Subs: 1 Anthony Williams (GK), 15 Mike Williams (69), 21 Marc Williams, 35 Stuart Nicholson, 37 Jeff Whitley (72).

Mark Jones

	Barnet	Wrexham
Shots on Goal:	15	10
Shots on Target:	11	6
Shots off Target	4	4
Possession:	50%	50%
Fouls Conceded:	18	13
Corners:	14	6
Yellow Cards:	0	0
Red Cards:	0	0

Phil Bolland (28) outjumps the 'Stags' defence and Neil Roberts to head at goal.

Coca Cola League 2: 1st April, 2008

Mansfield Town 2

Jefferson Louis 51p
John Mullins 54

Wrexham 1

Marc Williams 78

Referee: Nigel Miller (Durham)
Attendance (Away): 3,435 (601)

The Blue Square Premier looms closer than ever after Wrexham slumped to a 2-1 defeat in a game that neither side could afford to lose.

Failure to take anything from this six-pointer at Field Mill doesn't leave the Dragons any further from safety - still eight points behind third-bottom Notts County - but with games running out fast relegation is fast becoming a certainty.

Brian Little named a 4-4-2 formation with three changes from the defeat at Barnet

at the weekend and in an understandably tense and nervy opening period there was little to choose between the two struggling sides.

But boosted by a superb travelling support of over 600, the Dragons can justifiably claim to have edged the first half in terms of chances.

Leading scorer Michael Boulding had an early sight of goal for the home side when he headed straight at Gavin Ward, but it was Wrexham that settled the better.

Drewe Broughton fired a 20-yarder just wide, the same player saw another effort saved by veteran stopper Carl Muggleton, and Phil Bolland headed a Paul Hall corner agonisingly across the face of the goal and wide.

A timely intervention from Gareth Evans kept Matty Hamshaw at bay, and Stephen Dawson worried Ward with a curling effort that drifted just wide of the post.

Chris Llewellyn and Hall also went at the other end, but despite having slightly the better of the opening 45 minutes, Wrexham had to be content with a scoreless game at the interval.

It didn't remain that way for long, as the Stags opened the scoring in rather controversial circumstances. Hamshaw's corner led to a scramble in the Dragons' penalty area, and as Evans appeared to be pushed to the ground his hand struck the ball, and referee Nigel Miller instantly pointed to the spot. Jefferson Louis made no mistake from 12 yards to plunge the Dragons deeper in the mire.

Three minutes later it was 2-0 when Hamshaw's defence-slitting pass found an unmarked John Mullins to the right of goal who slotted the ball past Ward.

Wrexham struggled to pose any attacking threat, but gave themselves a brief glimmer of hope when Stuart Nicholson's shot was parried by Muggleton and substitute Marc Williams was in the right place to slot home from close range.

Unfortunately the hoped for onslaught never materialized, and time quickly counted down on the game and, probably, Wrexham's spell in the Football League!

"We will continue to have a go," declared a resolute Little afterwards. "We will roll our sleeves up. We have got a game on Saturday we have got to win. We will try our best."

Mansfield Town:
19 Carl Muggleton, 2 John Mullins, 3 Gareth Jelleyman, 4 Jonathan D'Laryea, 7 Matthew Hamshaw (87),8 Stephen Dawson, 11 Michael Boulding (90), 12 Jake Buxton, 13 Alex Baptiste, 16 Nathan Arnold, 20 Jefferson Louis (89).

Subs: 1 Jason White (GK), 10 Simon Brown, 26 Kevin Horlock (90), 27 Keith Briggs (87), 30 Rory Boulding (89).

Wrexham:
12 Gavin Ward, 2 Simon Spender, 9 Neil Roberts (64), 11 Chris Llewellyn, 15 Mike Williams, 24 Gareth Evans, 28 Phil Bolland, 29 Sam Aiston, 33 Paul Hall (64), 35 Stuart Nicholson, 39 Drewe Broughton (71).

Subs: 6 Richard Hope, 8 Danny Williams (64), 10 Michael Proctor (64), 20 Matty Done, 21 Marc Williams (71).

Stuart Nicolson takes control of the ball in an attack on the 'Stags' goal at Field Mill.

	Mansfield	Wrexham
Shots on Goal:	13	12
Shots on Target:	9	6
Shots off Target	4	6
Possession:	55%	45%
Fouls Conceded:	8	4
Corners:	6	8
Yellow Cards:	0	0
Red Cards:	0	0

Neil Roberts surges forward in an attempt to break down the 'Silkmens' rearguard.

Coca Cola League 2: 5th April, 2008

Wrexham 1   Macclesfield Town 1

Steve Evans 79   Jamie Tolley 52

Referee: Colin Webster (Tyne & Wear)

Attendance (Away): 3,993 (466)

Time is fast running out on Wrexham as another opportunity to put pressure on the teams above them was missed.

Let's face it; the fixture list has been kind with several home games in a short space of time against teams either in relegation trouble like ourselves, or with little to play for in mid-table.

But Bury apart, the Dragons haven't been able to turn draws into wins and consequently most fans in the near 4,000 crowd trudged away after the final whistle pretty mush resigned to the inevitable.

Danny Williams, Steve Evans and Neil Taylor all returned to the fold following spells on the treatment table, but couldn't inspire the Dragons to the level of performance required to prolong the club's proud 87-year stay in the Football League.

"The bottom line is that the quality you need to win a game of football is just lacking at the moment," was boss Brian Little's honest post-match assessment.

This lack of quality was never more evident than in the opening exchanges when the Dragons got into good positions on several occasions, but ultimately the final, decisive ball was a big let down. Good situations were therefore squandered with few questions asked of the Macclesfield defence.

So it was the visitors that posed the greater threat, and should have scored on 21 minutes when Richard Walker had a free header from a Neil Ashton free kick, but sent the ball wide.

The Silkmen's Gareth Evans stung Gavin Ward's hands with a powerful strike in the 26th minute, and Shaun Brisley steered a header wide moments later.

On 35 minutes it was Wrexham's turn to show. and Jonathan Brain had to be alert to tip Danny Williams' 25-yard free kick over for a corner.

Goalless at the break, but as at Field Mill in midweek the Dragons conceded early in the second half, when former Shrewsbury midfielder Jamie Tolley smashed a half-volley past Ward from just inside the area.

Tolley shot wide and Ward saved twice from the lively Francis Green as Macclesfield searched for a second goal,

and their profligacy in front of goal was punished 11 minutes from time when substitute Michael Proctor's long throw-in from the left was met by a looping header from Steve Evans that Brain couldn't keep out.

A fingertip save from Brain then denied Phil Bolland in the 88th minute, but even eight minutes of added-on time wasn't enough for Wrexham to find a winner.

"We have been bottom of the League for most of the season and that affects the players to a degree," added Little. "But we are bottom for a reason and after 40 games the table doesn't lie."

Wrexham:
12 Gavin Ward, 2 Simon Spender (72), 5 Steve Evans, 6 Richard Hope (69), 8 Danny Williams (69), 9 Neil Roberts, 11 Chris Llewellyn ▪, 21 Marc Williams, 25 Neil Taylor, 28 Phil Bolland, 39 Drewe Broughton.

Subs: 10 Michael Proctor (69), 20 Matty Done, 29 Sam Aiston (72), 33 Paul Hall, 35 Stuart Nicholson (69).

Macclesfield Town:
30 Jonny Brain, 3 Richard Walker, 4 Sean Hessey ▪, 5 Ryan Cresswell, 8 Francis Green (90), 11 Jamie Tolley, 12 Danny Thomas (66) ▪, 21 Neil Ashton, 25 Terry Dunfield, 26 Gareth Evans (90), 34 Shaun Brisley.

Subs: 2 Richard Edghill, 14 Michael Symes (90), 16 Izak Reid (66),19 James Jennings (90), 29 Scott Spencer

Wrexham's goalscorer Steve Evans in the thick of an aerial combat.

	Wrexham	Macclesfield
Shots on Goal:	8	7
Shots on Target:	2	2
Shots off Target:	6	5
Possession:	51%	49%
Fouls Conceded:	12	12
Corners:	7	2
Yellow Cards:	1	2
Red Cards:	0	0

The look on Gavin Ward and his defenders' faces says it all, after Danny Swailes' opening goal.

Coca Cola League 2: 8th April, 2008

MK Dons 4   Wrexham 1

Danny Swailes 2   Neil Roberts 59p
Aaron Wilbraham 10, 90
Sean O'Hanlon 75

Referee: Danny McDermid (London)
Attendance (Away): 8,646 (200)

Wrexham's first (and possibly last?) ever visit to the impressive Stadium:MK ended in disappointment as the home side continued their relentless march to promotion with a convincing victory.

It was always going to be a big ask of the Dragons to register a 'double' over Paul Ince's side, but the manner of this defeat is what most fans will find most galling.

For more slack defending allowed the home side to open up a two-goal lead inside the first ten minutes, and effectively kill the game as a contest almost before it had began.

For the next eighty minutes the Dragons gave as good as they got, and had Dons' central defender Carl Regan been quite rightly sent off when he hauled down Neil Roberts on 58 minutes it could have ended differently. Instead lenient referee Danny McDermid didn't even show a yellow card even though he correctly awarded a penalty.

Back to the start though, and it took only two minutes for the Dons to open the scoring when neither Gavin Ward or Steve Evans reacted to Dean Lewington's free kick, and defender Danny Swailes accepted the easy task of netting unmarked at the far post.

Eight minutes later the high-flying home side doubled their lead when Jemal Johnson was allowed to make progress far too easily down the left before picking out an unmarked Aaron Wilbraham who drilled the ball past Ward.

But the expected onslaught never materialised, though that probably had as much to with the Dons easing off as it did the Dragons rolling their sleeves up and getting down to business.

Neil Roberts drilled a 25-yard shot just wide and Willy Gueret saved from both Stuart Nicholson and Marc Williams as Wrexham rallied, but the Dons maintained their two-goal lead at the interval.

Wrexham started the second half brightly and got some reward when Roberts confidently dispatched the penalty kick past Gueret after Regan's misdemeanour.

Would the home side have wobbled then if down to ten men with their lead halved? Of course we'll never know, but had Mr.

McDermid correctly applied the letter of the laws then it could have been a far more interesting finish.

Instead the Dons were able to capitalise on their good fortune and reassert their superiority with a third goal when Lewington swung over a corner and Sean O'Hanlon was unmarked to head past Ward.

Wilbraham then merely rubbed even more salt into Wrexham's wounds in injury time when the defence went to sleep at a quickly-taken free kick, and the striker was able to waltz around Ward before slotting the ball into an empty net.

MK Dons:
12 Willy Gueret, 3 Dean Lewington■, 4 Keith Andrews, 6 Sean O'Hanlon, 11 Lloyd Dyer (85), 14 Mark Wright, 16 Aaron Wilbraham, 19 Carl Regan (79)■, 20 Alan Navarro■, 23 Jemal Johnson (66), 25 Danny Swailes.

Subs: 2 Jude Stirling (79), 8 Kevin Gallen (85), 18 John Miles (66)■, 29 Nathan Abbey (GK), 32 Jordan Hadfield.

Wrexham:
12 Gavin Ward, 2 Simon Spender, 5 Steve Evans, 6 Richard Hope, 8 Danny Williams (76), 9 Neil Roberts ■, 11 Chris Llewellyn, 21 Marc Williams, 24 Gareth Evans, 25 Neil Taylor, 35 Stuart Nicholson (72).

Subs: 10 Michael Proctor (72), 20 Matty Done (72), 29 Sam Aiston, 33 Paul Hall, 36 Jeff Whitley.

Neil Roberts fires the Dragons back into the game from the penalty spot, but to no avail.

Shots on Goal:	7	9
Shots on Target:	6	3
Shots off Target	1	6
Possession:	56%	44%
Fouls Conceded:	4	1
Corners:	9	9
Yellow Cards:	5	2
Red Cards:	0	0

Phil Bolland heads for goal in a rare Wrexham attack in a disappointing 'derby' defeat to Shrewsbury.

Coca Cola League 2: 13th April, 2008

Shrewsbury Town 3   Wrexham 0

Kevin McIntyre 7
Darren Moss 58
James Constable 68

Referee: Lee Mason (Lancashire)
Attendance (Away): 7,065 (1,242)

There's surely no one who hasn't **finally accepted that relegation is inevitable after this humiliating debacle at the New Meadow.**

Even in a season of many lacklustre and easily forgettable performances this was easily the worst of the lot! So much so that manager Brian Little revealed after the game that coach and Wrexham legend Joey Jones felt compelled to enter the dressing room after the game and spell out a few home truths.

"When a great hero and great friend of mine, Joey Jones, comes in and says the things he said, he was not very complimentary to the players," he said. "He had to say them and I'm delighted he did because it was true. It's a sad, bad day because we are virtually down now, and the players didn't do themselves justice either as individuals or collectively."

"I genuinely think the last 20 minutes today were the worst 20 minutes of my footballing career," he added. "Standing there on the sidelines looking at your team knowing they are not going to get anything out of the game, and that the chances are you are relegated out of the Football League, is probably the worst 20 minutes of my football career and I have not enjoyed it."

It wasn't much fun in the stands either, especially with the vociferous Shrews' fans understandably gloating with chants of "going down, going down, going down" in the adjacent stand.

What made the display even more shocking is that it came against a Shrewsbury side that hadn't won in any of their previous 15 games!

It took just seven minutes for the home side to open the scoring, in what can only be descried as farcical circumstances once again. Colin Murdock launched a free kick into the Dragons' penalty area. No danger you'd think, but both Gavin Ward and Richard Hope left it to each other and Kevin McIntyre nipped in to head over Ward and into the net.

Wrexham were so ineffectual for much of the game that they often made the home side, still not certain of safety themselves before the game, look like world-beaters.

Even so, Marc Williams could still have leveled things up in the dying seconds of the first half, but Shrews' keeper Scott Bevan saved well.

Defeat was effectively sealed when Wrexham-born Darren Moss got the better of Neil Taylor to head Marc Tierney' cross past convincingly past Ward.

Ten minutes later the penultimate nail was hammered into Wrexham's coffin when Phil Bolland was a little unlucky in fouling James Constable. Ward did well to save Dave Hibbert's spot kick, but Constable was quickest to react to net the rebound.

Then came that last, agonising 20 minutes!

Shrewsbury Town:
21 Scott Bevan, 2 Darren Moss, 5 Darren Kempson, 7 Marc Pugh (65), 9 Dave Hibbert■, 12 Ben Herd, 14 Ben Davies (70)■, 18 Steven Leslie, 22 Colin Murdock, 23 Marc Tierney, 28 Kevin McIntyre (80).

Subs: 1 Glyn Garner (GK), 10 James Constable (65), 17 Chris Humphrey (70), 19 Guy Madjo, 24 James Ryan (80).

Wrexham:
12 Gavin Ward, 2 Simon Spender■, 6 Richard Hope, 9 Neil Roberts■, 10 Michael Proctor (58), 20 Matt Done, 21 Marc Williams (68), 25 Neil Taylor, 28 Phil Bolland, 29 Sam Aiston (65), 39 Drewe Broughton■.

Subs: 5 Steve Evans, 8 Danny Williams (68)■, 15 Mike Williams, 33 Paul Hall (65), 36 Jeff Whitley.

Manager Brian Little puts his hands to his face in disbelief as his side concede yet another goal.

	Shrewsbury	Wrexham
Shots on Goal:	16	19
Shots on Target:	11	11
Shots off Target	5	8
Possession:	54%	46%
Fouls Conceded:	17	19
Corners:	8	5
Yellow Cards:	2	4
Red Cards:	0	0

Neil Roberts meets Wes Baynes' free-kick at the far post to volley in past Russell Hoult.

Coca Cola League 2: 19th April, 2008

Wrexham 1   Notts County 0

Neil Roberts 77

Referee: Anthony Bates (Staffordshire)
Attendance (Away): 4,076 (628)

Skipper Neil Roberts solitary goal delayed Wrexham's relegation from the Football League for at least another few days after a youthful Dragons' side conjured up an unlikely victory.

Wrexham had to win or hope that Dagenham lost at Rotherham (which they did incidentally) to retain even the slimmest of chances of holding on to their cherished League status.

Manager Brian Little had made wholesale changes from the side humiliated six days earlier. And, remarkably, he went with a side that only included one of the players that he brought to the club, namely goalkeeper Gavin Ward.

But despite the victory, welcome as it was, you can't say that the changes had a huge effect as the Dragons success owed as much to the inadequacies of the opposition as it did to a raised level of performance from the home side.

The work ethic was there in abundance though, and for that alone it's fair to say that the youthful Dragons' side deserved the three points.

The first half was one of those instantly for-gettable 45 minutes of football that has become so prevalent at the Racecourse in recent times, with the best of what few chances there were all going County's way.

Wes Baynes, who impressed with a whole-hearted display, had Wrexham's only effort of note in the first period, but Russell Hoult comfortably held his shot.

Danny Crow wasted the best chance of the half on 17 minutes, but was denied by the alertness of Ward and the striker was found wanting again with another opportunity on 34 minutes.

The second half surely had to be better and to the relief of the 4,000+ crowd it was. Baynes tried his luck again from distance, but failed to hit the target, and Stephen Hunt headed narrowly wide for the Magpies shortly afterwards.

Ryan Jarvis fired into the side netting, and Roberts cleared a Jason Lee header off the line as County continued to ask more of the questions.

Wrexham came more into it as time moved on and Baynes saw another 25-yard strike drift just wide.

Then came the breakthrough. Matty Done was fouled by Lee Canoville and Conall Murtagh's free kick was forced home at the far post by Roberts.

Ward superbly saved from Lee, and Hoult did likewise from Marc Williams, as the mood from the travelling contingent sudden-ly changed from that of mocking a Wrexham side probably still going down, to realising that defeat would leave them only two points clear of the drop themselves!

Now a win at Hereford on Tuesday is essential!

Wrexham:
12 Gavin Ward, 4 Shaun Pejic■, 5 Steve Evans, 9 Neil Roberts, 15 Mike Williams, 18 Levi Mackin (70), 19 Andy Fleming (70), 20 Matty Done (90), 21 Marc Williams, 25 Neil Taylor, 31 Wes Baynes■.

Subs: 8 Danny Williams (70), 10 Michael Proctor,13 Michael Jones (GK), 22 Connall Murtagh, 24 Gareth Evans (90).

Notts County:
25 Russell Hoult, 2 Lee Canoville■, 4 Mike Edwards, 8 Neil Mackenzie, 9 Jason Lee, 18 Stephen Hunt, 19 Danny Crow (51), 23 Richard Butcher, 27 Michael Johnson (46), 28 Ryan Jarvis (86), 30 Miles Weston.

Subs: 5 Adam Tann, 10 Lawrie Dudfield (51),15 Paul Mayo (46), 21 Spencer Weir-Daley, 29 Wayne Corden (86).

Wrexham's Wes Baynes forces his way through the 'Magpies' defence.

	Wrexham	Notts County
Shots on Goal:	12	10
Shots on Target:	6	3
Shots off Target	6	7
Possession:	52%	48%
Fouls Conceded:	12	11
Corners:	4	11
Yellow Cards:	2	1
Red Cards:	0	0

Neil Roberts battles it out with the 'Bulls' Dean Beckwith watched by Wes Baynes.

Coca Cola League 2: 22nd April, 2008

Hereford United 2   Wrexham 0

Gary Cooper 42
Theo Robinson 60

Referee: Keith Stroud (Hampshire)
Attendance (Away): 3,739 (478)

How ironic that exactly thirty years since probably the greatest day in Wrexham's long and proud history - when Rotherham were beaten 7-1 at the Racecourse to clinch promotion to the old Second - came the lowest point?

And adding to the irony is that it happened at the very ground where, a week after Rotherham were so clinically dispatched, the championship was clinched with a 1-1 draw.

Okay, so most fans had probably been gearing up for this moment for some time and, with having to beat promotion-chasing Hereford to keep survival hopes alive, most probably expected relegation to be confirmed at Edgar Street.

It didn't make it any easier to stomach though did it? Especially when Theo Robinson was put clear to beat Gavin Ward and make it 2-0 on the hour mark, and the grim reality of a future, for next season at least, in the Blue Square Premier.

"Que sera sera, whatever will be will be, we're going to Forest Green," sang a section of the travelling faithful in an attempt to make light of the predicament, but it still didn't make it any easier to take!

Brian Little persisted with his policy of giving youth its chance following the weekend defeat of Notts County. And the decision looked like it could pay off again in the early exchanges when Conall Murtagh shot straight at Wayne Brown inside 25 seconds. Matty Done also tested the ex-Chester 'keeper moments later.

Robinson missed a gilt-edge chance for the home side on four minutes, and Done tested Brown again before the 'keeper did even better to turn a powerful Neil Roberts drive round the post.

But the Bulls always looked dangerous, and started to hammer the final nail into the coffin just before the break when Robinson's clever back heel allowed Gary Hooper the space to shoot across Ward and into the corner of the net.

Robinson saw a 25-yard shot strike a post after the break, and Marc Williams was denied in style by Brown as the Dragons desperately searched for a goal.

But then came Robinson's crucial contribution, and the Dragons were left with the sorry task of playing out the last third of the game already knowing their fate.

"Wrexham 'til I die" was the defiant chant from the near-500 strong away following at the final whistle, no doubt realising that there will be plenty of hard work ahead to be ready for life in the BSP next season.

"There is a massive job for everybody - myself, the players, the fans and the people who own the club - but we're all in it together," said Little afterwards.

Keep the faith!

Hereford United:
1 Simon Brown, 2 Trent McClenahan, 4 Richard Rose, 6 Karl Broadhurst, 8 Ben Smith, 11 Clint Easton, 20 Toumani Diagouraga, 22 Theo Robinson, 25 Sammy Igoe, 28 Dean Beckwith, 29 Gary Hooper.

Subs: 10 Kris Taylor, 12 Trevor Benjamin, 18 Lee Collins, 23 Simon Johnson, 33 Ryan Esson (GK).

Wrexham: 12 Gavin Ward, 4 Shaun Pejic, 5 Steve Evans, 9 Neil Roberts, 15 Mike Williams, 18 Levi Mackin, 20 Matty Done, 21 Marc Williams (69), 22 Connall Murtagh (63)■, 25 Neil Taylor, 32 Wes Baynes (70).

Subs: 8 Danny Williams (63)■, 10 Michael Proctor (69), 13 Michael Jones (GK), 24 Gareth Evans, 35 Robbie Garrett (70).

The look says it all. With the final whistle signalling the end of Wrexham's 87 year Football League history.

Shots on Goal:	7	9
Shots on Target:	3	6
Shots off Target	4	3
Possession:	57%	43%
Fouls Conceded:	18	12
Corners:	8	6
Yellow Cards:	0	2
Red Cards:	0	0

Neil Roberts blasts home a consolation penalty goal after Wes Baynes was felled.

Coca Cola League 2: 26th April, 2008

Wrexham 1   Accrington Stanley 3

Neil Roberts 90 (pen)

Shaun Pejic 7 (og)
Peter Cavanagh 28
Shaun Whalley 72

Referee: Mark Haywood (West Yorkshire).
Attendance (Away): 3,657 (142)

It's a remarkable measure of how much the club means to the fans when over 3,500 still turn up despite relegation from the Football League being confirmed in midweek.

Maybe the thought of seeing the last Football League game at the famous old ground for who knows how long meant that the pilgrimage just had to be made.

Shame then that a goal as bizarre as any conceded in a season when farcical ones have been far too common place to be a recipe for success, knocked the stuffing out of another young Wrexham side, and gave the visitors the platform to stroll to an easy victory.

Scant consolation it may be, but at least the Dragons had the consolation of scoring the last goal of a sorry season at the Racecourse when Phil Edwards unceremoniously brought Wes Baynes' rampaging run to an end inside the penalty area four minutes into injury time, and Neil Roberts hammered the spot kick past Kenny Arthur.

"I can understand the fans' frustration, but it was a hard game for us to watch as well," admitted boss Brian Little in his post-match press conference.

"We were looking for the young lads to show us some glimpses of things we might be able to hang on to and help them with, but some of them failed that test today.

"We wanted to try and finish the season at home better than that because we haven't lost too many games here this year so it was disappointing."

The die was effectively cast in the seventh minute when the Dragons conceded another goal that will feature on the Christmas DVD extravaganza. Robert Grant's header shouldn't have posed a problem, but young 'keeper Michael Jones, given a first start since October, called for Shaun Pejic to leave the ball. The defender arced his body forwards to let the ball go, but it ricocheted off his back and rolled through the unsuspecting 'keeper's legs, and trickled over the goal line. Unbelievable!

Accrington compounded the Dragons' woes with a second goal; the lively Shaun

Whalley beating Steve Evans down the right, and his cross was parried by Jones into the path of Peter Cavanagh, who easily found the net from six yards out.

Chris Llewellyn should have pulled a goal back in the 57th minute when Gareth Evans' header put him clear with only Arthur to beat, but the Welsh international skied his shot over the crossbar.

Whalley made it 3-0 with a goal his performance deserved, racing onto Cavanagh's through ball to steer a shot with the outside of his right foot past Jones and into the bottom left-hand corner of the net.

Wrexham:
13 Michael Jones ,4 Shaun Pejic, 5 Steve Evans (46)■, 9 Neil Roberts, 11 Chris Llewellyn, 15 Mike Williams, 18 Levi Mackin, 19 Andy Fleming, 20 Matty Done, 23 Michael Carvill (46), 24 Gareth Evans.

Subs: 12 Gavin Ward, 21 Marc Williams, 22 Connall Murtagh, 25 Neil Taylor (46), 31 Wes Baynes (46).

Accrington Stanley: 1 Kenny Arthur, 2 Peter Cavanagh (77)■, 3 Leam Richardson, 6 Andrew Proctor, 7 Shaun Whalley■, 10 Paul Mullin, 12 Phil Edwards, 20 James Bell, 22 Robert Grant (69), 23 Ian Craney (78)■, 40 Peter Murphy.

Subs: 8 James Harris (69), 17 Graham Branch, 25 Ian Dunbavin (GK), 27 Andy Todd (77), 30 David Mannix (78).

Where's the ball?
The look on 'Carrots'
face says it all.

Shots on Goal:	8	5
Shots on Target:	2	3
Shots off Target	6	2
Possession:	38%	62%
Fouls Conceded:	6	15
Corners:	4	1
Yellow Cards:	1	3
Red Cards:	0	0

The future? Neil Taylor, Wes Baynes, Simon Spender and Andy Fleming celebrate Wes' second goal.

Coca Cola League 2: 4th May, 2008

Lincoln City 2

Steve Evans 39 (og)
Ben Wright 90

Wrexham 4

Levi Mackin 11
Wes Baynes 33, 88
Chris Llewellyn 90

Referee: Richard Beeby ()
Attendance (Away): 4,958 (597)

It was party time at Sincil Bank as Wrexham said farewell to the Football League in style, scoring more than two goals in a game for the first time this season, and recording a second 'double' of the campaign to boot.

Nearly 600 fans made the long journey across country - many in fancy dress - to again demonstrate just what the Club means.

Singing pretty much non-stop for the entire game, the fans were treated to an entertaining end-of-season game that was far more enjoyable than anybody could have predicted.

Wrexham opened the scoring when Wes Baynes (what a game he had!) whipped in a free kick after Marc Williams had been fouled, and Levi Mackin stooped eight yards out to head past Ayden Duffy and notch his first senior goal.

Suitably boosted by the goal, the Dragons stepped up a gear, and Baynes was denied by an alert Duffy who raced of his line to smother the ball at his feet.

The second goal the Dragons' enterprising play deserved came when Gary Croft handled just outside the box. Baynes took centre stage and drilled a low 20-yard free kick through the wall and past Duffy.

The party was now in full flow in the away section of the stand, and even when Steve Evans headed over the advancing Gavin Ward and into his own net from outside (yes, outside!) the penalty area, spirits remained high.

Chris Llewellyn wasted a great chance to restore the Dragons' two-goal lead a minute into the second half, but Paul Green was on hand to clear his tame effort off the line.

Lincoln began to put the Dragons' defence under sustained pressure with the returning Carl Tremarco clearing off the line from Louis Dodds, and Ben Wright putting the rebound over the bar from close range.

Ward then saved smartly from substitute Shane Clark and Wright missed the target with a volley before Baynes emphatically made it 3-1 with an even more powerful

free kick from just outside the penalty area after his surging run had been brought to a premature end by Clarke.

It just wouldn't be Wrexham though would it without a late twist, and Wright got between two defenders to pull a goal back in injury time.

Incredibly Lee Beevors then struck a post before Llewellyn made sure the party went on into the night by racing clear and lifting the ball over Duffy to make it 4-2.

Let's hope the memories of this day will give everyone a lift when it comes to preparing for life in the Blue Square Premier.

Lincoln City: 13 Ayden Duffy, 2 Paul Green, 3 Gary Croft (67), 5 Lee Beevers, 7 Lee Frecklington (28), 8 Jamie Forrester, 11 Scott Kerr, 15 Ben Wright, 19 Louis Dodds (74), 21 Gary King, 27 Daniel Hone.

Subs: 6 Nat Brown, 9 Mark Stallard, 17 Dany N'Guessan (74), 20 Owain Warlow (67), 23 Shane Clarke (28).

Wrexham: 12 Gavin Ward, 2 Simon Spender, 4 Shaun Pejic, 5 Steve Evans, 11 Chris Llewellyn, 18 Levi Mackin, 21 Marc Williams, 22 Conall Murtagh (68), 25 Neil Taylor, 31 Wes Baynes, 36 Carl Tremarco (90).

Subs: 13 Michael Jones (GK), 19 Andy Fleming (68), 23 Michael Carvill (90), 26 Robbie Garrett, 40 Alex Darlington.

Chris Llewellyn finely finishes Wrexham's fourth, and last ever goal in the Football League.

Shots on Goal:	17	12
Shots on Target:	8	7
Shots off Target:	9	5
Possession:	59%	41%
Fouls Conceded:	8	9
Corners:	5	6
Yellow Cards:	0	0
Red Cards:	0	0

Players Appearances & Goals 2007/08

Players	League & Cup Appearances						League & Cup Goals					
	Lge	LC	FAC	JPT	PC	Tot	Lge	LC	FAC	JPT	PC	Tot
Aiston, Sam	13/6					13/6						0
Baynes, Wes	10/2				1	11/2	2					2
Bolland, Phil	18				1	19						0
Broughton, Drewe	16					16	2					2
Carvill, Mike	5/3		1			6/3						0
Collins, Matt	2	1				3						0
Crowell, Matt	3/3		1			4/3						0
Done, Matty	13/11	1	1	1		16/11						0
Duffy, Rob	0/6					0/6						0
Evans, Gareth	11/2		1			12/2						0
Evans, Steve	29/1	1		1	1	32/1	3					3
Fleming, Andy	2/2					2/2						0
Garrett, Rob	9/3		1			10/3						0
Hall, Paul	7/4					7/4	1					1
Hope, Richard	33	1	1	1		36						0
Johnson, Josh	0/7	0/2				0/9						0
Jones, Mark	13/2	1			0/1	14/3						0
Jones, Michael	2	2				4						0
Llewellyn Chris	41/2	2	1	1	1	46/2	3			2		5
Mackin, Levi	9/1	2			1	12/1	1					1
Murtagh, Conall	3/1	1/1				4/2						0
Nicholson, Stuart	9/4					9/4						0
Pejic, Shaun	17/2	2	0/1	0/1	0/1	19/5						0
Proctor, Michael	20/17	2		0/1	1	23/18	11	1				12
Roberts, Neil	35/1	1	0/1		1	37/2	8		1			9
Sonner, Danny	9					9	1					1
Spann, Silvio	7/2		1	1		9/2	1					1
Spender, Simon	31/2	2	1		0/1	34/3	1					1
Taylor, Neil	22/5	0/1			1	23/6						0
Tremarco, Carl	10					10						0
Ugarte, Juan	0/1					0/1						0
Valentine, Ryan	14	2	1	1	1	19						0
Ward, Gavin	22				1	23						0
Whitley, Jeff	5/6					5/6						0
Williams, Anthony	22		1	1		24						0
Williams, Danny	11/4	1				12/4						0
Williams, Eifion	7/6	1	1	1		10/6	1					1
Williams, Marc	11/9	0/2	0/1	0/1		11/13	3					3
Williams, Mike	15/3			1	1	17/3						0
39 players used												

Reserves Review 2007-08
A Review of the Pontin's Holiday League Season 2007-08

The season brought a marked improvement results-wise on recent campaigns and Joey Jones' side were still in with a chance of making the play-off's with two games remaining, but ultimately had to settle for a commendable fifth place finish.

Unfortunately, those two games were both against Manchester City, who showed the strength of the squad at their disposal by naming two virtually different elevens for both games played just two days apart. Several members of their successful FA Youth Cup team featured, and demonstrated their quality with a 3-0 win at Globe Way, and a 6-3 success at Hyde United's Tameside Stadium.

There was little evidence in the opening games of the season to suggest the impressive run of results that would follow later, as the opening five games yielded just two points, and included heavy defeats against Blackpool, Burnley and Preston North End, the latter game being notable for Juan Ugarte's last goal in a Wrexham shirt!

The first win, 1-0 against Tranmere Rovers, arrived courtesy of Eifion Williams' first goal for the club. Marc Williams grabbed a second-half hat-trick as the Dragons came from 1-0 down at half time to win 3-1 at eventual champions Morecambe.

Brian Little's appointment saw numerous new faces arriving at the Racecourse during the January transfer window, which in turn saw many first team regulars from before Christmas featuring regularly in the second string after the festive period. Rob Duffy marked his debut for the club with a brace in a comfortable 3-0 victory at Rochdale, and followed this with another double in a 3-2 defeat at Tranmere.

The next eight games brought seven victories and a staggering 22 goals! Wes Baynes and Marc Williams were on target as Accrington Stanley were beaten at NEWI Cefn Druids' Plas Kynaston Lane, and the 'double' over Rochdale was emphatically completed with a five-goal rout at Globe Way.

Eifion's last goal for the club proved to be the winner in a 3-2 win at Bury before a remarkable game at Globe Way saw Morecambe edge a nine-goal thriller. The Dragons led 2-1 at the interval, but then found themselves 5-2 down before late goals by Wes Baynes and Josh Johnson almost led to a remarkable comeback.

Silvio Spann netted a brace as Accrington were brushed aside 3-0, and an Alex Darlington penalty earned a narrow win over Preston North End at Deepdale. The young striker, now playing for The New Saints in the Welsh Premier League, netted twice in a 2-0 success at Burnley before a strong side overcame stubborn resistance from a young Chester City side at Globe Way, Spann and Michael Proctor netting. With a play-off place was still a possibility, but the two Manchester City games proved to be two hurdles too far for Joey's side.

Pontins League Division One West

	P	W	D	L	F	A	GD	Pts
1 Morecambe	22	14	4	4	43	31	+12	46
2 Manchester City	22	13	3	6	61	35	+26	42
3 Carlisle United	22	11	5	6	43	30	+13	38
4 Preston North End	22	11	2	9	41	39	+2	35
5 Wrexham	**22**	**11**	**2**	**9**	**46**	**45**	**+1**	**35**
6 Burnley	22	10	4	8	37	33	+4	34
7 Blackpool	22	9	4	9	43	33	+10	31
8 Tranmere Rovers	22	9	2	11	23	31	-8	29
9 Bury	22	6	6	10	30	40	-10	24
10 Chester City	22	6	5	11	23	44	-21	23
11 Rochdale	22	6	3	13	41	46	-5	21
12 Accrington Stanley	22	5	2	15	29	53	-24	17

Pontin's Holidays League Division One West 2007-2008 — Facts & Stats

Date	Opp	V	Res	1	2	3	4	5	6	7	8	9	10	11	Sub	Sub	Sub	Sub	Sub
AUGUST																			
22	Blackpool	A	0-4	Maxwell	Price	Marriott	G Evans	L Jones	Crowell	Johnson	Murtagh	Ma Williams	Ugarte	Carvill	Matischok	Hunt(5)	Head (7)	Hurdman	M Stewart(10)
SEPTEMBER																			
5	**Carlisle United**	H	2-2	Mi Jones	Baynes	Marriott	G Evans	L Jones	Crowell	E Williams	Spann	Ugarte[2]	Ma Williams	Johnson	Matischok	Maxwell	Price	M Stewart(7)	Hunt
10	**Burnley**	H	1-3*	Mi Jones	Baynes	Marriott	Mi Williams	G Evans	Spann	Crowell	Mackin	Ugarte	Ma Williams	Johnson	P Williams(8)	Matischok	Price	M Stewart(10)	L Jones(5)
24	**Preston North End**	H	3-5	Mi Jones	Price	Marriott	Pejic	L Jones	Fleming[1]	Baynes[1]	Mackin	Roberts	Ugarte[1]	Johnson	Edwards(2)	Maxwell	M Stewart	P Williams	G Stewart
OCTOBER																			
10	Chester City	A	0-0	Mi Jones	Baynes	Mi Williams	Price	Marriott	Spann	Johnson	Mackin	Carvill	E Williams	Done	M Stewart(10)	P Williams	Hunt	G Stewart(9)	Hurdman
22	**Tranmere Rovers**	H	1-0	A Williams	Garrett	Marriott	Pejic	S Evans	Mackin	Johnson	Crowell	Ma Williams	E Williams[1]	Done	Baynes(2)	Maxwell	M Stewart(10)	L Jones	Price
NOVEMBER																			
28	Morecambe	A	3-1	Mi Jones	Spender	Valentine	G Evans	Mi Williams	Crowell	Fleming	Murtagh	Mackin	Ma Williams[3]	Johnson	Marriott	Maxwell	G Stewart(8)	Head	L Jones(6)
DECEMBER																			
5	**Bury**	H	3-2	Mi Jones	Spann	Mi Williams	G Evans	Spender	Mackin	Fleming	Murtagh	Carvill[2]	Crowell	G Stewart	Marriott(2)	Maxwell	L Jones	Anoruo(11)[1]	Price
17	**Blackpool**	H	0-2	Mi Jones	L Jones	Marriott	Mi Williams	G Evans	Mackin	Fleming	Murtagh	Ma Williams	Carvill	Done	Price	Maxwell	Anoruo	P Williams	G Stewart
JANUARY																			
9	Carlisle United	A	3-5	Mi Jones	Price	Hunt	L Jones	G Evans	Fleming[1]	Johnson	Murtagh	Reed[1]	Carvill[1]	Done	Edwards(4)	Maxwell	Matischok	Carding	Anoruo(2)
30	Rochdale	A	3-0	Mi Jones	Baynes	Marriott	Garrett	Mi Williams	L Jones	Carvill	Fleming	Duffy[2]	Ma Williams[3]	Aiston	P Williams(5)	Whelan	Head	M Stewart	Price(3)
FEBRUARY																			
6	Tranmere Rovers	A	2-3	Mi Jones	Baynes	Done	Pejic	Hope	Fleming	E Williams	Aiston	Duffy[2]	Ma Williams	Johnson	Edwards(7)	Maxwell	L Jones(5)	G Stewart(11)	Pearson
13	**Accrington Stanley**	H	2-1	Mi Jones	Baynes[1]	Done	Hope	Pejic	D Williams	Carvill	Spann	E Williams	Ma Williams[1]	Garrett	L Jones(6)	Whelan	P Williams	Price	Matischok(10)
18	**Rochdale**	H	5-0	Mi Jones	Garrett	Baynes	Pejic	D Williams	Fleming	Carvill[2]	Spann	E Williams[2]	Ma Williams	Done	L Jones(5)[1]	Maxwell	Edwards	Matischok	Anoruo(9)
27	Bury	A	3-2	Mi Jones	Garrett	Baynes	L Jones	Pejic	Fleming	Carvill	D Williams	Ma Williams[1]	E Williams[1]	Done[1]	Price	Whelan	Matischok	Hunt	Anoruo
MARCH																			
19	**Morecambe**	H	4-5	Maxwell	Garrett	Baynes[1]	Pejic	D Williams	Ma Jones	Carvill[1]	Spann	Reed	Ma Williams[1]	Johnson[1]	Darlington(6)	Price(9)	L Jones	Matischok	Matischok
26	Accrington Stanley	A	3-0	A Williams	Baynes	Marriott	Pejic	D Williams	Fleming	Spann[2]	Ma Jones	Ma Williams	Darlington	Johnson[1]	L Jones	Maxwell	Price	Matischok	Anoruo(10)
APRIL																			
2	Preston North End	A	1-0	A Williams	Garrett	Marriott	Pejic	S Evans	Ma Jones	Spann	Fleming	Duffy	Carvill	Johnson	Darlington(9)[1]	Maxwell	Price	Carding(11)[1]	Matischok
9	Burnley	A	2-0	A Williams	Garrett	Marriott	Pejic	Murtagh	Ma Jones	Spann	Fleming	Carvill	Darlington[1]	Johnson	Edwards(6)	Maxwell	Price(9)	P Williams	Hunt
16	**Chester City**	H	2-1	A Williams	Spender	Marriott	Bolland	Hope	Spann[1]	Darlington	Ma Jones	Proctor[1]	Carvill	Aiston	Price	Maxwell	L Jones	P Williams	Matischok
21	**Manchester City**	H	0-3	A Williams	Price	Marriott	Spender	Bolland	Whitley	Spann	Anoruo	Darlington	Johnson	Aiston	L Jones(7)	Maxwell	P Williams(8)	Matischok(PW)	G Stewart
23	Manchester City	A	3-6	A Williams	Spender[2]	Hunt	Bolland	L Jones	Whitley	Johnson	Matischok	Anoruo	Llewellyn	Aiston	Marriott	Maxwell	Head(10)[1]	Price	G Stewart(9)

* DENOTES OWN GOAL

Youth Review 2007-08

A Review of the Puma Youth Alliance North West Conference 2007-08

Steve Cooper's first full season in charge of the Centre of Excellence saw the under-18s finish their Puma Youth Alliance season in a worthy 10th place out of the 18 teams

The season actually promised more early on, as the young Dragons remained unbeaten until late October, a run of seven games bringing five wins and two draws. Goal scoring was spread throughout the team, and the defence stood firm during this period, conceding just two goals during the run!

Wigan Athletic brought the sequence to an end in the First Round of the League Cup and followed this with a 4-1 League win at Colliers Park a week later. Oldham Athletic were next up in the FA Youth Cup First Round and, in a repeat of the tie at Boundary Park two years earlier, the tie went all the way to extra time, and a penalty shoot out. Unfortunately the Dragons couldn't repeat their success and this time went out 3-2 on penalties after an entertaining 120 minutes' of football ended deadlocked at 1-1. After trailing at the break, Mark Stewart levelled, and the Dragons created enough chances thereafter to win the game, especially when the Latics went down to ten men following a sending-off in the closing stages of the 90 minutes. However, the Dragons failed to make the most of their numerical advantage, and in all truth never really looked like finding an extra time winner, and finally succumbed to defeat in the cruellest way possible. Steve Cooper was philosophical after the game: "While we improved in the second half, our display in the first half cost us the game," he declared. "The FA Youth Cup is all about the lads playing on the bigger stage. It's similar to if you go and make your first team debut. Therefore you look at individuals and while we did better in the second half, we still missed three or four chances and it has cost us."

But the youngsters put that disappointment quickly behind them with a 2-0 win at Shrewsbury Town the following weekend. Unfortunately a five-game run without a win followed, though this was in turn followed by a four-game unbeaten run that included a 3-0 defeat of Shrewsbury, and a superb 6-0 demolition of Accrington Stanley, both at Colliers Park. Inconsistency then seemed to be the word for the remainder of the campaign, but 10th place has to be a commendable effort in a tough League.

The end of the season saw the majority of the final year scholars released with just two, goalkeeper Chris Maxwell and defender Chris Marriott, offered one-year professional contracts.

Once again international honours came the club's way. Matt Hurdman and Kai Edwards were in the Wales U17 side that qualified for the Elite Stage of qualifying for the UEFA U17 Championships, with Kai captaining the side. Kai also joined up with Chris Maxwell in the Wales U19 squad for a qualifying tournament for the UEFA U19 Championships. Kai's progress was such that he was even named as a standby for the U21 squad for the friendly against England at the Racecourse back in May.

Puma Youth Alliance North West Fixtures 2008-09

Date		H/A	Opponents	Date		H/A	Opponents
Aug	16th	H	Chester City	Dec	6th	H	Stockport County
	23rd		In service training		13th	A	Walsall
	30th	A	Tranmere Rovers	Jan	10th	A	Chester City
Sept	6th	H	Port Vale		17th	H	Tranmere Rovers
	TBC	A	Stalybridge Celtic (FAYC)		24th		(NC3)
	13th	H	Shrewsbury Town		31st	A	Port Vale
	20th	A	Wigan Athletic	Feb	7th	A	Preston North End
	27th	H	Rochdale		14th	H	Oldham Athletic
Oct	4th	A	Macclesfield Town		21st	H	Morecambe
	11th	A	Carlisle United (NC1)		28th		(NC4)
	18th	H	Walsall	Mar	7th	H	Carlisle United
	25th	A	Stockport County		14th	A	Bury
Nov	1st	H	Wigan Athletic		21st	H	Burnley
	8th	A	Shrewsbury Town		28th	A	Blackpool
	15th	H	Macclesfield Town	Apr	4th	A	Rochdale
	22nd		(NC2)		18th	H	Accrington Stanley
	29th	A	Morecambe	May	2nd		In service training

Puma Youth Alliance North West Conference 2007-08

		P	W	D	L	F	A	GD	Pts
1	Walsall	27	18	5	4	61	34	+27	59
2	Wigan Athletic	27	17	5	5	65	25	+40	56
3	Carlisle United	27	16	4	7	61	37	+24	52
4	Macclesfield Town	27	15	5	7	61	32	+29	50
5	Blackpool	27	15	4	8	62	52	+10	49
6	Burnley	27	14	3	10	63	46	+17	45
7	Chester City	27	12	5	10	36	33	+3	41
8	Preston North End	27	12	3	12	51	50	+1	39
9	Tranmere Rovers	27	10	8	9	42	38	+4	38
10	Wrexham	27	10	7	10	40	35	+5	37
11	Oldham Athletic	27	11	4	12	60	63	-3	37
12	Port Vale	27	10	7	10	41	46	-5	37
13	Bury	27	11	4	12	47	54	-7	37
14	Stockport County	27	11	3	13	50	55	-5	36
15	Morecambe	27	5	5	17	42	64	-22	20
16	Accrington Stanley	27	5	4	18	32	83	-51	19
17	Rochdale	27	4	6	17	49	76	-27	18
18	Shrewsbury Town	27	4	4	19	27	67	-40	16

Puma Youth Alliance - North West 2007-2008 — Facts & Stats

Date	Opponent		Res	1	2	3	4	5	6	7	8	9	10	11	Sub	Sub	Sub	Sub	Sub
AUGUST																			
11	Macclesfield Town	A	1-1	Whelan	Edwards	Hunt	L Jones	Marriott	Matschok	G Stewart	Hurdman	Head¹	M Stewart	Carding	Price	Maxwell	Anoruo	Pearson (11)	J Jones(6)
18	Tranmere Rovers	H	2-0~	Maxwell	Edwards	Hunt	L Jones	Marriott	Matschok	G Stewart	Hurdman	Head	M Stewart	Carding	Price	Pearson (6)	Anoruo (9)¹	J Jones	Bainbridge
SEPTEMBER																			
1	Wigan Athletic	A	3-1	Maxwell	Price	Hunt	L Jones	Marriott	Matschok	G Stewart	Hurdman²	Head	M Stewart	Carding	J Jones (9)	Bainbridge	Pearson (11)¹	P Williams (6)	Edwards
8	Walsall	H	1-0	Maxwell	Price	Hunt	L Jones	Marriott	Matschok	G Stewart	Hurdman	Head	M Stewart¹	P Williams	Edwards (6)	J Jones (8)	Anoruo (9)	Bainbridge	Pearson
22	Port Vale	H	2-0	Maxwell	Price	Edwards	L Jones¹	Marriott¹	Matschok	G Stewart	Hurdman	Anoruo	M Stewart	P Williams	Pearson (6)	J Jones (8)	Head (9)	Bainbridge	
29	Stockport County	A	1-0	Maxwell	Price	Hunt	L Jones	Marriott	Matschok	G Stewart	Pearson	Head	M Stewart¹	P Williams	Anoruo (9)	J Jones (8)	Bainbridge	Clowes	
OCTOBER																			
13	Chester City	H	0-0	Bainbridge	Price	Hunt	L Jones	Marriott	Matschok	G Stewart	Pearson	Head	M Stewart	P Williams	Anoruo (9)	J Jones (8)	Hurdman (6)	Clowes	
20	Wigan Athletic (NC1)	H	0-2	Maxwell	Edwards	Hunt	L Jones	Price	Pearson	Carding	J Jones	Head	Anoruo	M Stewart	Marriott	Bainbridge	Penk	Rushton	
27	Wigan Athletic	A	1-4	Maxwell	Edwards	Hunt	Price	Marriott	L Jones	G Stewart	Hurdman	Head¹	M Stewart	Carding	Anoruo	Bainbridge	Pearson	J Jones	Clowes
31	Oldham Athletic (FAYC1)	A	1-1*	Maxwell	Edwards	Hunt	L Jones	Marriott	Hurdman	G Stewart	P Williams	Head¹	M Stewart¹	Pearson	Price (2)	Carding (11)	J Jones (9)	Bainbridge	Bainbridge
NOVEMBER																			
3	Shrewsbury Town	A	2-0~	Maxwell	Price	Hunt	L Jones¹	Marriott	J Jones	G Stewart	P Williams	Head¹	M Stewart	Carding	Anoruo (7)	Bainbridge	Pearson (3)	Gideon(RP)	Hurdman
10	Stockport County	H	1-3	Bainbridge	Price	Hunt	L Jones	Marriott	J Jones	G Stewart	Hurdman	Head	Anoruo	Gideon	Anoruo (11)	Pearson (6)	Griffiths (8)	Edwards	
17	Port Vale	A	1-1	Maxwell	Edwards	Hunt	L Jones	Marriott	Matschok	G Stewart	P Williams	Head¹	M Stewart	Carding	Price (2)	Pearson	Anoruo	Hurdman	Gideon
DECEMBER																			
1	Chester City	A	0-3	Maxwell	Edwards	Hunt	L Jones	Marriott	Matschok	G Stewart	J Jones	Head	Price	Carding	Clowes (10)	Anoruo (8)	Hurdman	Bainbridge	Quinn
15	Macclesfield Town	H	1-2	Maxwell	Price	Hunt	L Jones	Marriott	Hurdman	G Stewart	Pearson	Head	Anoruo¹	Carding	Matschok (6)	Kane (7)	P Williams (8)	J Jones	Clowes
JANUARY																			
5	Walsall	A	2-3	Maxwell	Price	Hunt	L Jones	Edwards	Matschok¹	G Stewart	P Williams	Head	Kane	Carding	Hurdman (7)	Whelan	Anoruo (9)¹	J Jones (8)	Clowes
12	Shrewsbury Town	H	3-0	Whelan	Price	Hunt	L Jones	Edwards	Matschok	Hurdman¹	P Williams	Anoruo¹	Kane¹	Carding	Clowes (8)	Pearson (6)	Head (9)	G Stewart	Maxwell
26	Rochdale	A	1-1	Maxwell	Price	Marriott	L Jones	Edwards¹	Matschok	P Williams	Hurdman	Anoruo	M Stewart	Carding	Hunt	Whelan	G Stewart (6)	Pearson (8)	Kane
FEBRUARY																			
5	Morecambe	H	1-1	Whelan	J Jones	Hunt	Price	Edwards	Matschok	G Stewart	P Williams	Anoruo	M Stewart	Carding	Hurdman (8)	Maxwell	Clowes	Head (10)	Kane (9)¹
9	Accrington Stanley	H	6-0	Maxwell	Price¹	Hunt	L Jones	Edwards	Matschok	G Stewart¹	P Williams¹	Kane²	M Stewart	Carding	J Jones	Whelan	Head (10)	Pearson (7)¹	Anoruo (9)
16	Blackpool	A	1-3	Whelan	Price	Hunt	L Jones¹	Edwards	Matschok	G Stewart	P Williams	Head	Kane	Carding	Maxwell	Pearson (9)	J Jones	Hurdman (8)	Anoruo (10)
23	Tranmere Rovers	A	1-1	Maxwell	Price	Hunt	L Jones	Edwards	Matschok	G Stewart	Hurdman¹	Anoruo	Kane	Carding	J Jones	Whelan	Pearson	Head	
MARCH																			
1	Burnley	H	1-2	Whelan	Price	Marriott	L Jones	Edwards	Matschok	G Stewart	J Jones	Anoruo¹	Kane	Pearson	Hurdman (8)	Maxwell	Head (10)	Hunt	Moss (6)
8	Bury	A	2-1~	Maxwell	Price	Hunt	Edwards	Marriott	Matschok	G Stewart	J Jones	Anoruo¹	Kane	Carding	Whelan	Pearson	Hurdman (11)	L Jones (7)	Head (10)
15	Carlisle United	H	0-2	Whelan	Price	Hunt	L Jones	Marriott	Matschok	G Stewart	J Jones	Head	Kane	Carding	Pearson (10)	Maxwell	Hurdman (7)	Clowes	Anoruo
29	Morecambe	A	1-2	Maxwell	Price	Hunt	L Jones	Marriott	Matschok	G Stewart	Hurdman	Anoruo¹	M Stewart	Carding	J Jones (7)	Pearson (10)	Head		
APRIL																			
5	Oldham Athletic	H	2-2	Maxwell	Price	Hunt	L Jones	Edwards	Matschok	J Jones¹	Hurdman	Anoruo	Rushton	Carding¹	Marriott (4)	Clowes	Moss	Kane (9)	Moss (6)
12	Blackpool	A	1-3	Maxwell	Price	Hunt	L Jones²	Marriott	Matschok	J Jones	Hurdman	Anoruo	Rushton	Carding	P Williams (7)	Moss (8)	Head (10)	G Stewart	Head (10)
19	Preston North End	A	1-2	Maxwell	Price	Hunt	L Jones	Marriott	Matschok¹	P Williams¹	Hurdman	Head	Anoruo	Carding	J Jones (8)	M Stewart (10)	G Stewart (11)	Pearson	Edwards

~ denotes own goal   * denotes lost 3-2 on penalties (L Jones & Hunt scored)